where LOCALS ➜hike

✵ ✵ IN THE Canadian Rockies ✵ ✵

the **PREMIER** trails IN
KANANASKIS COUNTRY
near CANMORE + CALGARY

➤➤ Boot-tested and written by

KATHY + CRAIG COPELAND

hiking camping.com

Heading outdoors eventually leads you within.

The first people on earth were hikers and campers. So today, when we walk the earth and bed down on it, we're living in the most primitive, elemental way known to our species. We're returning to a way of life intrinsic to the human experience. We're shedding the burden of millennia of civilization. We're seeking catharsis. We're inviting enlightenment.

Rawson Lake below, Mt. Sarrail right, Mt. Foch beyond, from Sarrail Ridge (Trip 25)

Mount Kidd, above the Kananaskis River, from Highway 40

MEMBER

FOR THE

PLANET

Businesses donating 1% of their sales to the natural environment
www.onepercentfortheplanet.org

Copyright © 2005 by Kathy and Craig Copeland
All Rights Reserved
1st edition June 2002; 2nd edition Aug 2005
3rd edition May 2008; updated 3rd edition July 2009

Photographs and layout by the authors
Maps by Angela Lockerbie
Production by C.J. Poznansky, giddyupgraphics@mac.com
Cover and interior design by Matthew Clark,
  www.subplot.com
Printed in China by Asia Pacific Offset

Published in Canada by hikingcamping.com, inc.
P.O. Box 8563, Canmore, Alberta T1W 2V3 Canada
fax: 403.678.3343 email: nomads@hikingcamping.com

Library and Archives Canada - Cataloguing in Publication

Copeland, Kathy, 1959-
  Where locals hike in the Canadian Rockies: the premier trails in
Kananaskis Country, near Canmore & Calgary / boot-tested and written
by Kathy & Craig Copeland. — 3rd ed., May 2008.

Includes index.   ISBN 978-0-9783427-4-6

  1. Hiking—Alberta—Kananaskis Country—Guidebooks. 2. Trails—
Alberta—Kananaskis Country—Guidebooks. 3. Kananaskis Country
(Alta.)—Guidebooks. I. Copeland, Craig, 1955- II. Title.

GV199.44.C22K36 2008   796.522'097123'32   C2008-901713-7

Front cover photo: Ascending Tent Ridge (Trip 8)

Back cover photos, from top to bottom: Ascending to Piper Pass (Trip 27),
Atop Northover Ridge (Trip 24), Descent to Aster Lake (Trip 24),
Ascending King Creek Ridge (Trip 19)

Contents

What's with the Weird Name? 4 / Land of Many Uses, and a Few Abuses 4 / Shoulder-Season Hiking 8 / Frontcountry Camping 8 / Backcountry Camping 9 / Maps, Elevations, Distances 10 / Carry a Compass 11 / Placate the Weather Gods 12 / Wilderness Ethics 13 / Leave Your Itinerary 17 / Hiking with Your Dog 17 / Physical Capability 17 / Wildlife 18 / Ticks 18 / Bears 20 / Cougars 23 / Lightning 24 / Hypothermia 26

Mt. Joffre and Northover tarns, from Northover Ridge (Trip 24)

North America's Preeminent Alps

The tour buses go to Banff National Park. The ten-year-old Subaru wagons go to Kananaskis Country. But the mountains themselves, regardless of geopolitical distinctions, are all part of the same range. Welcome to the Canadian Rockies, North America's preeminent alps.

Mountain freaks living nearby in Calgary and Canmore cherish their backyard wilderness. They call it K-Country. Yet hikers from afar remain unaware of it. Confession: we were among them.

We first hiked in the Canadian Rocky Mountain national parks while travelling from the U.S. during the late 1980s. We were astounded. Though we'd previously hiked much of the world's vertical topography, here we felt like pious peasants stumbling upon Chartre Cathedral. We were compelled to immigrate.

The first several years we lived in Calgary, however, our intent to explore the national parks was so fundamentalist that we largely ignored K-Country. Friends said we were crazy to spend every weekend driving to Banff, Kootenay, Yoho and Jasper national parks. We thought they were lazy, settling for K-Country because it was close.

Not until long after the publication of *Don't Waste Your Time*® *in the Canadian Rockies*, our first hiking guidebook on the national parks, did we turn our attention to K-Country. Once again, we were astounded. And this time, chagrined as well.

Like the rest of the Canadian Rockies, the mountains of K-Country are among this planet's most scenically captivating. Its foothills afford splendid shoulder-season hiking starting in May and continuing into late October. On summer weekends, locals flock to a few popular K-Country trails, but you'll never encounter hordes like those that unceasingly throng Banff's Lake Louise and Moraine Lake.

Every trail in this book leads to sensational scenery. The rapture you'll experience on these hikes trivializes the effort you'll expend. The drama usually unfolds soon: the rewards generously dispensed well before arrival at the destination. You'll be inspired by immense forests, piercing peaks, tumbling glaciers, sheer cliffs, rowdy creeks, sprawling meadows, psychedelic wildflowers. Awaiting you are climactic vistas with startling impact.

You now hold in your hands the key to K-Country's superlative day-hikes and backpack trips. We never intended this to be an encyclopedically exhaustive volume. Books that detail every wretched, obscure scratch in the dirt overburden and confuse the vast majority of hikers, therefore failing to guide them. By definition, a guidebook should winnow and recommend, sparing the reader unnecessary, tedious decision-making. It should also be eloquent. *Guide*books have languished too long as a knuckle-dragging subspecies of literature. So, our goal is to write superior, discerning guidebooks—accurate of course, but also lucid, as well as entertaining—that local or visiting hikers will find helpful and enjoyable.

What's not in this book? Punishing, dreary, sketchy trips, mostly. Their appeal is limited to inveterate explorers and intrepid mountaineers. The average hiker would find these journeys frustrating, disappointing,

or overwhelming. We've also omitted several valley-bottom trails in southern K-Country that are lackluster compared to those we did include. Presenting inferior options would be to advocate hiking exclusively in K-Country, which is ridiculous when just up the highway are dozens more premier trails in the same mountain range, albeit in the national parks.

Now you can quickly, easily choose a K-Country hike, confident that each one in this book offers a fulfilling experience. Most of the trails are well constructed and maintained. A few are rougher—unmaintained routes, bootbeaten paths—but they lead to especially gratifying destinations. Our precise *By Vehicle* and *On Foot* directions, and the maps accompanying each trip, ensure you'll get there and back without difficulty.

We hope *Where Locals Hike* compels you to get outdoors more often and stay out longer. Do it to cultivate your wild self. It will give you perspective. Do it because the backcountry teaches simplicity and self-reliance, qualities that make life more fulfilling. Do it to remind yourself why wilderness needs and deserves your protection. A deeper conservation ethic develops naturally in the mountains. And do it to escape the cacophony that muffles the quiet, pure voice within.

What's with the Weird Name?

Kananaskis was a legendary Indian who survived an axe-blow to the head. The name Kananaskis means *meeting of the waters*. Captain John Palliser, leader of a British scientific expedition in the mid-1800s, bestowed the name on a river and two passes in the heart of this region: the Kananaskis River, as well as North and South Kananaskis passes. Later, the name was also given to a pair of the area's largest bodies of water: Upper and Lower Kananaskis lakes.

Land of Many Uses, and a Few Abuses

K-Country is not one big park. It's a recreation area comprising several provincial parks and protected wildlife areas. Unlike the Canadian Rocky Mountain national parks, K-Country has a multiple-use policy that extends far beyond hiking. Restricted but permissible activities include mountain-biking, horseback riding, fishing, hunting, snowmobiling, power boating, logging, oil and gas exploration, hydro-electric power generation, free-range cattle grazing, and the operation of a golf resort. Most of these activities are severely limited. Some are confined to specific, small, remote areas.

Most hikers believe that multiple use is eroding the integrity of the remaining wilderness. Environmental organizations like the Kananaskis Coalition and the Canadian Parks and Wilderness Society are working to reduce K-Country development and resource extraction. The Friends of Kananaskis welcome your interest in protecting K-Country. Call them to learn about current campaigns. Their volunteer Trail Care group needs help maintaining trails. They're listed in the back of this book, under *Info Sources*.

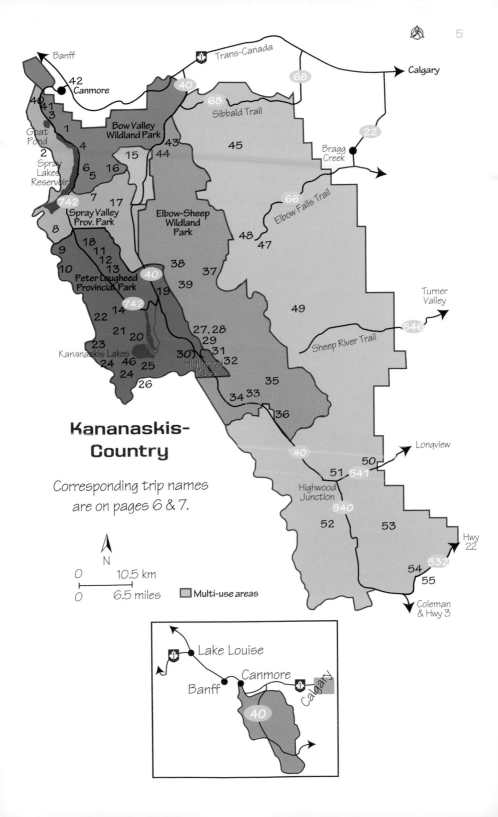

5

Banff
42 Canmore
40
41
3
Goat
Pond
1
Bow Valley
Wildland Park
Trans-Canada
40
68
Calgary
68
Sibbald Trail
2
Spray
Lakes
Reservoir
4
15
43
44
45
Bragg
Creek
22
6
5
16
7
17
742
Spray Valley
Prov. Park
Elbow-Sheep
Wildland
Park
66
Elbow Falls Trail
48 47
8
9
18
11
12
13
38
37
39
Turner
Valley
10
Peter Lougheed
Provincial Park
40
19
546
22
14
742
49
Sheep River Trail
21
20
23
Kananaskis Lakes
27, 28
29
31
32
30
Highwood
Pass
24 46 25
24
26
35
34 33
36

Kananaskis-
Country

Corresponding trip names
are on pages 6 & 7.

N

0   10.5 km
0   6.5 miles   Multi-use areas

40
50
51 541
Highwood
Junction
940
Longview

52
53
Hwy
22
54 532
55
Coleman
& Hwy 3

Lake Louise
Canmore
Banff   Calgary
40

Trips at a Glance   *Trips in each category are listed according to geographic location: starting in the north and moving roughly from west to east, then south. After the trip name, the round-trip distance is listed, followed by the elevation gain.*

Dayhikes & Backpack Trips

1	Middle Sister	19 km	(11.8 mi)	/	1419 m	(4654 ft)
2	Old Goat Glacier	10.5 km	(6.5 mi)	/	620 m	(2034 ft)
3	Three Sisters Pass	6 km	(3.7 mi)	/	610 m	(2000 ft)
4	West Wind Pass	6 km	(3.7 mi)	/	378 m	(1240 ft)
5	Sparrowhawk Tarns	10 km	(6.2 mi)	/	680 m	(2230 ft)
6	Read's Tower	9.1 km	(5.6 mi)	/	1125 m	(3590 ft)
7	Buller Passes	14 km	(8.6 mi)	/	670 m	(2198 ft)
8	Tent Ridge	10.6 km	(6.6 mi)	/	780 m	(2560 ft)
9	Birdwood Traverse	18.3 km	(11.3 mi)	/	620 m	(2034 ft)
10	Burstall Pass	15 km	(9.3 mi)	/	470 m	(1542 ft)
11	Chester Lake	9 km	(5.6 mi)	/	315 m	(1030 ft)
12	Headwall Lakes	14 km	(8.7 mi)	/	430 m	(1410 ft)
13	James Walker Creek	17 km	(10.5 mi)	/	510 m	(1673 ft)
14	Black Prince Cirque	10 km	(6.2 mi)	/	590 m	(1934 ft)
15	Mt. Allan	14.4 km	(8.9 mi)	/	1314 m	(4309 ft)
16	Memorial Lakes	16 km	(10 mi)	/	759 m	(2490 ft)
17	Galatea Lakes	17 km	(10.5 mi)	/	670 m	(2198 ft)
18	Rummel Lake	8.6 km	(5.3 mi)	/	355 m	(1164 ft)
19	King Creek Ridge	7 km	(4.3 mi)	/	729 m	(2390 ft)
20	Mt. Indefatigable	7.6 km	(4.7 mi)	/	920 m	(3018 ft)
21	Invincible Lake	14 km	(8.7 mi)	/	635 m	(2082 ft)
22	North Kananaskis Pass	34.4 km	(21.3 mi)	/	660 m	(2165 ft)
23	South Kananaskis Pass	24.8 km	(15.4 mi)	/	610 m	(2000 ft)
24	Northover Ridge	33.7 km	(20.9 mi)	/	1180 m	(3870 ft)
25	Rawson Lake	7.8 km	(4.8 mi)	/	300 m	(984 ft)
26	Elk Lakes / Petain Basin	29.4 km	(18.2 mi)	/	846 m	(2775 ft)
27	Elbow Lake / Piper Pass	19.2 km	(11.9 mi)	/	617 m	(2024 ft)
28	Tombstone Lakes	22.1 km	(13.7 mi)	/	545 m	(1988 ft)
29	Rae Lake	17.2 km	(10.7 mi)	/	366 m	(1200 ft)
30	Pocaterra Ridge	9.3 km	(5.8 mi)	/	550 m	(1804 ft)
31	Ptarmigan Cirque	4.5 km	(2.8 mi)	/	214 m	(702 ft)
32	Little Arethusa	5.4 km	(3.3 mi)	/	559 m	(1832 ft)

Shoulder-Season Dayhikes

En route to North Kananaskis Pass (Trip 22)

Mist Mtn, from Mist Ridge (Trip 35)

Shoulder-Season Hiking

Mid-July through mid-October is prime hiking season in the Rockies. That's when alpine trails will most likely be snow-free. Shoulder-season trails are at lower elevations where strong sun exposure allows snow-free hiking earlier and later in the year: perhaps starting in late March, often continuing into November. Shoulder-season options are fewer and shorter than the choices available to you in summer, but some offer stirring scenery.

Frontcountry Camping

K-Country has several vehicle-accessible campgrounds. After April 1, you can reserve sites at Bolton Creek campground, in Peter Lougheed Park, by calling 1-866-366-2267. The reservation fee is non-refundable. Sites at other campgrounds (except those set aside for groups) are available first come-first, first-served. Most sites accommodate two tents. Visit www.kananaskiscountrycampgrounds.com for details.

Overflow camping is available at Pocaterra campground near the junction of Hwy 40 and Kananaskis Lakes Trail. The luxurious, privately owned Mt. Kidd RV Park, near Ribbon Creek, is more expensive. To reserve, call (403) 591-7700 or visit www.mountkiddrv.com.

Backcountry Camping

You need a permit to pitch your tent at a backcountry campground in K-Country. The per-person, per-night permit fee applies to anyone age 16 or older. You'll also have to pay an administration fee. If you plan your entire summer's backpack trips and book them all at the same time, you'll only pay the admin fee once. You can reserve up to a year in advance. Permits are available at the Barrier Lake, Peter Lougheed Provincial Park, and Elbow Valley visitor information centres. To purchase your permit via phone and credit card, and receive it via fax, call (403) 678-3136, (You can reach this number toll-free by first dialing 310-0000, if calling from within Alberta.) Need to change or cancel your reservation? They'll ding you for another reservation fee, but they'll refund your permit fee.

All the sites at backcountry campgrounds are reservable. By early summer, those at Elbow Lake, The Forks, Three Isle Lake, Aster Lake, Turbine Canyon, Ribbon Lake, and west shore of Upper Kananaskis Lake, tend to be fully booked for the season's remaining weekends. So reservations are a necessary form of trip insurance. Hey, the world's just too crowded.

Northover Ridge (Trip 24)

Maps, Elevations, Distances

There is no definitive source for accurate trail distances and elevations in K-Country. Maps, brochures, and trail signs state conflicting figures more often than they agree. But the discrepancies are usually small. And most hikers don't care whether an ascent is 715 m (2345 ft) or 720 m (2362 ft), or a trail is 8.7 km (5.4 mi) or 9 km (5.6 mi). Still, we made a supreme effort to ensure accuracy. Our directions are also precise—written in a way that should help you visualize the terrain without referring to a map.

You might want topo maps, however, for several reasons. (1) After reaching a summit, say Tent Ridge (Trip 8), a topo map will enable you to interpret the surrounding geography. (2) On particularly rough, long hikes, such as Northover Ridge (Trip 24), a topo map will make it even easier to follow our directions. (3) If you're intrigued by the country through which you're hiking, a topo map ensures a more fulfilling experience.

The Surveys & Mapping Branch of the Department of Energy, Mines and Resources (DEMR) prints 1:50 000 topographic maps covering the province. They're sold at outdoor shops and bookstores. We've listed the applicable DEMR topo maps for each trip in this book. These maps can be frustrating, however, because DEMR doesn't update all the information, such as trail locations. Narrower, less popular trails are not always indicated, even though the trails themselves are distinct on the ground. DEMR maps are also expensive, and you'll often need two or three for a single backpack trip.

Gem Trek Publishing prints several topographic maps for K-Country, as well as the national parks. We list the appropriate one for each trip. The contour intervals are 25 or 40 meters. All trails and distances are indicated. Their maps are printed on water- and tear-resistant paper. They're the most helpful maps for hikers. Buying one Gem Trek map saves you the expense of several DEMR maps. They're sold at outdoor shops, bookstores, and park info centres.

Friends of Kananaskis Country, in partnership with Alberta Tourism, Parks, Recreation and Culture, publishes brochures for K-Country areas.

Elk

They cost a couple dollars apiece. Each has a topo map, as well as a chart listing trails, distances, elevation gains, and trailhead access. The maps, however, are so small that they're no more helpful than a sketch.

Modestly-priced Alberta road maps are available at Tourist Info Centres in towns and cities throughout the province. If you live out-of-province, Travel Alberta (open weekdays, 8:30 a.m. to 5 p.m. MST) will mail you a free Alberta road map. Call 1-800-661-8888 from anywhere in North America, or (403) 678-5277 from overseas.

Summit cairn, Junction Hill (Trip 51)

Carry a Compass

Left and *right* are relative. Any hiking guidebook relying solely on these inadequate and potentially misleading terms should be shredded and dropped into a recycling bin. You'll find all the *On Foot* descriptions in this book include frequent compass directions. That's the only way to precisely, accurately, reliably guide a hiker.

What about GPS? Compared to a compass, GPS units are heavier, bulkier, more fragile, more complex, more time consuming, occasionally foiled by vegetation or topography, dependent on batteries, and way more expensive.

Keep in mind that the compass directions provided in this book are of use only if you're carrying a compass. Granted, our route descriptions are so detailed, you'll rarely have to check your compass. But bring one anyway, just in case. A compass is required hiking equipment—anytime, anywhere, regardless of your level of experience, or your familiarity with the terrain.

Clip your compass to the shoulder strap of your pack, so you can glance at it quickly and easily. Even if you never have to rely on your compass, occasionally checking it will strengthen your sense of direction—an enjoyable, helpful, and conceivably life-saving asset.

Keep in mind that our stated compass directions are always in reference to true north. In the Canadian Rockies, that's 19° left of (counterclockwise from) magnetic north. If that puzzles you, read your compass owner's manual.

Invincible Lake and Spray Mountains

Placate the Weather Gods

The volatility of the Rocky Mountain climate will have you building shrines to placate the weather gods.

Summer is pitifully short. Don't count on more than two-and-a-half months of high-country hiking. Alpine passes can be blanketed in white until late July. Snowfall is possible on any day, and likely at higher elevations after August.

We've included sixteen shoulder-season trips that enable you to hike as early as April and as late as November. These trails are snow-free sooner and longer than others, because they're east of the Front Range, at low elevation, exposed to frequent wind and ample sunlight.

For weather forecasts and trail-condition reports, contact the Barrier Lake, Peter Lougheed Provincial Park, or Elbow Valley visitor information centres. They're listed in the back of this book, under *Info Sources*.

Regardless of the forecast, always be prepared for heavy rain, harsh wind, plummeting temperatures, sleet, hail: the whole miserable gamut. Likewise, allow for the possibility of scorching sun and soaring temperatures. The weather can change dramatically, with alarming speed. A clear sky at dawn is often filled with ominous black clouds by afternoon. Storms can dissipate equally fast.

Statistics indicate that, throughout the Canadian Rockies, you can expect a third of summer days to be rainy. The average monthly maximum and minimum temperatures reveal the following. In June, highs along the Front Range (the eastern edge of the Rockies) reach about 20 C (67 F), and the lows stay just above freezing. July is usually the hottest month. August can be almost as hot as July, but generally isn't. September tends to be slightly warmer than May. Summer highs in the Rockies average 24° C (75° F), lows average 7° C (45° F). By September, highs in the Rockies are about 17° C (65° F), while the lows hover just above freezing.

Fall is touted by many as the ideal time to hike in the Rockies. Bugs are absent then, weekend crowds diminish, larch trees turn golden. Most of the trips in this book should be hikeable until early October. But the days are shorter, the nights noticeably colder. We prefer the long days and warm nights of mid-summer.

Wilderness Ethics

We hope you're already conscientious about respecting nature and other people. If not, here's how to pay off some of your karmic debt load:

Let wildflowers live. They blossom for only a few fleeting weeks. Uprooting them doesn't enhance your enjoyment, and it prevents others from seeing them at all. We've heard parents urge a string of children to pick as many different-colored flowers as they could find. It's a mistake to teach kids to entertain themselves by pillaging nature.

Give the critters a break. The wilderness isn't a zoo. The animals are wild. Recognize that this is their home, and you are an uninvited guest. Behave accordingly. Allow all of them plenty of space. Most are remarkably tolerant of people, but approaching them to take a photograph is harassment and can be dangerous. Some elk, for example, appear docile but can severely injure you. Approaching any bear is suicidal. Read our *Bears* section.

Stay on the trail. Shortcutting causes erosion. It doesn't save time on steep ascents, because you'll soon be slowing to catch your breath. On a steep descent, it increases the likelihood of injury. When hiking cross-country in a group, spread out to soften your impact.

Roam meadows with your eyes, not your boots. Again, stay on the trail. If it's braided, follow the main path. When you're compelled to take a photo among wildflowers, try to walk on rocks.

Basin beneath Mt. Bogart (Trip 5)

Leave no trace. Be aware of your impact. Travel lightly on the land. At campgrounds, limit your activity to areas already denuded. After a rest stop, and especially after camping, take a few minutes to look for and obscure any evidence of your stay. Restore the area to its natural state. Remember: tents can leave scars. Pitch yours on an existing tentsite whenever possible. If none is available, choose a patch of dirt, gravel, pine needles, or maybe a dried-up tarn. Never pitch your tent on grass, no matter how appealing it looks. If you do, and others follow, the grass will soon be gone.

Avoid building fires. A few backcountry campgrounds in K-Country supply firewood for established fire pits. Even where allowed, however, fires are a luxury, not a necessity. Don't plan to cook over a fire; it's inefficient and wasteful. If you pack food that requires cooking, bring a stove. If you must indulge in a campfire, keep it small. Use an existing fire ring made of rocks. If no rings are present—which unfortunately is rare—build yours on mineral soil or gravel, not in the organic layer. Never scorch meadows. Below a stream's high-water line is best. Garbage with metal or plastic content will not burn; pack it all out. Limit your wood gathering to deadfall about the size of your forearm. Wood that requires effort (breaking, chopping, dragging) is part of the scenery; let it be. After thoroughly dousing your fire, dismantle the fire ring and scatter the ashes. Keep in mind that untended and unextinguished campfires are the prime cause of forest fires.

Be quiet at backcountry campgrounds. Most of us are out there to enjoy tranquillity. If you want to party, go to a pub.

Pack out everything you bring. Never leave a scrap of trash anywhere. This includes toilet paper, nut shells, even cigarette butts. People who drop butts in the wilderness are buttheads. They're buttheads in the city too, but it's worse in the wilds. Fruit peels are also trash. They take years to decompose, and wild animals won't eat them. If you bring fruit on your hike, you're responsible for the peels. And don't just pack out *your* trash. Leave nothing behind, whether you brought it or not. Clean up after others. Don't be hesitant or oblivious. Be proud. Keep a small plastic bag handy, so picking up trash will be a habit instead of a pain. It's infuriating and disgusting to see what people toss on the trail. Often the tossing is mindless, but sometimes it's intentional. Anyone who leaves a pile of toilet paper and unburied feces should have their nose rubbed in it.

Poop without impact. Use the outhouses at trailheads and campgrounds whenever possible. Don't count on them being stocked with toilet paper; always pack your own in a plastic bag. If you know there's a campground ahead, try to wait until you get there.

In the wilds, choose a site at least 60 m (66 yd) from trails and water sources. Ground that receives sunlight part of the day is best. Use a trowel to dig a small cat hole—10 to 20 cm (4 to 8 inches) deep, 10 to 15 cm (4 to 6 inches) wide—in soft, dark, biologically active soil. Afterward, throw a handful of dirt into the hole, stir with a stick to speed decomposition, replace your diggings, then camouflage the site. Pack out used toilet paper in a plastic bag. You can drop the paper (not the plastic) in the next outhouse you pass. Always clean your hands with anti-bacterial moisturizing lotion. It's sold in drugstores.

Urinate off trail, well away from water sources and tent sites. The salt in urine attracts animals. They'll defoliate urine-soaked vegetation, so aim for dirt or pine needles.

Keep streams and lakes pristine. When brushing your teeth or washing dishes, do it well away from water sources and tentsites. Use only biodegradable soap. Carry water far enough so the waste water will percolate through soil and break down without directly polluting the wilderness water. Scatter waste water widely. Even biodegradable soap is a pollutant; keep it out of streams and lakes. On short backpack trips, you shouldn't need to wash clothes or yourself. If necessary, rinse your clothes or splash yourself off—without soap.

Mt. Kidd, from Highway 40

Respect the reverie of other hikers. On busy trails, don't feel it's necessary to communicate with everyone you pass. Most of us are seeking solitude, not a social scene. A simple greeting is sufficient to convey good-will. Obviously, only you can judge what's appropriate at the time. But it's usually presumptuous and annoying to blurt out advice without being asked. "Boy, have you got a long way to go." "The views are much better up there." "Be careful, it gets rougher." If anyone wants to know, they'll ask. Some people are sly. They start by asking where you're going, so they can tell you all about it. Offer unsolicited information only to warn other hikers about conditions ahead that could seriously affect their trip.

Leave Your Itinerary

Even if you're hiking in a group, and especially if you're going solo, it's prudent to leave your itinerary in writing with someone reliable. Agree on precisely when they should alert the authorities if you have not returned or called. Be sure to follow through. Forgetting to tell your contact person that you've safely completed your trip would result in an unnecessary, possibly expensive search. You might be billed for it. And a rescue team could risk their lives trying to find you.

Hiking With Your Dog

Dogs are allowed throughout K-Country—in day-use areas, frontcountry campgrounds, backcountry campgrounds, and on backcountry trails—but must be leashed at all times. This could change, however, because dogs remain a controversial issue. Confirm current dog policies at the visitor information centres. They're listed in the back of this book, under *Info Sources*.

Even if K-Country continues to allow dogs on trails, bring yours hiking only after serious consideration.

Most dog owners believe their pets are angelic. But other people rarely agree, especially hikers confined overnight in a backcountry campground where someone's brought a dog. The reasons are numerous. A barking dog can be outrageously annoying. A curious dog, even if friendly, can be a nuisance. An untrained dog, despite its owner's hearty reassurance that "he won't hurt you," can be frightening. Many owners ignore their responsibility to keep dogs from polluting streams and lakes, or fouling campgrounds.

Dogs in the backcountry are a danger to themselves. For example, they're likely to be spiked by porcupines that prowl campgrounds at night. Even worse, they can endanger their owners and other hikers, because dogs infuriate bears. If a dog runs off, it might reel a bear back with it.

If you must hike with your dog, never unleash it.

Physical Capability

Until you gain experience judging your physical capability and that of your companions, these guidelines might be helpful. Anything longer than an 11-km (7-mi) round-trip dayhike can be very taxing for someone who doesn't hike regularly. A 425-m (1400-ft) elevation gain in that distance is challenging but possible for anyone in average physical condition. Very fit hikers are comfortable hiking 18 km (11 mi) or more and gaining 950-plus meters (3100-plus feet) in a single day.

Backpacking 18 km (11 mi) in two days is a reasonable goal for most beginners. Hikers who backpack a couple times a season can enjoyably manage 27 km (17 mi) in two days. Avid backpackers should find 38 km (24 mi) in two days no problem. On three- to five-day trips, a typical backpacker prefers not to push beyond 16 km (10 mi) a day. Remember: it's always safer to underestimate your limits.

Watch for moose in boggy, marshy areas.

Wildlife

It's possible to see all kinds of animals—big and small—throughout the Canadian Rockies. Deer, chipmunks, squirrels, raccoons, skunks, bats and owls, you might expect. But also be on the lookout for eagles, elk, mountain goats, bighorn sheep, moose, coyotes, black bears and grizzlies. In the evening, watch for porcupines waddling out of the forest and beavers cruising ponds. On alpine trails, you're likely to see pikas and marmots. It's a rare and fortunate hiker who glimpses a wolf, wolverine, or cougar.

Ticks

Ticks are vile, insidious creatures, but slow and easily thwarted if you're vigilant. In the Canadian Rockies, they're active from early April to mid-June.

Look at your pinky fingernail. Wood ticks are generally smaller than that. They have dark, reddish-brown bodies with eight legs. Their protruding mouths have barbs too small to see. Ticks are arachnids but lack the speed and seeming intelligence of spiders. They climb onto grass and shrubs. When an animal or a hiker brushes past, the tick slides off the vegetation and clings to its victim. It spends three or more hours crawling upward, searching for moist flesh. Upon choosing a drilling site, it secretes a kind of glue, then bites—painlessly, unnoticed—and begins sucking blood. It drops off when gorged.

Mountain goat in Three Lakes Valley (Trip 11)

A tick bite can cause Rocky Mountain spotted fever or tick paralysis. Neither has been reported in the Canadian Rockies for many years. Lyme disease is not yet evident here. Ticks don't transmit disease immediately upon biting; it takes hours.

Spotted fever is potentially fatal. Symptoms include fever, headache, chills, muscular pain, coughing, and a spreading rash. Symptoms of tick paralysis are numbness, drowsiness and loss of coordination, all of which can disappear soon after the tick is removed. If you suspect any of these maladies, see a doctor fast. With early detection, antibiotics are highly effective. But not all ticks carry disease. Even the carriers don't transmit disease immediately upon biting; it takes hours.

Learn to recognize tick habitat. They thrive on sunny, grassy slopes below 2000 m (6560 ft), especially those frequented by large mammals such as deer, elk or bighorn sheep. The Mt. Lady Macdonald (Trip 42), Bull Creek Hills (Trip 50), and Junction Hill (Trip 51) trails cross prime tick territory. To sprawl or even sit in ticky terrain is to offer yourself for dinner. Inspect your clothing and your body occasionally while hiking. Do it again thoroughly at day's end. Ticks will favour your groin, armpits, neck and scalp, but can bite almost anywhere. Ask a companion to check your head and back. If you're hiking with a dog, inspect it as well. Dogs can transfer ticks to people and into your vehicle or home.

Finding and removing ticks before they bite is easy. If you discover one burrowed into your skin, the sooner you detach it, the safer you are. Let a doctor do this. If you attempt it yourself, forget about suffocating the tick

Grizzly bear

with Vaseline, or burning its butt with a match. You'll only make the tick regurgitate and defecate, increasing the likelihood of disease transmission. Don't use normal tweezers; they're too big and might crush the tick, spurting its gut contents into your wound. And don't use your fingers, or you might contaminate whatever else you touch. If you do touch it, wash your hands afterward.

You want to remove the entire tick—mouth and all. Use fine-pointed sliver grippers, or a specialized tick-removal tool. Gently hold the tick by its mouth without grabbing or squeezing the body. Lightly, steadily, pull it directly back until your skin "tents." Hold it there, perhaps several seconds, until the tick lets go. If its mouth breaks off and remains attached, pull it out like a splinter. Drop the tick into an empty film canister along with a damp scrap of paper to keep it hydrated, in case your doctor wants a laboratory analysis. Clean your tick removal tool. Wash your wound with soap and water, rub it with an antiseptic wipe, then bandage it. Record the date and time you were bitten. Monitor yourself for signs of disease.

Bears

Bears are rarely a problem in the Canadian Rockies. But oblivious hikers can endanger themselves, other people, and the bears. If you're prepared for a bear encounter and know how to prevent one, you can hike confidently, secure in the understanding that bears pose little threat.

Black bear

Only about 50 grizzly bears roam K-Country. There are many more black bears here, but no study has accurately estimated the number. You're more likely to see a bear while driving Hwy 40 than while hiking most backcountry trails. The visitor information centres (listed in the back of this book, under *Info Sources*) post trail reports that include bear warnings and closures. Check these before your trip; adjust your plans accordingly.

Grizzlies and blacks can be difficult for even an inexperienced observer to tell apart. Both species range in colour from nearly white to cinnamon to black. Full-grown grizzlies are much bigger, but a young grizzly can resemble an adult black bear, so size is not a good indicator. The most obvious differences are that grizzlies have a dished face; big, muscular shoulder humps; and long, curved front claws. Blacks have a straight face; no hump; and shorter, less visible front claws. Grizzlies are potentially more dangerous than black bears, although a black bear sow with cubs can be just as aggressive. Be wary of all bears.

Any bear might attack when surprised. If you're hiking, and forest or brush limits your visibility, you can prevent surprising a bear by making noise. Bears hear about as well as humans. Most are as anxious to avoid an encounter as you are. If you warn them of your presence before they see you, they'll usually clear out. So use the most effective noisemaker: your voice. Shout loudly. Keep it up. Don't be embarrassed. Be safe. Yell louder near streams, so your voice carries over the competing noise. Sound off more frequently when hiking into the wind. That's when bears are least able to hear or smell you coming.

Bears' strongest sense is smell. They can detect an animal carcass several kilometers (miles) away. So keep your pack, tent and campsite odor-free. Double or triple-wrap all your food in plastic bags. Avoid smelly foods, especially meat and fish. On short backpack trips, consider eating only fresh foods that require no cooking or cleanup. If you cook, do it as far as possible from where you'll be sleeping. Never cook in or near your tent; the fabric might retain odor. Use as few pots and dishes as you can get by with. Be fastidious when you wash them. At night, hang all your food, trash, and anything else that smells (cooking gear, sunscreen, bug repellent, toothpaste) out of bears' reach. Use the metal food-caches provided at some provincial-park backcountry campgrounds. Most backcountry camp-grounds in Peter Lougheed Provincial Park have poles with cables, designed for hanging food. Elsewhere, a tree branch will suffice. Bring a sturdy stuffsack to serve as your bear bag. Hoist it at least 5 meters (16 feet) off the ground and 1.5 meters (5 feet) from the tree trunk or other branches. You'll need about 12 meters (40 feet) of light nylon cord. Clip the sack to the cord with an ultralight carabiner.

Backpackers who don't properly hang their food at night are inviting bears into their campsite, greatly increasing the chance of a dangerous encounter. And bears are smart. They quickly learn to associate a particular place, or people in general, with an easy meal. They become habituated and lose their fear of humans. A habituated bear is a menace to any hiker within its range.

If you see a bear, don't look it in the eyes; it might think you're challenging it. Never run. Initially be still. If you must move, do it in slow motion. Bears are more likely to attack if you flee, and they're fast, much faster than you. A grizzly can outsprint a racehorse. And it's a myth that bears can't run downhill. They're also strong swimmers. Despite their ungainly appearance, they're excellent climbers too. Still, climbing a tree can be an option for escaping an aggressive bear. Some people have saved their lives this way. Others have been caught in the process. To be out of reach of an adult bear, you must climb at least 10 meters (33 feet) very quickly, some-thing few people are capable of. It's generally best to avoid provoking an attack by staying calm, initially standing your ground, making soothing sounds to convey a nonthreatening presence, then retreating slowly.

What should you do when a bear charges? If you're certain it's a lone black bear—not a sow with cubs, not a grizzly—fighting back might be effective. If it's a grizzly, and contact seems imminent, lie face down, with your legs apart and your hands clasped behind your neck. This is safer than the fetal position, which used to be recommended, because it makes it harder for the bear to flip you over. If you play dead, a grizzly is likely to break off the attack once it feels you're no longer a threat. Don't move until you're sure the bear has left the area, then slowly, quietly, get up and walk away. Keep moving, but don't run.

Arm yourself with pepper spray as a last line of defense. Keep it in a holster, on your hip belt or shoulder strap, where you can grab it fast. Many people have successfully used it to turn back charging bears. Cayenne pepper, highly irritating to a bear's sensitive nose, is the active ingredient. Without causing permanent injury, it disables the bear long enough to let you escape. But vigilance and noise making should prevent you from ever having to spray. Do so only if you really think your life is at risk. You can buy pepper spray at outdoor stores. *Counter Assault* and *Bear Scare* are reputable brands.

Remember that your safety is not the only important consideration. Bears themselves are at risk when confronted by people. Whenever bears act aggressively, they're following their natural instinct for self preservation. Often they're protecting their cubs or a food source. Yet if they maul a hiker, they're likely to be killed, or captured and moved, by wildlife management officers. Protecting these beautiful, magnificent creatures is a responsibility hikers must accept.

Merrily disregarding bears is foolish and unsafe. Worrying about them is miserable and unnecessary. Everyone occasionally feels afraid when venturing deep into the mountains, but fear of bears can be tempered by knowledge and awareness. Just take the necessary precautions and remain guardedly alert. Experiencing the grandeur of the Canadian Rockies is certainly worth risking the remote possibility of a bear encounter.

Cougars

You'll probably never see a cougar. But they live in the Canadian Rockies, and they can be dangerous, so you should know a bit about them.

Elsewhere referred to as a *puma, mountain lion,* or *panther,* the cougar is an enormous, graceful cat. An adult male can reach the size of a big human: 80 kilos (175 pounds), and 2.4 meters (8 feet) long, including a 1-meter (3-foot) tail. In the Canadian Rockies, they tend to be a tawny grey.

Nocturnal, secretive, solitary creatures, cougars come together only to mate. Each cat establishes a territory of 200 to 280 square kilometers (77 to 108 square miles). They favour dense forest that provides cover while hunting. They also hide among rock outcroppings and in steep canyons.

Habitat loss and aggressive predator-control programs have severely limited the range of this mysterious animal that once lived throughout North America. Still, cougars are not considered endangered or threatened. Cougars appear to be thriving in the West Kootenay.

Cougars are carnivores. They eat everything from mice to elk, but prefer deer. They occasionally stalk people, but rarely attack them. In folklore, cougars are called *ghost cats* or *ghost walkers,* and for good reason. They're very shy and typically avoid human contact. Nevertheless, cougars have attacked solo hikers and lone cross-country skiers.

Cougar sightings and encounters are increasing, but it's uncertain whether that's due to a larger cougar population or the growing number of people visiting the wilderness. If you're lucky enough to see a cougar, treasure the experience. Just remember they're unpredictable. Follow these suggestions:

Never hike alone in areas of known cougar sightings. Keep children close to you; pick them up if you see fresh cougar scat or tracks. Never approach a cougar, especially a feeding one. Never flee from a cougar, or even turn your back on it. Sudden movement might trigger an instinctive attack. Avert your gaze and speak to it in a calm, soothing voice. Hold your ground or back away slowly. Always give the animal a way out. If a cougar approaches, spread your arms, open your jacket, do anything you can to enlarge your image. If it acts aggressively, wave your arms, shout, throw rocks or sticks. If attacked, fight back. Don't play dead.

Lightning

Many of our recommendations take you to high ridges, open meadows and mountain peaks where, during a storm, you could be exposed to lightning. Your best protection is, of course, not being there. But it's difficult to always avoid hiking in threatening weather. Even if you start under a cloudless, blue sky, you might see ominous, black thunderheads marching toward you a few hours later. Upon reaching a high, thrilling vantage, you could be forced by an approaching storm to decide if and when you should retreat to safer ground. Try to reach high passes early in the day. Rain and lightning storms tend to develop in the afternoon.

The power of nature that makes wilderness so alluring often presents threats to your safety. The following is a summary of lightning precautions recommended by experts. These are not guaranteed solutions. We offer them merely as suggestions to help you make wise choices and reduce your chance of injury.

A direct lightning strike can kill you. It can cause brain damage, heart failure or third-degree burns. Ground current, from a nearby strike, can severely injure you, causing deep burns and tissue damage. Direct strikes are worse but far less common than ground-current contact.

To avoid a direct strike, get off exposed ridges and peaks. Even a few meters off a ridge is better than right on top. Avoid isolated, tall trees. A clump of small trees or an opening in the trees is safer.

To avoid ground current, stay out of stream gullies and away from crevices, lichen patches, or wet, solid-rock surfaces. Loose rock, like talus, is safer.

Crouch near a highpoint at least 10 meters (33 feet) higher than you. Sit in the **low-risk area**: near the base of the highpoint, at least 1.5 meters (5 feet) from cliffs or walls.

If your hair is standing on end, there's electricity in the air around you. Get outa there! That's usually down the mountain, but if there's too much open expanse to traverse, look for closer protection.

Once you choose a place to wait it out, squat with your feet close together. To prevent brain or heart damage, you must stop the charge from flowing through your whole body. It helps to keep your hands and arms away from rocks. Several books say to insulate yourself by crouching on a dry sleeping pad, but we wonder, how do you do this if it's raining and you're not in a tent or cave?

Petain Basin (Trip 26)

Stay at least 10 meters (33 feet) from your companions, so if one is hit, another can give cardiopulmonary resuscitation.

Deep caves offer protection, but stay out of shallow or small caves because ground current can jump across openings. Crouch away from the opening, at least 1.5 meters (5 feet) from the walls. Also avoid rock overhangs. You're safer in the low-risk area below a highpoint.

Hypothermia

Many deaths outdoors involve no obvious injury. "Exposure" is usually cited as the killer, but that's a misleading term. It vaguely refers to conditions that contributed to the death. The actual cause is hypothermia: excessive loss of body heat. It can happen with startling speed, in surprisingly mild weather—often between 0 and 10° C (30 and 50°F). Guard against it vigilantly.

Cool temperatures, wetness (perspiration or rain), wind, or fatigue, usually a combination, sap the body of vital warmth. Hypothermia results when heat loss continues to exceed heat gain. Initial symptoms include chills and shivering. Poor coordination, slurred speech, sluggish thinking, and memory loss are next. Intense shivering then decreases while muscular rigidity increases, accompanied by irrationality, incoherence, even hallucinations. Stupor, blue skin, slowed pulse and respiration, and unconsciousness follow. The heartbeat finally becomes erratic until the victim dies.

Avoid becoming hypothermic by wearing synthetic clothing that wicks moisture away from your skin and insulates when wet. Read *Prepare For Your Hike*, in the back of this book, for a description of clothing and equipment that will help you stay warm and dry. Food fuels your internal fire, so bring more than you think you'll need, including several energy bars for emergencies only.

If you can't stay warm and dry, you must escape the wind and rain. Turn back. Keep moving. Eat snacks. Seek shelter. Do it while you're still mentally and physically capable. Watch others in your party for signs of hypothermia. Victims might resist help at first. Trust the symptoms, not the person. Be insistent. Act immediately.

Create the best possible shelter for the victim. Take off his wet clothes and replace them with dry ones. Insulate him from the ground. Provide warmth. A pre-warmed sleeping bag inside a tent is ideal. If necessary, add more warmth by taking off your clothes and crawling into the bag with the victim. Build a fire. Keep the victim conscious. Feed him sweets. Carbohydrates quickly convert to heat and energy. In advanced cases, victims should not drink hot liquids.

Staying warm on a frigid day at Headwall Lakes (Trip 12)

Dayhikes and Backpack Trips

The sink lake at the mouth of Sparrowhawk-tarns cirque (Trip 5)

TRIP 1
Middle Sister

LOCATION	Bow Valley Wildland Provincial Park
ROUND TRIP	19 km (11.8 mi)
ELEVATION GAIN	1419 m (4654 ft)
KEY ELEVATIONS	trailhead 1350 m (4428 ft), summit 2769 m (9085 ft)
HIKING TIME	6 to 8 hours
DIFFICULTY	challenging
MAPS	Gem Trek Best of Canmore, Gem Trek Canmore and Kananaskis Village

Opinion

Like satellite dishes precisely positioned for optimal reception, Canmore's posh chalets are aimed at the Three Sisters, so the image of this striking trinity comes beaming in through their cathedral windows. And all the outdoor athletes in this mountain-mad town have clambered atop the sisters. Little Sis is a climb. Big Sis is a moderate scramble. Middle Sis is a hike.

But "hike" doesn't mean easy. You'll trudge the length of a violently-gouged canyon, boulder-hop through a bleak basin, then slog across talus and scree to the summit, which lacks a full panorama because the dominant sibling obscures the western horizon. You'll ascend a cartilage-crunching 1419 m (4654 ft) in the process—mostly on a route, mind you, not a trail. You'll probably be chipping away at this chore, up and back, for at least six hours. And the exploit begins and ends with a half-hour road-walk.

So it's not a premier trip. It's a worthwhile trip to a Bow Valley icon. We've included it in this book, despite the poor effort/reward ratio, because the central sister is a magnetic destination. Her popularity, however, is due only to her membership in the celebrated sorority, her showy visage, and her convenient location on the edge of Canmore.

You're going anyway? Then go for the going's sake. Challenging workouts can be fun if challenge itself is the prize. You can earn a powerful sense of athletic accomplishment here. The terrain you'll traverse—Stewart Creek canyon and basin—is not classically beautiful, but it is feral, gnarly, turbulent, which can stimulate an active mind. It's like picking your way through the debris of a recent cataclysm: neither soothing nor boring.

Because this is a route, be more attentive than you would on a trail. Watch for the sporadic cairns, so you'll stay oriented. Guard against ankle injury by using trekking poles. Stay hydrated by carrying at least three litres of water per person. Stewart Creek is feeble and unreliable up-canyon. You'll find no water in the basin above.

Back side of Middle Sister,
at the head of Stewart Creek ravine

Summit of Middle Sister is upper right

Fact

By Vehicle

From downtown **Canmore**, at the east end of Main Street, go left (south) on 8th Ave. Cross the Bow River bridge, bear left on Rundle Drive, then ascend left on Three Sisters Drive. Where Spray Lakes Road forks right, bear left (south). At the four-way intersection turn left (east) onto Three Sisters Parkway. Reach a stop sign at the next four-way intersection. Reset your trip odometer to 0 here and proceed straight (southeast).

From the Three Sisters Parkway overpass spanning the **Trans-Canada** (Hwy 1), drive uphill (southwest) to a stop sign at a four-way intersection. Reset your trip odometer to 0 here, turn left and proceed southeast.

From **either approach**, go straight through the roundabout at 0.5 km (0.3 mi) where right leads to Stewart Creek golf course. Continue straight again at 0.7 km (0.4 mi). Beyond 0.9 (0.6 km) the road is unpaved and blocked. Park here, well off the road, at 1350 m (4428 ft).

On Foot

Follow the **unpaved road** east-southeast. Little Sister is visible right (southwest). Your immediate goal, the mouth of Stewart Creek canyon, is visible right (south-southeast). Ignore any spurs. Stay on the main road, curving right (south-southeast).

Reach a **fork** at 1.7 km (1.1 mi). The main road continues left (east-southeast). Turn right (west) onto the smaller road (chained to prevent vehicle traffic). Just beyond the chain, ignore a right (north) spur. Continue the gentle ascent west.

After passing right and left spurs, the road curves left (south-southwest). You're entering **Stewart Creek canyon**. Reach **road's end** at 2.3 km (1.4 mi),

*Middle Sister left, Big Sister right,
above Cougar Creek neighbourhood*

Three Sisters Blvd

soon ends

Stewart Creek Golf Course

weir

N

0   0.5 km

0   0.3 mile

Trail closed
May 1 to June 15

TRIP 1

Stewart Creek

Little Sister ▲

Middle Sister ▲

Big Sister ▲

1424 m (4670 ft), on the east bank of **Stewart Creek**. If you cycled here, stash and lock your bike, because the terrain ahead resembles what you see upstream: a jumbled chaos of boulders and trees.

Continue by crossing to the creek's far (west) bank. It's easy if the two planks are still in place atop the weir that partially obstructs the creek. Once across, follow a bootbeaten path northwest up to a **former road**, then turn left (south) and follow the road south-southwest.

In about ten minutes, re-cross to the creek's left (east) bank, rejoin the former road, and continue upstream (south). About 15 minutes farther, reach a fork. Right (southwest) descends to the creek. Go left (south) and ascend.

Up-canyon, follow sections of bootbeaten route and the occasional cairn. Your mission: head generally southwest by keeping to Stewart Creek's **main ravine**. Most of the year, the creek is dry in its upper reaches, so it poses no obstacle. Ignore a tributary drainage (left / south) and later a talus-filled gully (right / northwest).

Where the main ravine deepens, the hike becomes more challenging. Steep, narrow paths skirt the roughest, rockiest sections. But it's also possible to scramble directly through the **bedrock dryfalls**. Whichever feels most comfortable for you is the way forward. If you're unable to either negotiate or bypass the dryfalls… checkmate. Game over. Thanks for coming out to play. Time to the return to the trailhead.

Summiting Middle Sister

Canmore and the Bow Valley, from summit of Middle Sister

Eventually the gap between Little and Middle Sister is visible (right / northwest). Be aware that's not your goal. Your ascent route is farther: between Middle and Big Sister.

Above the bedrock dryfalls, follow the obvious, comfortable route boot-beaten into scree on the ravine's left (southeast) bank. It soon switchbacks, vaulting you above the ravine near where it pinches out at 2170 m (7118 ft). You've entered a broad, desolate **basin**, brimming with industrial-size talus.

Middle Sister is right (north) above you, about one hour distant. You'll reach it from left (south) to right (north) via the escarpment ahead (west). Ascend the talus. Aim for where you can easily surmount the **escarpment**. You'll soon see a distinct, bootbeaten route funneling hikers upward. Follow it.

Tan scree is visible on the summit ridge (north-northeast). The route climbs to that scree. A rapidly improving view of the peaky horizon is your motivation. Step onto the 2769-m (9085-ft) summit of **Middle Sister** at 9.5 km (5.9 mi). Moderately strong hikers will arrive within 3½ hours of departing the trailhead and will need about 2½ hours for the return trip.

Little Sister is nearby (northeast). Beyond it, across the Bow Valley, is the Fairholme Range. Big Sister is also nearby (southwest). Mount Lawrence Grassi is northwest. Mt. Lougheed is southeast. Numerous other peaks are visible and, with map in hand, easy to identify.

TRIP 2
Old Goat Glacier

LOCATION	Spray Valley Provincial Park
ROUND TRIP	10.5 km (6.5 mi)
ELEVATION GAIN	620 m (2034 m)
KEY ELEVATIONS	trailhead 1720 m (5640 ft)
	end of moraine 2340 m (7675 ft)
HIKING TIME	3 to 3½ hours
DIFFICULTY	moderate
MAP	Gem Trek Canmore and Kananaskis Village

Opinion

Glaciers are like dull, rusty knives. They don't merely slice the earth's skin. They rip it, tear it, hack it, leaving a gash as appalling as any wound a man ever suffered. Exploring these gaping lacerations is fascinating. This one, the hanging canyon gouged by Old Goat Glacier, is little known and seldom visited. Yet you can hike there and back in just three hours. And the trailhead is only a 20-minute drive from Canmore.

The climactic sight on this gratifying excursion is the canyon's southwest wall, which is also the northeast face of 3110-m (10,200-ft) Old Goat Mtn, highest peak in the Goat Range. The lengthy, soaring, vertical wall is much more impressive than Old Goat Glacier, which is now a tiny remnant of the implacable force that long ago slashed open the canyon.

The hike, entirely on an adequate trail, is rewarding from the start. The short, forested approach is mostly creekside. You'll soon burst into a basin beneath an imposing headwall. Then you'll ascend a steep talus slope, enjoying rapidly expanding views of Spray Lakes Reservoir and the Three Sisters massif (Trip 1). Once you surpass the trees and enter the canyon, the crest of a moraine offers a gentle ascent probing the realm of rock and ancient ice.

Before scampering up Mount Rundle's south summit (Trip 40), Ha Ling Peak (Trip 41), or Mt. Lady Macdonald (Trip 42), Canmore's three most popular hiking destinations, ask yourself: "Would I prefer solitude today?" If your answer is "yes," you're much more likely to find it in Old Goat Glacier canyon.

Fact

By Vehicle

From downtown Canmore, follow signs leading uphill to the Canmore Nordic Centre. Reset your trip odometer to 0 at the Nordic Centre turnoff. Continue ascending on Smith-Dorrien / Spray Trail (Hwy 742). Pavement

Spray Lakes Reservoir and Big Sister, from trail to Old Goat Glacier

ends at 1.2 km (0.7 mi). The road levels in Whiteman's Gap then descends south. At 10.2 km (6.3 mi) cross the bridge over the Goat Pond outlet canal. At 13.6 km (8.4 mi) pass the ranger station. Slow down. At 13.8 km (8.6 mi) pass a sign for Spray Lake West. Turn right 100 m (110 yd) farther and proceed across the dam. At 14.5 km (9 mi) turn left and follow the west-shore road past numerous campsites. At 15.8 km (9.9 mi)—just before a culvert and directly across the road from campsites 16 and 17—turn right (west) into a small clearing. At the entrance is a sign indicating that fires and camping are prohibited. There's room for two vehicles in the clearing. A third vehicle could park just past the entrance, on the right, before the culvert. The elevation here is 1720 m (5640 ft).

On Foot

Follow the trail into the forest, along the creek's right (northwest) bank. Head upstream, south-southwest. In two minutes, ignore a right fork; bear left on the main trail beside the creek. Within ten minutes, the striking wall of Old Goat Mtn is visible ahead.

About 20 minutes from the trailhead, the ascent route is in view south-southwest. It's between the prow of a cliff (left), and the forested headwall (right). You'll ascend the talus slope just left of the forest, ultimately gaining the canyon now hidden by the prow.

The grade is negligible for about 35 to 40 minutes, until a moderate ascent begins at 1845 m (6052 ft). Soon reach a creek and **avalanche run-out** beneath the headwall. The run-out might be snow-covered through July, but that shouldn't impede your progress. Angle left (south) and hop the creek. A path bootbeaten through the alders will be evident if enough snow has melted. Cairns and bits of flagging might also mark the way.

Beyond the run-out, look for a cairn at the base of the **steep slope** ahead. Close inspection will reveal that a discernible, bootbeaten, cairned path continues upward— just left of the forest, just right of the giant boulders. It initially climbs southeast. Thanks to this path, the ascent is surprisingly merciful.

At 2060 m (6757 ft), about an hour from the trailhead, a big, **solitary spruce tree** with draping branches offers a respite from sun or rain. The path continues on the grass-and-dirt margin between rock and trees. Behind you, Spray Lakes Reservoir is visible. Beyond and above it looms the Three Sisters massif (Trip 1). Another ten minutes of anti-gravity effort will bring you to the edge of the glacier-gouged

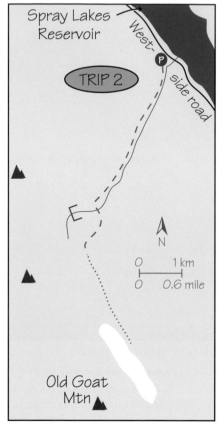

hanging **canyon** bound by 700-m (2296-ft) walls.

The path, ascending gently now, continues south-southeast beside a cordon of trees on a grassy ramp. Here you can begin to appreciate the long, towering, sheer face of **Old Goat Mtn**, on the far side of the canyon. A rain-storm will set off a dozen cascades in the mountain's natural spillways. Old Goat's 3110-m (10,200-ft) summit, however, is never visible from within the canyon. To see it all, ascend Read's Tower (Trip 6), on the east side of Spray Lakes Reservoir.

The ramp ends within eight minutes, at 4.8 km (3 mi), 2300 m (7544 ft). But the path resumes atop the nearby **moraine**. Angle right, drop into the shallow gully (snow filled into July), then gain the crest of the moraine. Proceed south-southeast.

About seven minutes farther, the moraine widens and is nearly level. It's a good place to lounge while you survey the surrounding desolation and try to fathom how the diminutive **Old Goat Glacier** once had the crushing mass to grind this canyon into existence. Beyond, the moraine crest narrows again but affords another 15 minutes of easy hiking deeper into the canyon.

TRIP 3
Three Sisters Pass

LOCATION	Spray Valley Provincial Park
ROUND TRIP	6 km (3.7 mi)
ELEVATION GAIN	610 m (2000 ft)
KEY ELEVATIONS	trailhead 1677 m (5500 ft), pass 2287 m (7500 ft)
HIKING TIME	4 to 4½ hours
DIFFICULTY	moderate
MAP	Gem Trek Canmore and Kananaskis Village

Opinion

Calling it a *pass* strains the definition. Nobody would dare plunge over the abyss into the Bow Valley unless pursued by the Mounties or an irate griz. But it's hikeable from the west. And the steep east edge of this dubious pass affords a reach-out-and-touch-it view of the Three Sisters massif, plus an aerial perspective of the Bow Valley near Canmore.

You'll ascend a mostly dry gorge violently ripped out of the mountainside by sporadic raging water. It's inhospitable terrain. Even with trekking poles—a requirement here—the uneven footing can seem a cantankerous struggle. With a monkish, nonjudgmental attitude, you'll find it a rugged but fascinating challenge. Think of this stony gauntlet as an edifying metaphor for life.

Ideally, the weather should be cool and dry. A hot day will bake your enchilada, because shade is nil and all the rocks reflect heat. Stay away during rain. If wet, the boulders will be slippery as politicians.

If you're seeking a short excursion near Canmore, West Wind Pass (Trip 4) offers more pleasant hiking and superior views. Opt for Three Sisters Pass only if you want to dial up your workout.

Fact

By Vehicle

From downtown **Canmore**, follow signs leading uphill to the Canmore Nordic Centre. Reset your trip odometer to 0 at the Nordic Centre turnoff. Continue ascending on Smith-Dorrien / Spray Trail (Hwy 742). Pavement soon ends. After crossing Whiteman's Gap, proceed generally southeast to 12 km (7.4 mi).

From the **junction of Hwy 40 and Kananaskis Lakes Trail** (50 km / 31 mi south of Trans-Canada Hwy 1, or 17 km / 10.5 mi north of Highwood Pass), turn southwest onto Kananaskis Lakes Trail. Reset your trip odometer to 0. At 2.2 km (1.4 mi) turn right (northwest) onto unpaved Smith-Dorrien / Spray Trail (Hwy 742). Continue to 51.4 km (31.9 mi).

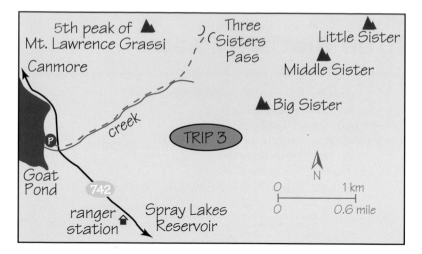

From **either approach**, park in the small pullout on the west side of the road. It's 1.6 km (1 mi) north of the Spray Lake ranger cabin. There's a sign NO CAMPING / NO FIRES. Elevation: 1677 m (5500 ft).

On Foot

From the pullout, walk 90 paces south along the east side of the road, to the wide, dry creekbed. Turn left and walk 210 paces up the left side of the deep, **rocky drainage**. Then go left, up the embankment. Look for a faint, boot-beaten path in the dryas (short, leafy ground-cover). Your general direction of travel is and will remain northeast.

Follow the path over rock and dryas, through small trees on the north side of the drainage. Watch for cairns. Near where you turn away from the creekbed, you might also notice a rougher path paralleling the edge of the embankment, but it peters out sooner.

Within 20 minutes, at 1770 m (5810 ft), cross a short stretch of rocks, then resume on path. Several minutes farther, it veers left into a dense stand of scrawny trees. At 1841 m (6040 ft) cross a short rockslide. Drop slightly off the bench to pick up a path again. At about 35 minutes, pass a short, slabby, side canyon (possible cascades) on the right. Continue ascending the main, narrowing gorge.

About an hour up, the gorge is walled in by cliffs. Large rock slabs cover the bottom. In a year of average rainfall, water will fill these **natural basins**, requiring you to work your way right, around the pools. Then cross left to pick up a path. At one point, it's easiest to go between the wall and a boulder. Soon proceed over rockslides that have tumbled down both walls.

At 1976 m (6480 ft), ascend a particularly rough, slippery section of dirt and loose rock on the left side of the gorge. After 30 m (100 ft), the steepness abates. At 2037 m (6680 ft), having hiked about an hour and 20 minutes, the route is in the middle of the drainage, near trees. Stay in the main gorge. Pass a side canyon and a rock band, both on the right. The route then favours the left side. Soon enter trees. The final ascent is north, on a narrow path in a tiny watercourse through low trees.

Big Sister, from Three Sisters Pass

After hiking about two hours, enter **Three Sisters Pass** at 3 km (1.9 mi), 2287 m (7500 ft). Trees extend nearly to the pass. Patches of dryas soften the rocky terrain. Talus flows down both sides. Mt. Lawrence Grassi is left (northwest). The Three Sisters peaks are right (east and southeast). Canmore is northeast, in the Bow Valley. The Fairholme Range is across the valley.

Ascending another 30 m (100 ft) will improve your view of the Sisters and the canyon below. Go left (west-northwest), up talus to a little bench that allows easier walking. Bear right (north) for several minutes along the edge of the bench.

Rimwall borders West Wind Pass (Trip 4).

TRIP 4
West Wind Pass / Windtower

LOCATION	Spray Valley Provincial Park
	northeast shore of Spray Lakes Reservoir
ROUND TRIP	4.2 km (2.6 mi) to pass, plus 6.4 km (4 mi) to tower
ELEVATION GAIN	378 m (1240 ft) to pass, plus 610 m (2000 ft) to tower
KEY ELEVATIONS	trailhead 1707 m (5600 ft), pass 2085 m (6841 ft)
	tower 2695 m (8842 ft)
HIKING TIME	1¼ to 1¾ hours for pass
	plus 2¾ to 3¾ hours for tower
DIFFICULTY	easy to pass, moderate to tower
MAPS	Gem Trek Canmore and Kananaskis Village;
	Spray Lakes Reservoir 82 J/14

Opinion

Most of us have no idea where the heck we are.

If we walked beyond sight of familiar features, we'd become disoriented and would soon be lost.

We don't know where nearby rivers come from, or where they flow to. What's over the next hill? Well, uh, hmmm, we're really not quite sure. If asked to describe what's visible from the nearest mountaintop, we'd be flummoxed.

We're ignorant of geography because it seems irrelevant. Who cares about geography when 99% of our travel is in automobiles, perhaps GPS equipped, on paved roads bristling with directional signs? Getting lost is unlikely, a momentary frustration at worst.

For most of human history, however, we either walked or rode horses, and to do either without meeting our demise required us to be keenly aware of our location, our destination, and what lay between. Geographic knowledge was mission critical.

Prior to books and maps, that knowledge was sometimes passed along in conversation, but often we had to earn it by climbing high, peering in all directions, and memorizing what we saw as if our lives depended on it—because they did.

Mountain passes and peaks afforded opportunities to gain invaluable insight. Today, the value of that insight has diminished, but gaining it can still be intriguing, challenging, gratifying, and just plain fun.

Plus it acquaints you with some astounding people: relatives of yours. The strongest and bravest of your ancestors. The ones who sought vantage points so their genes might live on in you.

The Canadian Rockies offer countless places to ascend in their footsteps. One of the most convenient and scenically rewarding is also among

Ascending from Spray Lakes Reservoir to West Wind Pass

the easiest: the trail to West Wind Pass and the route continuing up Windtower.

Swift hikers can reach the pass, fully appreciate the expansive view, and return to the trailhead within two hours. The trail climbs aggressively but rewards quickly and generously.

Broad, grassy, West Wind Pass invites you to lie about, gazing at sights near and far, below and above. The northeast side of the pass is sheer, granting an aerial view of Wind Ridge, Wind Valley, and the Bow Valley. Turn around, and you'll see most of the Spray Valley. Look up and there's Rimwall and Windtower.

Many hikers imagine themselves quickly dispatching the remaining ascent to the tower. Then they roll over and resume their idle reverie at the pass. But if you're fit and capable, jump up and press on, because you *will* dispatch it quickly. You'll be in open, subalpine terrain, clambering over ledges, striding along benches, gazing at distant peaks. After surmounting treeline, you'll tweak the nose of mighty Mt. Lougheed, then—ta da!—step onto the summit of Windtower.

The panorama includes Canmore, the Bow Valley beyond, and all the mountains on both sides. And if the wind isn't molesting you, it's possible to linger long up here, because the descent can take as little as 1½ hours: one hour back to West Wind Pass, then 30 minutes down to the trailhead.

Fact

Before your trip

Though the trail to West Wind Pass is usually snow-free by mid-April, it's closed when bighorn sheep are lambing: April 1 through June 15. This closure also helps prevent hikers from encountering the grizzlies that frequent the area during the birthing season.

If you intend to summit Windtower, pause before departing the trailhead. You'll save time and energy later by orienting yourself now. West Wind Pass is left (northeast), hidden in forest. Mt. Lougheed is right (east). Windtower is between them. Beneath the tower and the mountain, notice how the upper edge of the treeline appears to form an arc.

At the apex of that arc—right of the rockbands, beneath Lougheed's left shoulder—you can see the bootbeaten route ascending into the scree. If you prefer to hike rather than scramble, *that's* how far right (south) you must traverse from the pass before making any significant elevation gain to Windtower.

By Vehicle

From downtown Canmore, follow signs leading uphill to the Canmore Nordic Centre. Reset your trip odometer to 0 at the Nordic Centre turnoff. Continue ascending on Smith-Dorrien / Spray Trail (Hwy 742). Pavement soon ends. After crossing Whiteman's Gap, proceed generally southeast. Park in the pullout (right / west) just before Spurling Creek, at 18.5 km (11.5 mi), 1707 m (5600 ft).

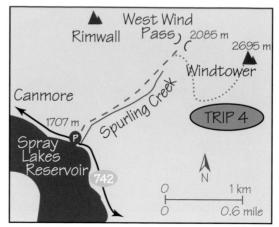

On Foot

The trail starts on the east side of the road, across from the north edge of the pullout. It ascends steeply above Spurling Creek. Your general direction of travel will be northeast all the way to the pass.

Soon attain views. The Goat Range is southwest, beyond Spray Lakes Reservoir. Break out of the trees to enter **West Wind Pass** at 3 km (1.9 mi), 2085 m (6841 ft). Swift hikers will be here in less than an hour.

The northeast edge of the pass plunges into Wind Valley. Wind Ridge forms the valley's northwest wall. The pass is between the vertical faces of Rimwall (left / northwest) and Windtower (right / east).

Just below the west edge of West Wind Pass, where the trail levels in grass, look right. You'll see a right (east) fork curving and ascending right (southeast); that's the route to Windtower. A few paces farther, ignore another right fork descending south into forest.

The Windtower route is evident most of the way to the summit. Where the path fades, watch for cairns. If the route is unapparent, carry on as long as the going is reasonably easy. If you feel the hike is becoming a continuous scramble, you're off course. Back up and find a more inviting way forward. The correct route poses no serious obstacles.

The first leg is a long southward traverse, well below and far past the Windtower summit. Your elevation gain will remain gradual except where you must surmount low, rocky outcrops. Be patient. Keep hiking generally south.

At 2260 m (7415 m), about 50 minutes after departing West Wind Pass, angle left (east) and temporarily aim for Mt. Lougheed. Begin a more aggressive ascent now, because you can do so without your feet needing assistance from your hands.

Soon reach the section of route, bootbeaten into scree, that you saw from the trailhead. After a steep pitch, the route turns north, directly toward Windtower. It's a scree slope the rest of the way, but the grade eases and remains consistently efficient. Arrive at the 2695-m (8842-ft) **summit** about 1¾ hours after departing West Wind Pass.

TRIP 5
Sparrowhawk Tarns

LOCATION	Bow Valley Wildland Park
	east of Spray Lakes Reservoir
ROUND TRIP	10 km (6.2 mi)
ELEVATION GAIN	680 m (2230 ft)
KEY ELEVATIONS	trailhead 1720 m (5642 ft)
	upper tarns 2400 m (7872 ft)
HIKING TIME	5 to 6 hours
DIFFICULTY	moderate
MAPS	Gem Trek Canmore and Kananaskis Village;
	Spray Lakes Reservoir 82 J/14

Opinion

Wandering is to hiking what scat singing is to music.

When you wander, you're improvising a jazz solo with your feet instead of your voice: *Bippity-bippity-doo-wop-razzamatazz-skoobie-doobie-bee-bop-a-lula-shabazz*. And a beautiful place to do it is the alpine cirque harbouring the Sparrowhawk Tarns.

Though it starts at an official day-use area, the Sparrowhawk trail dwindles about halfway. A discernible route continues only briefly, but that's enough. From there, you can wander all afternoon in a secretive, tarn-dappled enclave ringed by lofty peaks.

A *tarn* is a small, water-retaining depression left behind by a retreating glacier. Think of it as a high-elevation mountain pond. The half-dozen or so here punctuate a cirque that can be as vividly green as Ireland.

The tarns diminish, however, by the end of a hot, dry summer. Some years they evaporate entirely. The cirque is still beautiful in autumn; it just lacks exclamation marks. A sprinkling of golden larches will do their best to compensate.

The tarns are at the back of the cirque, 720 m (2362 ft) directly beneath towering Mt. Bogart. Mt. Sparrowhawk is linked to Mt. Bogart and is within view of the tarns, but it's 3 km (1.9 mi) distant. So why weren't these named the *Bogart Tarns*? Or better yet, the *Casablanca Tarns*? Call them what you will, just don't leave without seeing them.

Upon surpassing treeline, it might appear the entire area is visible. Not true. Proceed—on rock and grass, over slabs and ledges, along miniature waterways, past dainty wildflowers—into the cirque's deepest corners. Only by wandering can you appreciate the oddly harmonious mixture of the delicate and awesome that makes this such a compelling destination.

About halfway to Sparrowhawk tarns, you'll gaze up at the alplands between Read's Tower and Mt. Sparrowhawk. Sporting an *S* on your chest and a cape billowing from your shoulders, you might have energy to venture in that direction after visiting the tarns. If not, make mental note to return, next time following the directions for Read's Tower (Trip 6).

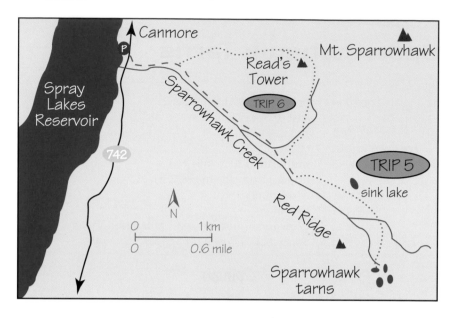

Fact

By Vehicle

From downtown **Canmore**, follow signs leading uphill to the Canmore Nordic Centre. Reset your trip odometer to 0 at the Nordic Centre turnoff. Continue ascending on Smith-Dorrien / Spray Trail (Hwy 742). Pavement soon ends. After crossing Whiteman's Gap, proceed generally southeast 22.7 km (14.1 mi).

From the **junction of Hwy 40 and Kananaskis Lakes Trail** (50 km / 31 mi south of Trans-Canada Hwy 1, or 17 km / 10.5 mi north of Highwood Pass), turn southwest onto Kananaskis Lakes Trail. Reset your trip odometer to 0. At 2.2 km (1.4 mi) turn right (northwest) onto unpaved Smith-Dorrien / Spray Trail (Hwy 742). Continue to 40.7 km (25.2 mi).

From **either approach**, turn west into the trailhead parking lot at Sparrowhawk day-use area. Elevation: 1720 m (5642 ft).

On Foot

From the parking lot, head east and cross the road. North of Sparrowhawk Creek, the trail angles up the denuded roadside slope, enters forest, and begins a moderate ascent generally east. Gradually curve southeast.

Within twelve minutes the ascent eases. A couple minutes farther, at 0.7 km (0.4 mi), 1878 m (6160 ft), bear right where a cairned left **fork** begins ascending northeast to Read's Tower (Trip 6). Ahead, the Sparrowhawk trail skirts left of a chaotic jumble of deadfall.

At 2027 m (6650 ft), about 40 minutes from the trailhead, break into the **subalpine zone**. Cliffs are now visible on both sides of the canyon. You can also glimpse Spray Lakes Reservoir northwest.

The trail fades among scattered, young trees atop an open, rocky, gentle knoll. Proceed up-canyon, generally southeast, into sparse forest. The

Looking northwest from the mouth of Sparrowhawk-turns cirque

sketchy trail soon drops to intersect a **draw** at the base of a steep, bouldery, trail-less slope.

Cairns suggest a route upward, among the boulders. It's easier to turn right, briefly follow the draw, then turn left and ascend southwest where the slope is greener, thus avoiding the rougher terrain. On the stone-and-dryas covered slope above, pass between a big boulder on a knob (left) and a talus slope (right).

Continue toiling upward among larches, on dirt and dryas. At 2280 m (7478 ft), about 1¾ hours from the trailhead, crest a **rib** overlooking a **sink lake** (east). You've entered the **cirque** beneath Bogart Tower (east), Mt. Bogart (east-southeast), and Red Ridge (south-southwest). South, below Red Ridge, is the creek that drains the uppermost tarns. They're still above you, out of sight.

To ramble deeper into the cirque, initially head southeast. The terrain is convoluted, necessitating frequent ups and downs. But navigation is easy because you're well into the alpine zone, with no trees to obstruct your view. Follow your bliss. The **Sparrowhawk tarns** are numerous, scattered throughout the farthest reaches of the cirque. Their namesake, Mt. Sparrowhawk, is north, linked to Mt. Bogart by a long, southeast-trending ridge.

After gaining more elevation, try curving east-southeast, to the tarns near the cirque's southeast wall, beneath Mt. Bogart. After that, turn around. Head east, then ascend generally southwest over slabs and ledges to the uppermost tarns. They're terraced at about 2400 m (7872 ft), below the cirque's

The sink lake at the mouth of Sparrowhawk-tarns cirque. Mt. Bogart beyond.

southwest wall. Finally, descend to the creek draining the uppermost tarns. Turn south in this lush, grassy basin. Work your way back to the rib above the sink lake. You're now on familiar ground. Return the way you came.

When you reach the open, flat area where defined trail resumes, pause. Study the slopes rising northeast toward 3121-m (10,237-ft) Mt. Sparrowhawk. Left of it, directly north, is 2625-m (8610-ft) **Read's Tower** (Trip 6). Ascending between them offers an arduous but enjoyable day of exploration.

TRIP 6
Read's Tower

LOCATION	Bow Valley Wildland Provincial Park
CIRCUIT	7.8 km (4.8 mi), plus 1.3 km (0.8 mi) detour on tower
ELEVATION GAIN	1125 m (3590 ft) up and around tower
KEY ELEVATIONS	trailhead 1720 m (5642 ft), tower 2610 m (8561 ft)
	col behind tower 2565 m (8413 ft)
	Sparrowhawk ridge 3000 m (9840 ft)
HIKING TIME	5 to 7 hours
DIFFICULTY	challenging
MAPS	page 42; Gem Trek Canmore & Kananaskis Lakes

Opinion

Comfort is a narcotic. Partake sparingly. It's sweetest not when you wallow in it, by relaxing all weekend, but when it washes over you after a challenging achievement like the completion of this circuit on the largely untracked west flank of Mt. Sparrowhawk.

Actually, Read's Tower—the centerpiece of the circuit—poses only a minor challenge compared to the other, increasingly demanding (and commensurately rewarding) options available here. After setting out on the Sparrowhawk tarns trail (Trip 5), you'll veer onto a steep route on a broad ridge leading to the base of the tower. Rapidly expanding views of the Spray Valley will fuel your motivation as you surge above treeline into trail-less terrain. Then it's up the tower—an even steeper grunt culminating in a terrific view from the tiny, airy summit. The panorama includes the Goat Range, Mt. Assiniboine, Sparrowhawk tarns basin, and Mt. Sparrowhawk.

After a quick descent back to the tower's base, your next challenge is to reach the alpine col behind the tower. This too requires a taxing, off-trail ascent, but it's a necessary leg of the journey if you want to enjoy a full day's adventure. Attaining the col allows you to circle back to the trailhead via Sparrowhawk Creek canyon, marveling at new terrain rather than retracing your steps. The col also serves as launch pad for those with the verve to march all the way up 3121-m (10,237-ft) Mt. Sparrowhawk. Scramblers think it's easy, but the 1401-m (4595-ft) elevation gain and loss (bypassing Read's Tower) is formidable.

Departing the col, you'll careen cross-country into Sparrowhawk Creek canyon to intersect the Sparrowhawk tarns trail. The challenging option here is to lengthen the day and boost your fulfillment by ascending to the tarns and roaming the virginal basin beneath Mt. Bogart. Daylight permitting, do it. Read Trip 5 for a pep talk. Or simply cruise the trail down-canyon toward whatever small but prized comforts (a bag of chips? a cold beer?) you left in your vehicle to enjoy upon returning.

Spray Lakes Reservoir and Old Goat Mtn (Trip 2), from Read's Tower

Fact

By Vehicle

Follow the directions for Sparrowhawk tarns (Trip 5). Read's Tower and Sparrowhawk tarns share the same trailhead, at 1720 m (5642 ft).

On Foot

From the parking lot, head east and cross the road. North of Sparrowhawk Creek, the trail angles up the denuded roadside slope, enters forest, and begins a moderate ascent generally east.

Within twelve minutes the ascent eases. A couple minutes farther, at 0.7 km (0.4 mi), 1878 m (6160 ft), look for a **cairned left fork**. A distinctive, **white rock** is imbedded in the trail immediately before the fork. The rock's exposed surface is about the size of two boots. Abandon the Sparrowhawk tarns trail here. Go left (northeast) onto the cairned path and begin a steep, rough ascent.

Though merely a boot-trodden route, the path is discernible. It's also sporadically cairned and flagged. Follow it generally east-northeast. About 22 minutes up, attain a grand view west and southwest across Spray Lakes Reservoir. Five minutes farther, the path fades. Look right (south). See the talus just beyond the trees? The path resumes above it, turning left (northeast) and ascending steeply.

Read's Tower, from Sparrowhawk tarns basin (Trip 5)

Emerge from forest at 2080 m (6822 ft), about 40 minutes from the trailhead. You're now ascending on scree, dryas, and tufts of grass. Though still evident, the path is now unnecessary. The way forward is simply up.

At 2207 m (7240 ft), about 50 minutes from the trailhead, reach the first **level reprieve**, behind a couple stunted trees. Read's Tower is visible ahead (east-southeast). Mt. Sparrowhawk, the blocky summit on the far, rounded ridge, is east-northeast. The Goat Range is west. Spray Lakes Reservoir stretches from Mt. Shark in the south, to the Three Sisters in the north.

Continue ascending the ridge. Proceed through a stand of trees. Keep following the crest southeast. Reach a **big cairn** where the ridge climaxes at 2.3 km (1.4 mi), 2341 m (7680 ft), immediately below Read's Tower. About one hour from the trailhead, this is a comfortable place to shed packs, relax, appreciate your accomplishment, and survey the terrain ahead. All while you savour a nip of that dark chocolate you remembered to bring.

Aiming for Read's Tower? The summit is only .65 km (0.4 mi) distant, requiring a mere 30-minute surge of energy. Drop into the **saddle**, curve left, and ascend east on the talus-strewn southwest face. The grade is steep, relentless, but strong hikers will find it simply spurs them to maintain an efficient assault. Step onto the 2610-m (8561-ft) apex of **Read's Tower** about 1½ hours after departing the trailhead. You're surrounded by mountains near and far. Prominent among them are Mt. Assiniboine (west) and, slightly left of it, Mt. Eon.

After descending back to the **saddle** immediately below Read's Tower, you can of course retrace your steps: up to the cairn, then down the ridge to the trailhead. But you're within 0.7 km (0.4 mi) of the col behind Read's Tower. To complete a circuit through the col, don't return to the cairn on the ridge. Instead, from the lowpoint in the saddle, turn right (northeast). Descend into the **basin** below the tower's northwest face, then curve east and ascend out of it.

The col is obvious: left of and directly below Read's Tower, right of the steep slope rising to Mt. Sparrowhawk. A route bootbeaten into the talus should be evident. But because the route is in a **gully** shaded by the tower, it can remain snow-covered well into July. The slope is precipitous. A long, sliding fall on icy snow could leave you in a battered heap. Assess snow conditions before proceeding.

About 30 minutes after departing the saddle, crest the 2565-m (8413-ft) **col behind Read's Tower**. From here, you can continue ascending 1.8 km (1.1 mi) east-northeast to 3121-m (10,237-ft) **Mt. Sparrowhawk**. It's a long, tiring, but straight-forward slog. Beneath the summit block, round the right (south) side. The final ascent is from the east. The new view comprises 3107-m (10,191-ft) Mt. Lougheed (north, across Spencer Creek basin).

Back at the col behind Read's Tower, resume the circuit by descending south, cross-country, on the steep, dryas- and scree-covered slope. For an aerial view of the scoured, terraced basin on Mt. Sparrowhawk's lower reaches, detour left (southeast). But return to the right (west) side of the stream that courses through the drainage you're descending, so you'll avoid a very steep thrash through krummholz below.

After dropping into the mouth of the **scoured basin**, bear right (southwest). The gentle grade allows easy striding to the basin lip, where you'll peer southwest down the final, untracked, steep slope. Below is Sparrowhawk Creek canyon. Your immediate goal: intersect the Sparrowhawk tarns trail (Trip 5). See the lightly treed area? On its far side is a nearly naked berm. You'll find the trail on the crest of that berm. Now, over the lip you go, southwest. Aim for the berm but favour the left (southeast) side of the slope.

It takes about 30 minutes to hike the 2.1 km (1.3 mi) from the col to where you'll intersect the **Sparrowhawk tarns trail** at 2010 m (6593 ft). Left ascends southwest to the tarns. Turn right to descend Sparrowhawk Creek canyon northwest. The grade is gentle the rest of the way.

Within 30 minutes, having hiked another 2 km (1.2 mi), pass the cairn marking the Read's Tower route. You're now on familiar ground. Proceed straight. The **trailhead** is just 0.7 km (0.4 mi) farther west. You'll arrive there in about twelve minutes.

Fireweed

TRIP 7
Buller Passes

LOCATION	Spray Valley Provincial Park
ROUND TRIP	14 km (8.6 mi) to Buller Pass
CIRCUIT	17.3 km (10.7 mi) including unnamed summit beyond North Buller Pass
ELEVATION GAIN	670 m (2198 ft) to Buller Pass
	1070 m (3510 ft) to unnamed summit (includes regaining losses)
KEY ELEVATIONS	trailhead 1815 m (5953 ft), Buller Pass 2485 m (8150 ft) unnamed summit 2750 m (9020 ft)
HIKING TIME	4 to 5 hours for Buller Pass
	7 to 8 hours for unnamed summit
DIFFICULTY	easy to Buller Pass, challenging to unnamed summit
MAPS	Gem Trek Canmore and Kananaskis Village Spray Lakes Reservoir 82 J/14

Opinion

Coldwell Banker, in its marketing materials, proclaims that "Purchasing a home is the most important thing people will do in their lives." Wow. What small, narrow lives they assume we're living. Surely, becoming capable, creative, wise and compassionate, by pursuing imaginative, challenging, fulfilling, meaningful endeavours, is what's most important in life. And along the way developing the confidence and flexibility to feel at home wherever we are. Judged by this loftier definition, going hiking is far more important than buying a home. So, off you go. On an adventurous, rewarding dayhike through the Buller passes, and up to an unnamed summit with a walloping view of Rocky Mountain wilderness.

You have several options here. Whichever you choose, only the first and last hour of the day will be in heavy timber. You'll mostly be above treeline, with the surrounding mountains in view. To make this a shorter, easier round trip, turn back at Buller Pass. The view from the pass—across Ribbon Lake basin to Guinn's Pass (Trip 17)—is outstanding, but the hike itself is merely worthwhile. The longer circuit, looping back via North Buller Pass, is preferable, adding a little more scenery and a lot more excitement— routefinding and cross-country travel. But if you want a panoramic vista that will blow open your doors and windows, detour about 40 minutes beyond North Buller Pass to an airy, unnamed summit high above the Sparrowhawk tarns (Trip 5). Given one of Alberta's famous blue skies, you'll see much of the Great Divide between Mt. Assiniboine and Mt. Rundle, including most of Spray Lakes Reservoir.

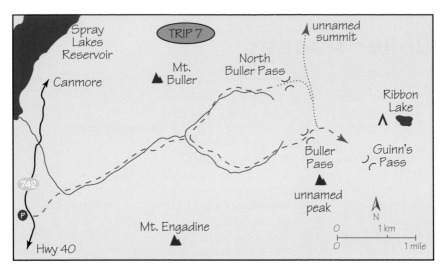

Wait until late July before attempting the circuit. A snow cornice tends to linger long on the east side of North Buller Pass. Keep in mind, you'll be hiking a defined trail only as far as Buller Pass. Shortly beyond, you'll navigate trail-less, alpine terrain. The unnamed peak demands a short, steep ascent on talus and scree. But it's not a scramble, and it poses no exposure. North Buller Pass is also steep and rocky. Descending its west side is an exercise in slide-control. You'll quickly drop to walkable terrain, however, where navigation is simple: just head down-valley. A path soon develops. You'll re-join the main trail within 45 minutes of departing North Buller Pass.

Might North Buller or the unnamed summit outstrip your desire or ability? No worries. Examine them both after crossing Buller Pass and beginning the circuit. If they look too formidable, you can about face and head home via Buller Pass. So start early intending to do it all.

Fact

By Vehicle

From downtown **Canmore**, follow signs leading uphill to the Canmore Nordic Centre. Reset your trip odometer to 0 at the Nordic Centre turnoff. Continue ascending on Smith-Dorrien / Spray Trail (Hwy 742). Pavement soon ends. After crossing Whiteman's Gap, proceed generally southeast. At 31.4 km (19.5 mi) turn right (west) into Buller Mtn day-use-area parking lot. Elevation: 1815 m (5953 ft).

From the **junction of Hwy 40 and Kananaskis Lakes Trail** (50 km / 31 mi south of Trans-Canada Hwy 1, or 17 km / 10.5 mi north of Highwood Pass), turn southwest onto Kananaskis Lakes Trail. Reset your trip odometer to 0. At 2.2 km (1.4 mi) turn right (northwest) onto unpaved Smith-Dorrien / Spray Trail (Hwy 742) and drive generally northwest. At 32.2 km (20 mi) turn left (west) into Buller Mtn day-use-area parking lot. Elevation: 1815 m (5953 ft).

Buller Pass (left) and North Buller Pass (right), from Guinn's Pass (Trip 17)

On Foot

Return to the highway and cross it. The trail begins on the east side. Immediately cross a small bridge, enter forest, and curve northeast. This will remain your general direction of travel for the first hour.

Within 15 minutes, cross a bridge to Buller Creek's north bank. The trail ascends moderately then contours for nearly 1 km (0.6 mi) through pleasant Engelmann spruce forest. At 2.8 km (1.7 mi), 1985 m (6510 ft), cross a bridge to the creek's south bank. Ascend more steeply, then enjoy a level reprieve. Where the forest opens, you can look up both valleys: right (east-southeast) leads to Buller Pass; left (northeast) leads to North Buller Pass. Mt. Buller is farther left (directly north).

At 2100 m (6888 ft), about an hour from the trailhead, pass a turquoise pool where the creek cascades into a rock bowl. Then cross a footlog over the creek's south fork. One minute beyond, watch closely for a **fork** near a tree blazed *N-S*. Here, at 3.7 km (2.3 mi), the narrow trail to North Buller Pass veers left (northeast). For Buller Pass, bear right (southeast) on the main trail. If you opt for the circuit linking both passes, you'll loop back to this fork.

Proceeding on the main trail, within 15 minutes ascend past an interesting gorge on the right and attain a view of cliffs. Larches appear in the upper subalpine zone. The trail begins curving northeast. At 2240 m (7347 ft) Buller Pass is visible ahead.

Basin below Buller passes, from Guinn's Pass

Ascending gently into the upper basin, the trail grazes a creeklet and small cascade. Then it climbs the steep, rocky headwall, gaining 160 m (525 ft), to crest **Buller Pass** at 7 km (4.3 mi), 2485 m (8150 ft), about two hours from the trailhead. Ribbon Lake is visible east, in the basin far below the pass. Behind it is 2959-m (9705-ft) Mt. Kidd. North of the lake is 3144-m (10,315-ft) Mt. Bogart.

A rough trail descends the east side of the pass. It reaches a junction in 2 km (1.2 mi). From there, right climbs south to Guinn's Pass. Left goes north then west to arrive at Ribbon Lake in 1.5 km (0.9 mi). For details about Ribbon Lake, and the trail descending northeast along Ribbon Creek to Hwy 40 near Kananaskis Village, read *Beyond Guinn's Pass* in Trip 17.

North Buller Pass

To complete a circuit via North Buller Pass, or to ascend the unnamed summit beyond it, descend the rocky trail east-northeast from Buller Pass. In about 15 minutes, near 2280 m (7580 ft), turn left (north) at the bottom of the chunky rocks, just above krummholz. Proceed onto smooth, leafy dryas. Dip into a depression, then ascend the dryas-covered slope. At 2420 m (7940 ft), hike north between **grassy knobs**.

To attain a panoramic vista atop the unnamed summit on the ridge north of North Buller Pass, continue reading the next section *Unnamed Summit*.

For **North Buller Pass**, curve left (northwest) before losing significant elevation. Ascend steep talus to crest the 2477-m (8125-ft) pass. You've hiked 1.7 km (1.1 mi) from Buller Pass. Skip below to *Circuit via North Buller Pass* for directions down-valley to the trailhead.

Spray Lakes Reservoir and the Goat Range, from the unnamed summit beyond North Buller Pass

Unnamed Summit

From the **grassy knobs** between Buller and North Buller passes, it's another 40 minutes to the panoramic vista atop the unnamed summit on the ridge north of North Buller Pass.

Drop into the **draw** below the east side of North Buller Pass. Then ascend north on the **grassy rib** right of the dry rocky gully. When grass and dryas end, keep toiling upward on steep scree until you surmount the **ridge**. Bear right and follow the crest generally north to the 2750-m (9020-ft) **unnamed summit** at the north end of the ridge north of North Buller Pass. You've hiked 9.5 km (5.9 mi) from the Buller Mtn trailhead. You're 1050 m (3444 ft) above Spray Lakes Reservoir. Spectacles are near and far in every direction.

Mt. Bogart is nearby northeast. The Sparrowhawk tarns (Trip 5) are north-northeast, 350 m (1148 ft) below you. North, past the tarns, is 3121-m (10,237-ft) Mt. Sparrowhawk, and beyond it is 3108-m (10,194-ft) Mt. Lougheed. Red Ridge is north, immediately below you. Northwest, past Spray Lakes Reservoir and Goat Pond, is Mt. Rundle. Below Rundle's northeast side, the Banff Springs Hotel is discernible. Mt. Assiniboine and her satellite peaks, Eon Mtn and Mt. Aye, are west-southwest. The beginning of Bryant Creek valley is southwest. The Tower is south-southwest. Guinn's Pass is south-southeast. Mt. Kidd is southeast. The Opal Range is farther southeast, beyond Hwy 40.

Departing the unnamed summit, after retracing your steps generally south along the ridgecrest, you have two choices. It's easier and more pleasant but longer to simply continue reversing your ascent route, dropping into

Ascending the unnamed summit beyond North Buller Pass

the draw below the east side of North Buller Pass. From there, ascend west on steep talus to the 2477-m (8125-ft) pass. The other option is shorter and entails no elevation loss but is more challenging: traverse directly from the ridgecrest down to the pass, across an excruciatingly steep slope. Traction is awkward in the loose talus and negligible on the cement-like dirt. But it's doable if you're a mountain goat. It's 1.3 km (0.8 mi) from the unnamed summit to North Buller Pass via the traverse.

Circuit via North Buller Pass

From North Buller Pass, you'll hike 2.6 km (1.6 mi)—about 45 minutes— to intersect the main trail to Buller Pass.

Carefully work your way down the chunky scree littering the steep, west side of North Buller Pass. Reach flatter ground at 2325 m (7626 ft). Continue cross-country, generally west, occasionally on scraps of route beaten into the rocky, shrubby terrain. The cliffs in this valley are less dramatic than those en route to Buller Pass.

Curve southwest, staying north of the **creek**. A snippet of trail in the creek gully leads up and out, skirting a waterfall in a small **box canyon**. A divided trail begins on the right, above the waterfall. It leads through trees to creekside willow flats. Proceed southwest, briefly through willows. At 2205 (7232 ft) cross to the creek's southeast bank. In another 1 km (0.6 mi) intersect the **main trail to Buller Pass**, just above the turquoise pool where the creek cascades into a rock bowl. You're now on familiar ground. If you detoured to the unnamed summit, your total mileage here is 13.3 km (8.3 mi). Turn right. In a minute, cross a footlog over the creek's south fork. Follow the trail 3.7 km (2.3 mi), generally southwest, back to the trailhead.

TRIP 8
Tent Ridge

LOCATION	Spray Valley Provincial Park
LOOP	10.6 km (6.6 mi)
ELEVATION GAIN	780 m (2560 ft)
KEY ELEVATIONS	trailhead 1900 m (6232 ft)
	east-arm summit 2480 m (8136 ft)
	saddle 2386 m (7828 ft)
	west-arm summit 2540 m (8333 ft)
HIKING TIME	5 to 6 hours
DIFFICULTY	challenging due to light scrambling and brief route-finding
MAPS	Gem Trek Canmore and Kananaskis Village
	Gem Trek Kananaskis Lakes

Opinion

Imagine the earth's topography is a physical manifestation of sound. Hills would be yawns. Bigger mountains would be yells. And the peaks you'll see from Tent Ridge would be screams, howls, shrieks, screeches and roars.

This is the K-Country climax. Horseshoe-shaped Tent Ridge appears to have been tossed up against it: clang! The highpoint of the ridge bellows back in the fearsome north face of Mt. Smuts. Just beyond, numerous, massive, lofty summits—including Mounts Birdwood and Sir Douglas—riot for your attention. To oblige, bring a topo map. It will enhance your trip.

Unglue your gaze from the nearby peaks on the Great Divide, and you'll overlook Spray Lakes Reservoir, you'll survey most of the Spray and Bryant Creek valleys, you'll peer into the basins harbouring Rummel (Trip 18) and Chester lakes (Trip 11), and you'll see the route up Mt. Chester.

The loop described here follows the entire ridgecrest: south along the east arm, north along the west arm. Though you'll stride effortlessly much of the way, light scrambling is briefly necessary. In particular, surmounting the east arm demands skill and cool. Scrambling up is almost always easier than down, so looping clockwise is preferable.

Tent Ridge basin—a utopian meadow cloistered within the embrace of the ridge—is itself worth visiting should you decline the ridgecrest. You'll likely find solitude at the small ponds beneath the headwall. But the ridge is a vastly more exciting venture. If you're a sure-footed hiker with a little scrambling and routefinding experience, give it a go. If you're daunted by the initial ascent, you can retreat into the basin having wasted little time.

Bear in mind, the beginning of this trip is not clear-cut, because it immediately enters a clearcut. Just follow the detailed *On Foot* description and know that this less-than-auspicious start belies the wonders awaiting you atop Tent Ridge.

Fact

By Vehicle

From downtown **Canmore**, follow signs leading uphill to the Canmore Nordic Centre. Reset your trip odometer to 0 and continue ascending on Smith-Dorrien / Spray Trail (Hwy 742). Pavement soon ends. After crossing Whiteman's Gap, proceed generally southeast. At 35 km (21.7 mi) turn right (west) at the signs for Mt. Shark and Engadine Lodge.

From the **junction of Hwy 40 and Kananaskis Lakes Trail** (50 km / 31 mi south of Trans-Canada Hwy 1, or 17 km / 10.5 mi north of Highwood Pass), turn southwest onto Kananaskis Lakes Trail. Reset your trip odometer to 0. At 2.2 km (1.4 mi) turn right (northwest) onto unpaved Smith-Dorrien / Spray Trail (Hwy 742). At 28.6 km (17.7 mi) turn left (west) at the signs for Mt. Shark and Engadine Lodge.

From **either approach**, reset your trip odometer to 0. Pass Mt. Engadine Lodge. Cross the bridge over Smuts Creek. At 0.8 km (0.5 mi) bear right. Reach the trailhead parking area—the grassy clearing on the right—at 1.8 km (1.1 mi), 1900 m (6232 ft).

On Foot

Before departing the trailhead, look northwest. Just beyond where you parked, you'll see a grassy, former logging road intersecting the main road. That's the way you'll return upon completing the clockwise loop described here.

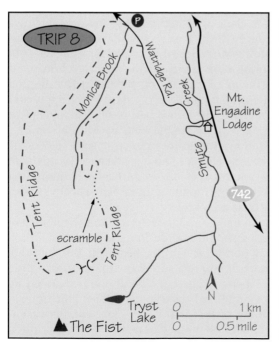

To begin, go in the opposite direction. Walk back (south-southeast) on the main road 200 m/yd to the steep, grassy, former **logging road** on the right (west). It's initially a broad, sloping swath. Ascend right (northwest) on the path bootbeaten through the grass. In a few minutes, the road curves left (south). Enter a re-growing **cutblock** and proceed south. Tent Ridge is visible west and southwest above the forest.

Quickly reach a **fork** on level ground. Straight proceeds south along the forest edge. Turn right (southwest) onto a route marked by a cairn and a crude teepee of logs. Ascend through young trees and slash. The route remains obvious, climbing the left (east) side of a draw. Spray Lakes Reservoir is visible north. Mt. Sparrowhawk is northeast.

Soon enter forest. Where deadfall blocks your progress, the route swerves around it. Ascend generally southwest. About 30 minutes from the trailhead, reach a small, level **clearing** at 2076 m (6800 ft). Five minutes farther, arrive at a **T-junction** with a well-trod trail running southeast / northwest. Go left (southeast).

After hiking about 45 minutes, overlook the forested **Monica Brook drainage**. The brook is audible but not visible. You're now among alpine larch. Go left (south) up the draw.

At 2.7 km (1.7 mi), 2155 m (7070 ft), enter the spacious, inviting meadow of **Tent Ridge basin**. Hiking time: about one hour. The two north-trending arms of Tent Ridge wrap around the basin, forming a horseshoe. Wildflowers are abundant here in early summer.

Continue about 100 m/yd into the meadow. Look left (east) along the forest margin for a distinct, bootbeaten path. Follow it left, ascending north-northeast among trees. About 10 minutes farther, at 2205 m (7234 ft), it curves right (south). The **east arm of Tent Ridge** is now immediately ahead. The ridgecrest route is apparent. Proceed upward. Spray Lakes Reservoir dominates the view behind you (north).

The grade steepens and, for the next 30 minutes or so, the hike becomes a scramble. Exposure is mild. Hand- and foot-holds are prevalent and "juggy"—big and sturdy. Crest the 2480-m (8136-ft) **east-arm summit** about

West arm of Tent Ridge. Mount Nestor and Old Goat Mountain are beyond Spray Lakes Reservoir.

On the east arm of Tent Ridge. Spray Lakes Reservoir beneath Mount Nestor and Old Goat Mtn in the Goat Range

two hours from the trailhead. It's crowned with weather-recording equipment housed in an orange, fiberglass shell. Visible across the Spray Valley are Mt. Chester east-southeast, and Rummel Pass (Trip 18) east-northeast.

Resume right (west), descending on scree into the 2386-m (7828-ft) **saddle** linking the two arms of Tent Ridge. Total distance: 4.7 km (2.9 mi). Right (north) is Tent Ridge basin. Left (south) is Tryst Lake basin. On the far side of Tryst Lake basin is The Fist. Nearby, south-southwest, is 2939-m (9640-ft) Mt. Smuts.

From the saddle, ascend west. About 2½ hours from the trailhead, top-out at 2540 m (8333 ft). This is the **west-arm summit**, the Tent Ridge climax, and the supreme hiker-accessible vantage of Mt. Smuts. A topo map is invaluable for interpreting the mountain vastness extending in all directions. A few of the highlights include heavily forested Bryant Creek Valley (northwest), glacier-laden, 3407-m (11,175-ft) Mt. Sir Douglas (south) and, just beyond it, 3097-m (10,158-ft) Mt. Birdwood.

Light scrambling briefly ensues as you continue north atop the **west arm of Tent Ridge**. About 8 minutes farther, at 2480 m (8136 ft), easily skirt a short cliff by dropping left, southwest of the crest. The ridge broadens beyond and carefree hiking resumes. A gentle ascent leads to a 2520-m (8268-ft) **bump**, about 3½ hours from the trailhead.

Near the **west arm's north end**, at 7.1 km (4.4 mi), the route angles right and begins descending north-northeast. About five minutes down, at 2380 m (7808 ft), it veers right (southeast), back toward the east arm. About ten minutes farther, at 2318 m (7605 ft), just before the route ascends slightly, abandon it.

Ascending the west arm of Tent Ridge, from the saddle linking the two arms

Go left (northeast), dropping through **stunted, open forest**. In a couple minutes, bear left (north) across a **bare slope**. Two minutes farther, turn right (north-northeast) and descend a **larch-filled gully**. Smith-Dorrien / Spray Trail (Hwy 742) is visible far below.

Two minutes farther, intersect a bootbeaten **trail** at 2238 m (7343 ft). Follow it right (east). One minute farther, the trail turns sharply left (north), continuing the steep descent. Stay on it.

Heading south on west arm of Tent Ridge

Intersect a grassy, former **logging road** at 1930 m (6332 ft). You've now hiked about 4 ½ hours from the trailhead. Turn right (southeast) and walk the old road. A few minutes farther you'll see the main road ahead (southeast) and the trailhead parking area just beyond. Swift striders complete the 10.6-km (6.6-mi) loop in about 4¾ hours.

TRIP 9
Birdwood Traverse

LOCATION	Spray Valley Provincial Park
SHUTTLE TRIP	18.3 km (11.3 mi)
ELEVATION GAIN	620 m (2034 ft)
KEY ELEVATIONS	trailhead 1865 m (6117 ft)
	Smuts Pass 2335 m (7660 ft)
	Birdwood Pass 2460 m (8069 ft)
HIKING TIME	8 to 9 hours
DIFFICULTY	moderate
MAPS	Gem Trek Kananaskis Country
	Spray Lakes Reservoir 82 J/14

Opinion

"The universe resounds with the joyful cry 'I am!'" The musician Soriabin said it. Live with an open heart, and you'll witness it. Hike the Birdwood Traverse, and you'll participate in it. This is an exalting journey. At its climax, you'll certainly feel "I am!"

You'll hike up one luxuriant valley and down another. Between, you'll cruise through four, closely-linked passes while marveling at brazen peaks near and far. You'll dip into a virginal alpine lake basin. You'll rub shoulders with giants: Mt. Smuts and Snow Peak. You'll tickle the belly of Mt. Bird wood, whose distinctively long, northwest ridge is a K-Country landmark. The traverse, beneath Birdwood's west face, is the hidden, trail-less crux of this inconspicuous trip. Yet it's surprisingly easy. So is the rest of the route. The elevation gain is piddling in light of the astonishment and gratification it avails.

Easy is relative, however. Novices will be overwhelmed here. You must be a strong hiker and competent navigator. Though the *On Foot* directions are detailed, and the routefinding is across open terrain, bring a topo map. If you must be reminded to bring a compass, sit in the corner with your back to the class.

To spare you a long, boring tramp, the *By Vehicle* directions disregard the official trailhead, suggesting instead that you park on the road and take a shortcut. You'll start cross-country, then follow bits of old logging road. Soon tag onto the trail ascending Commonwealth Creek valley to Smuts Pass. From there, it's a two-hour, off-trail ramble to Burstall Pass (Trip 10). Trail then resumes, allowing a straightforward descent of Burstall Creek valley (photo on page 65) to the road.

You've rarely ventured off trail? Attaining the col beyond Smuts Pass, above Birdwood Lakes, is a rational but fruitful goal. Birdwood Pass is then in view, as are the alplands you must traverse to reach it. If you hesitate to

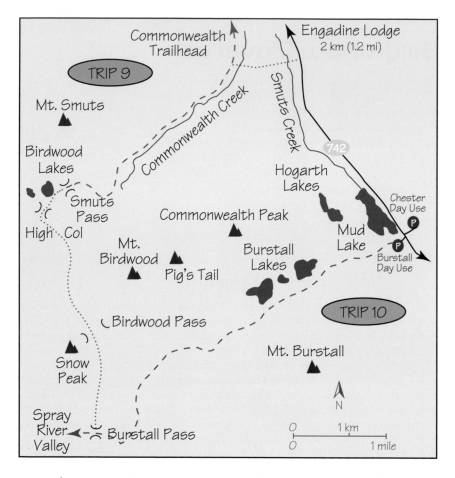

Commonwealth
Trailhead

Engadine Lodge
2 km (1.2 mi)

TRIP 9

Mt. Smuts

Commonwealth Creek

Smuts Creek

Birdwood
Lakes

Hogarth
Lakes

742

Chester
Day Use
P

Smuts
Pass

Commonwealth Peak

Mud
Lake

High Col

Mt.
Birdwood

P
Burstall
Day Use

Pig's Tail

Burstall
Lakes

Birdwood Pass

TRIP 10

Snow
Peak

Mt. Burstall

N

Spray
River
Valley

Burstall Pass

0   1 km

0   1 mile

proceed, trust your instinct; turn around. If you continue despite qualms, look back every few minutes. You'll feel more secure knowing retreat is always viable.

It's safest to wait until the high-country snow has melted before attempting this trip. Early August is a good bet. The south slope of Birdwood Pass will probably retain snow longest, and it's not visible until you're there. You can get a sense for it, though, by surveying nearby Burstall Pass and the shoulder of Snow Peak, which are visible from upper Chester Creek (Trip 11).

Finally, while most hikes are simply less genial during rain, a few—like this one—are a mistake. Rain will make the cross-country travel slippery. It will probably ruin the scenery. And low cloud might seriously hamper navigation. Save the Birdwood Traverse for when a high-pressure system settles over the Rockies.

Nearing Birdwood Pass, after traversing from the col (left) above Birdwood Lake

Fact

Before your trip

Be prepared to ford Smuts Creek almost immediately. Though neither deep nor broad, it's frigid, and the bottom is rocky. River sandals or neoprene socks will spare you a few minutes of pain—if you don't mind hauling them the rest of the day. Definitely bring a bandana to dry your feet before rebooting.

By Vehicle

From Calgary, this trip's starting point is nearly the same distance via Hwy 40 or Canmore. But the Hwy 40 approach is quicker and easier. It avoids Canmore congestion and is paved farther.

From the **junction of Hwy 40 and Kananaskis Lakes Trail** (50 km / 31 mi south of Trans-Canada Hwy 1, or 17 km / 10.5 mi north of Highwood Pass), turn southwest onto Kananaskis Lakes Trail. Reset your trip odometer to 0. At 2.2 km (1.4 mi) turn right (northwest) onto unpaved Smith-Dorrien / Spray Trail (Hwy 742). At 22.2 km (13.8 mi) pass Mud Lake parking lot, on the left (west). Leave one vehicle here to arrange a shuttle. At 26.4 km (16.4 mi)—near a yellow sign, 70 m (77yd) after the metal guardrail starts—pull off the road and park.

From downtown **Canmore**, follow signs leading uphill to the Canmore Nordic Centre. Reset your trip odometer to 0 at the Nordic Centre turnoff.

Continue ascending on Smith-Dorrien / Spray Trail (Hwy 742). Pavement soon ends. After crossing Whiteman's Gap, proceed generally southeast. At 35 km (21.7 mi) pass the turnoff for Mt. Shark and Engadine lodge. At 37 km (23 mi)—near a yellow sign, 70 m (77yd) before the metal guardrail ends—pull off the road and park. To arrange a shuttle, leave one vehicle 4.2 km (2.6 mi) farther south, at Mud Lake parking lot, on the right (west).

From **either approach**, you're now at 1865 m (6117 ft), across the main valley from the tributary valley of Commonwealth Creek. You'll start hiking cross-country, but the route is visible below. Take time to survey it before setting out.

On Foot

From the guardrail at the parking spot, you have an unobstructed view southwest up Commonwealth Creek valley to Smuts Pass. The mountain swooping down to the pass from the left (south) is Mt. Birdwood. Grassy-sloped Tent Ridge (Trip 8) is visible directly west. In the valley below is Smuts Creek. See the short section of creek with gravel on both banks? That's your initial goal. Also fix in your mind the indented clearing in the forest just beyond the creek's gravelly west bank.

Descend west from the road. At the bottom of the slope, the valley floor is soggy but hikeable. Ford **Smuts Creek** where both banks are gravel. Elevation: 1840 m (6035 ft). From the west bank, proceed through the indented clearing in the forest. It's still boggy here. Curve right (northwest). Pass a faded metal blaze high on a tree. A bootbeaten route follows the path of least resistance through the brush and trees. Curve west and ascend slightly into a regrowing **cutblock**. Go left (south), gradually curving southwest along the edge of the cutblock. Ascend to a clearing and intersect an old **logging road**.

Turn right (north), following the road as it winds southwest down to a **creeklet**. Cross the creeklet on a footlog and continue following the road. It curves west and ascends to intersect another old **logging road** at 1 km (0.6 mi), about 12 minutes from Smuts Creek. This road runs north / south. Right (north) leads to Commonwealth trailhead. Turn left (south). The old road gradually dwindles to defined **trail**. Follow it into Commonwealth Creek drainage, where it turns right (southwest).

Hike the trail upstream, along the right (northwest) bank of moss-lined **Commonwealth Creek**, through beautiful forest. Soon pass a small cascade. The trail is narrow, rooty, and probably muddy. It's on a steep slope with rock outcrops. About 20 minutes upstream, the creek narrows and is lined by willows. The trail levels and improves upon entering a willowy meadow at the mouth of **Commonwealth Creek valley**. Having ascended little, you're now at 1900 m (6232 ft). Ahead (southwest) is the headwall below Smuts Pass. Rising above it is 3098-m (10,161-ft) Mt. Birdwood. Left of it is Pig's Tail. Left of that is Commonwealth Peak.

Proceed through luxuriant meadow. Cow parsnip (tall, with white flowers) flourishes here. Re-enter forest. Ascend northwest over a rockslide. Return to forest. At 2020 m (6626 ft), about 45 minutes up-valley, reach the base of the **headwall**. The trail to Smuts Pass ascends generally the middle

Birdwood Lake

of the headwall—on heather and grass, and through patchy krummholz (stunted trees). In season, flowers colour the slope. Visible to either side are paths in talus.

At 5.3 km (3.3 mi), about an hour from the base of the headwall, reach 2335-m (7660-ft) **Smuts Pass**. Right (north) is the Mt. Smuts summit ridge. Left (southeast) is the Mt. Birdwood summit ridge. Visible southwest is a smooth break in the ridge. That's the col you'll cross to traverse Mt. Birdwood's west face. Ahead (west), in the basin 30 m (100 ft) below, is the first and biggest of the two Birdwood Lakes. The second lake is on a terrace just beyond.

Descend to the south shore of **Birdwood Lake**. An easy, ten-minute ascent southwest leads to the 2390-m (7839-ft) **col**. Visible southeast is Birdwood Pass, with its rock slabs and grass. Survey the terrain between the col and Birdwood Pass, to plan your route and look for bears. Make noise to warn grizzlies of your presence. Bear diggings are common here.

From the col, drop left (east). Contour near treeline on a game trail. In a few minutes reach rock outcroppings. Descend southwest, on the right side of a chute. About 12 minutes beyond the col, pick up another game trail. Where the route is obscure, in thick vegetation and profuse flowers, briefly contour at about 2280 m (7478 ft). An obvious trail will resume. Then head south-southeast toward the pass. Forested Spray River valley is visible west below this upper basin.

About 20 minutes from the col, reach a rocky gully. Descend it to grass and krummholz. Continue to the head of **Birdwood Creek basin**. Mount a low, slabby rib. Hike among larches toward Birdwood Pass. Cross a creeklet in a small defile. Heading south-southeast, traverse meadows. Soon hop over another creek in a defile. Ascend a grassy depression.

Assault either side of the pass—left or right. We were pulled right, toward the black wall, rather than the gray one. If you are too, climb the scree gully right of the mound in the middle of the pass. About an hour from the col, arrive atop the mound in **Birdwood Pass**, at 9.3 km (5.8 mi), 2460 m (8069 ft). Visible north-northwest, more than 20 km (12.4 mi) distant, is Mt. Assiniboine. East-northeast, below you, is Burstall Creek valley, which you'll exit from Burstall Pass.

The terrain between Birdwood and Burstall passes is the trip's most precipitous. If all the snow has melted, however, surefooted hikers will encounter no danger. From the southwest edge of Birdwood Pass, traverse the grassy, gravelly slope south beneath the east face of **Snow Peak**. Contour at about 2430 m (7970 ft). Visible northeast, beyond Hwy 742, is Mt. Chester (Trip 11).

About 15 minutes south of Birdwood Pass, abandon the plunging slope. Angle southwest on narrow, rocky, grassy ledges. Ascend about 15 m (49 ft) to surmount the shoulder of Snow Peak. It descends south, in steps. Reach **Burstall Pass** at 10.8 km (6.7 mi), 2380 m (7806 ft).

A sign here states trail distances to destinations in Banff National Park. Right descends generally west, intersecting the Spray River Valley trail in 4.7 km (2.9 mi). From there, right (north-northwest) leads to Bryant Creek; left (southeast) crosses Palliser Pass. Another trail leads west 1 km (0.6 mi) to Leman Lake. If you started this trip early, and at least four hours of daylight remain, you have time to proceed 1.6 km (1 mi) generally south along the inviting, alpine ridge to South Burstall Pass.

As for the Burstall Pass view, south-southeast is glacier-laden, 3407-m (11,175-ft) Mt. Sir Douglas. West, beyond and above Leman Lake, is Mt. Leval. North is Birdwood Pass. North-northeast is Mt. Birdwood, and just right of it is Commonwealth Peak. Northeast, beyond Hwy 742, is Mt. Galatea.

From Burstall Pass, a trail leads 7.5 km (4.7 mi) generally northeast through Burstall Creek valley. After descending 465 m (1525 ft), it ends at Mud Lake parking lot, on Hwy 742, where your shuttle vehicle awaits. The following directions are minimal. Read Burstall Pass (Trip 10) for details.

Descend the trail east-southeast from Burstall Pass. It gradually curves north into **Burstall Creek valley**. Within 15 minutes it levels, heading east through a subalpine meadow at 2131 m (6990 ft). About 30 minutes from the pass, enter forest. A ten-minute descent ends on an **alluvial flat** at 2000 m (6560 ft). The braided stream-channels often flood, but not so deeply as to prevent you from crossing. Robertson Glacier is visible south-southeast. Signs with red blazes lead east, across the flat. The trail re-enters forest and heads generally northeast. It soon widens into an old **logging road**. Follow it out to **Hwy 742**.

TRIP 10
Burstall Pass

LOCATION	Peter Lougheed Provincial Park, Hwy 742
ROUND TRIP	15 km (9.3 mi)
ELEVATION GAIN	470 m (1542 ft)
KEY ELEVATIONS	trailhead 1910 m (6265 ft), pass 2380 m (7256 ft)
HIKING TIME	5 to 7 hours
DIFFICULTY	easy
MAPS	page 62; Gem Trek Kananaskis Lakes
	Spray Lakes Reservoir 82 J/14

Opinion

Ask local hikers to regale you about favourite destinations in their coveted backyard wilderness, and Burstall Pass is likely to fulfill the promise of its name. It continually bursts through layers of ever-thickening memory and leaps off the tongue.

You'll warm up striding easily on an old road, probing a forested valley beneath pewter peaks. After hopping across (or de-booting and sloshing through) shallow stream channels, you'll ascend to a hanging, subalpine valley. Then you'll proceed up the headwall to Burstall Pass, where exhilarating mountain scenery extends in all directions. You'll see saber-sharp peaks slicing the sky. You'll peer over the pass into the southern reaches of Banff Park. You'll have enough visual stimuli to expand your emotions to full capacity.

The grassy alpine environs of the pass will prod you to explore, or induce you to lie down and let your mind walk the lush, lonesome bear haven of the Spray River Valley below. Try to keep moving. The ridge southwest of the pass is an easy, exciting, off-trail ramble where the panorama continues to unfold. In particular, glacier-chested Mt. Sir Douglas appears more imposing the farther you go.

Fact

By Vehicle

From downtown **Canmore**, follow signs leading uphill to the Canmore Nordic Centre. Reset your trip odometer to 0 at the Nordic Centre turnoff. Continue ascending on Smith-Dorrien / Spray Trail (Hwy 742). Pavement soon ends. After crossing Whiteman's Gap, proceed generally southeast. At 41.5 km (25.7 mi), immediately past Mud Lake, turn right (west) into the Burstall day use area, at 1910 m (6265 ft). This is across from the Chester Lake trailhead parking lot.

From the **junction of Hwy 40 and Kananaskis Lakes Trail** (50 km / 31 mi south of Trans-Canada Hwy 1, or 17 km / 10.5 mi north of Highwood Pass),

Burstall Pass alplands

turn southwest onto Kananaskis Lakes Trail. Reset your trip odometer to 0. At 2.2 km (1.4 mi) turn right (northwest) onto unpaved Smith-Dorrien / Spray Trail (Hwy 742). At 22.2 km (13.8 mi), turn left (west) into the Burstall day use area, at 1910 m (6265 ft).

On Foot

The trail departs the north end of the parking lot, where there are no trees. Go left (west), past the gated road, up onto the berm. Follow the berm southwest, passing Mud Lake (right). Proceed onto a gravel road curving left (south). Within 70 m (77 ft), where the gravel road continues straight (south-southeast), fork right (south-southwest) onto a narrower, dirt road. Cross another berm, this one channeling French Creek (left) into a culvert. Ignore a faint right (southwest) fork. Ascend south, following hiker signs. Just above, where a trail forks left (southeast), stay on the road curving right (southwest). You've hiked just five minutes from the trailhead. From here on, the navigating is more straightforward.

Follow the road southwest along the north slopes of Mt. Burstall. Commonwealth Peak is right (north) across Burstall Creek valley. At about 2.5 km (1.6 mi) pass Burstall Lakes on your right (north). The road soon tapers to trail. At 3.6 km (2.2 mi) cross braided, shifting, sometimes flooded stream channels in an alluvial flat. It's wettest in early summer. Expect to wade. The water is shallow, the current gentle, the bottom muddy, so it's not dangerous, just cold. Robertson Glacier is visible left (south).

At 4 km (2.5 mi) begin climbing. Ascend west through dense forest about 30 minutes to emerge in subalpine meadows. The trail bends southwest here. After a brief, level respite, the ascent resumes—south, curving northwest. Reach 2380 m (7256 ft) **Burstall Pass** at 7.5 km (4.7 mi).

Mt. Birdwood, from above Burstall Pass

North of the pass is Snow Peak. North-northeast are, from left to right, Birdwood Pass (Trip 9), 3097-m 10,158-ft Mt. Birdwood, Pig's Tail, and Commonwealth Peak. Distant northeast, beyond the trailhead, is the 3000-m (9840-ft) Fortress. South-southwest is 3406-m (11,172-ft) Mt. Sir Douglas.

Continue through the pass, around a sinkhole, to overlook upper Spray Valley. Leman Lake is west across the valley. Distant northwest is 3611-m (11,845-ft) Mt. Assiniboine.

For the optimal view, proceed cross-country, ascending about 235 m (720 ft) to the **ridgecrest** southwest of the pass. You'll see a huge expanse of Spray Valley, from Bryant Creek in the north to Palliser Pass in the south. Belgium Lake is just north of Palliser Pass. Mts. King Albert and Queen Elizabeth are immediately west of Belgium Lake. Roam the crest south, where Mt. Sir Douglas appears much closer.

If you're backpacking over Burstall Pass into Banff Park, follow cairns into a gully descending northwest. The trail is initially faint but improves as it steepens, switchbacking westward into the Spray River Valley. Intersect the Palliser Pass trail 4.7 km (2.9 mi) from and 476 m (1560 ft) below Burstall Pass. The valley bottom elevation is 1890 m (6200 ft).

Right (north-northwest) arrives at the south end of Spray Lakes Reservoir in 13.3 km (8.3 mi). Left (south-southeast) crosses Banff Park's south boundary in Palliser Pass at 6.4 km (4 mi). Straight leads 1 km (0.6 mi) generally southwest to Leman Lake, at 1935 m (6347 ft). Burstall campground is a few minutes north of the lake.

TRIP 11
Chester Lake / Three Lakes Valley

LOCATION	Peter Lougheed Provincial Park, Hwy 742
ROUND TRIP	9 km (5.6 mi) to Chester, 13.5 km (7.4 mi) to third lake
ELEVATION GAIN	315 m (1030 ft) to Chester, 555 m (1820 ft) to third lake
KEY ELEVATIONS	trailhead 1910 m (6265 ft), Chester Lake 2220 m (7280 ft)
	third lake 2460 m (8070 ft)
HIKING TIME	3 to 4 hours for Chester, 4 to 5 hours for third lake
DIFFICULTY	easy
MAPS	Gem Trek Kananaskis Lakes
	Spray Lakes Reservoir 82 J/14

Opinion

Countless Calgarians have hiked to Chester Lake. Many have done it repeatedly. It's the most popular trail in K-Country. For good reason: the difficulty / reward ratio is out of whack. A child can do it. Yet even mountaineers are moved by the splendour of the lake setting. Be thankful camping is prohibited. Otherwise a tribe of devoted Chesterites would establish a tent city here every summer.

Upon arrival at Chester Lake, most hikers stop and plop. It *is* a premier destination, particularly if you lack time or energy for a more vigourous, solitudinous outing, or if you're a parent toting infants or herding youngsters. But adventures beckon beyond. After admiring Chester Lake, persist to Three Lakes Valley, The Fortress, or Mt. Chester.

The initial 2 km (1.2 mi) to Chester Lake is on a former logging road reincarnated as a hiking and ski trail. It's broad, smooth, not too steep, quickly and easily dispatched while enjoying occasional mountain views. Above the regenerated clearcut, enter mature forest. The way finally levels out in meadows known for their dazzling, late-June display of glacier lilies and alpine buttercups. Autumn oranges and mauves are also delightful here. Approaching Chester Lake, the alps forming the cirque are visible ahead. Visual tension—stark, imposing cliffs, contrasting with lush, welcoming meadows—creates a scene of compelling drama.

Venturing north to Three Lakes Valley should be compulsory. A mere two-hour round trip from Chester Lake, it doubles the day's scenic reward. This intimate-but-awesome enclave is guarded by soaring Mt. Galatea and patrolled by stolid mountain goats. The lakes are small, just tarns really, and the third is often dry. But the first two are lovely. And the second offers a superb view of grand, glacier-laden peaks on the Great Divide. En route, you'll pass a heap of colossal boulders. Scurry onto a flat one to lounge in the sun, relish your red-pepper hummus, or evade marmots jostling for attention. Bring your rock shoes for a little bouldering.

Glacier lilies

The canyon northeast above Chester Lake leads to The Fortress—a distinctive, lofty bastille that, from Hwy 40, appears unassailable. But from this side, it's simply a moderate scramble to the big-grin view on top. Allow a full day. From the summit-ridge col, keen explorers loop back to the trailhead via Headwall Lakes (Trip 12). Even if your goal isn't The Fortress, nipping into the canyon is worthwhile. A 1½ -hour round-trip from Chester Lake allows you to appreciate the fetching, grassy environs of upper Chester Creek.

Swooping above Chester Lake's southeast shore is Mt. Chester. Where the trail to the lake crosses the last meadow, look right (southeast). The Mt. Chester scramble begins up that draw. It's a rugged ascent, gaining 834 m (2736 ft) from the meadow. If you're capable, however, you'll need no directional advice; it's straightforward. The summit panorama includes an arresting view of the Great Divide.

Fact

By Vehicle

From downtown **Canmore**, follow signs leading uphill to the Canmore Nordic Centre. Reset your trip odometer to 0 at the Nordic Centre turnoff. Continue ascending on Smith-Dorrien / Spray Trail (Hwy 742). Pavement soon ends. After crossing Whiteman's Gap, proceed generally southeast. At 41.5 km (25.7 mi)—just past Mud Lake, and across from Burstall day use area—turn left (east) into the enormous Chester Lake trailhead parking lot, at 1910 m (6265 ft).

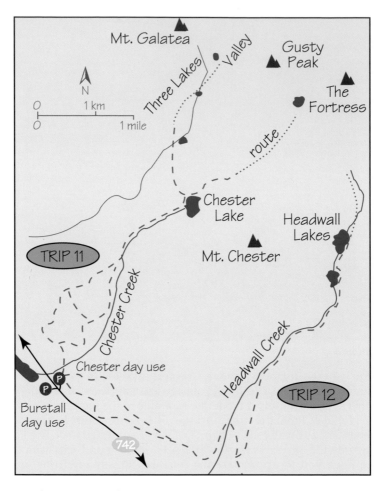

From the **junction of Hwy 40 and Kananaskis Lakes Trail** (50 km / 31 mi south of Trans-Canada Hwy 1, or 17 km / 10.5 mi north of Highwood Pass), turn southwest onto Kananaskis Lakes Trail. Reset your trip odometer to 0. At 2.2 km (1.4 mi) turn right (northwest) onto unpaved Smith-Dorrien / Spray Trail (Hwy 742). At 22.2 km (13.8 mi)—just before Mud Lake, and across from Burstall day use area—turn right (east) into the enormous Chester Lake trailhead parking lot, at 1910 m (6265 ft).

On Foot
From the northeast corner of the parking lot (above the toilets and info kiosk), follow the unpaved road northeast. Pass a gate in 40 m/yd. Quickly reach a fork. The narrow, overgrown road (right / east) leads to Headwall Lakes. For Chester Lake, bear left (north) on the broad, gravel road and immediately cross a bridge over **Chester Creek**. Likewise, go left at all subsequent junctions. The road climbs at a moderate grade through forest of primarily Engelmann spruce and alpine fir.

Chester Lake, from Mt. Chester summit

At 1942 m (6370 ft), about ten minutes up, reach a signed junction. Turn left (northwest), as the hiker sign directs. At 2073 m (6800 ft), about 30 minutes up, French Creek is visible south. Burstall Pass (Trip 10) is southwest. Just north of it is Smuts Pass (Trip 9).

A few minutes farther, bear left (northeast) at the next junction where right leads south. Your general direction of travel is northeast. At 2.2 km (1.4 mi) the **road narrows to a wide trail**. It soon levels at 2140 m (7020 ft) in a small meadow. You've now hiked about 45 minutes. Ups and downs are few and gentle the rest of the way. Meadows and trees alternate.

Descend into a large, tussocky meadow at 2.7 km (1.7 mi). Looking north-northeast you can see 3185-m (10,447-ft) Mt. Galatea at the head of Three Lakes Valley. From the next meadow, Mt. Chester is visible east. The trail then slips back into forest for 10 minutes before emerging in another meadow. Lavender fleabane (daisy shaped) thrive here.

At 4 km (2.5 mi) enter a sweeping, willowy **meadow below Mt. Chester**. The alps forming Chester Lake cirque are in view. Left (north-northeast, between Chester Lake and Three Lakes Valley) is 2985-m (9791-ft) Gusty Peak. Ahead (northeast) is the 3000-m (9840-ft) Fortress. Right (east) is 3054-m (10,017-ft) Mt. Chester. The scramble route up Chester begins in the conspicuous draw southeast. Behind you (south-southwest) is French Glacier, between Mt. Robertson and Mt. French.

An elevated pit toilet on the left heralds your arrival at **Chester Lake**. Reach the southwest shore, near a footlog over the outlet stream, at 4.5 km (2.8 mi), 2220 m (7282 ft). Fleet-footed hikers eager to explore farther will be here about 1¼ hours after leaving the trailhead.

Three Lakes Valley

From Chester Lake to the third and highest lake in Three Lakes Valley is a 4.5 km (2.8 mi) round trip gaining 240 m (787 ft). Start at the footlog over the outlet stream on Chester Lake's southwest shore. Follow the trail left, around the west shore. In 60 m (66 yd) turn left (northwest) and ascend the first of two forks. The shoreline trail leads to upper Chester Creek. The two ascending forks soon merge. Proceed uphill among larches. At 2238 m (7340 ft), about five minutes above the lake, emerge from forest and encounter an array of **giant boulders**. It's reminiscent of southern California's Joshua Tree National Park. The trail passes left of the boulders.

In another five minutes, at 2256 m (7400 ft), enter a meadowy basin harbouring a stream-fed pond. The trail curves right (north-northeast) into **Three Lakes Valley**. Zigzag up rocky steps. Attain a view southwest to Burstall Pass (Trip 10) and, just north of it, the distinctively long, northwest ridge of Mt. Birdwood (Trip 9). The slopes here are lush green, adorned with wildflowers including yellow columbine and white Sitka valerian.

Though called *lakes*, the pools in this valley are actually small tarns. Reach the **first tarn** at 2287 m (7500 ft). Round its left side to ascend a narrow trail north through a grassy depression between trees on the left and rock slabs on the right. Where the trail fades above, pick your way over the slabby hump.

About 10 minutes above the first, reach the **second tarn** at 2410 m (7900). Gusty Peak forms the valley's right (east) wall. South-southwest is an excellent view of the Great Divide. The highest peak in that direction is 3407-m (11,175-ft) Mt. Sir Douglas.

Gazing at the Great Divide, from the second lake in Three Lakes Valley

Grass and moss campion (tight, green cushions, studded with tiny pink flowers) enliven the slabby terrain en route to the **third tarn**. Though shallower than the others and often dry, this last tarn, at 2460 m (8070 ft), is a worthy goal. It's deeper in the valley, where you can fully appreciate the intricacies and magnitude of 3185-m (10,447-ft) Mt. Galatea, directly north. The head of the valley, above the third tarn, is an austere, gray, talus bowl.

Upper Chester Creek

Follow the trail left, around the northwest shore. Bear right (east), passing two left forks that ascend to Three Lakes Valley. Climb into the forest on a rough, twisting path. From here on, your general direction of travel is northeast. At 2223 m (7290 ft), drop to and cross a meadow. Ascend the grassy slope beneath the scree on the left (north). At 2271 m (7450 ft), about ten minutes up, you're among larches, near **treeline**. Chester Lake is visible below. Among many notable landmarks on the Great Divide, Burstall Pass is southwest. Just north of it, is the distinctively long, northwest ridge of Mt. Birdwood (Trip 9). At 2363 m (7750 ft), about 20 minutes up, The Fortress is visible northeast. Over the next rocky rib, you can see deeper into the canyon. The meadows here are small, delicate, exquisitely picturesque. Hints of bootbeaten path continue. **Upper Chester Creek** is above ground for only about 50 m (55 yd), at 2400 m (7872 ft). Strong hikers will be here within 30 minutes of departing Chester Lake. Negotiating the bouldery expanse beyond is no fun, but it's necessary if proceeding to The Fortress or Headwall Lakes (Trip 12).

The Fortress

About 2 km (1.2 mi) up the canyon northeast above Chester Lake, turn right (east) and scramble up steep scree to the 2710-m (8889-ft) **col**. You're now 490 m (1607 ft) above Chester Lake; 290 m (951 ft) below The Fortress. Turn left (north-northeast) and ascend the **ridgecrest**. Loose scree atop rock slabs demands attention. The ridge then widens and the angle of ascent eases. Toil onward. The angle further relaxes, but the crest narrows. Bear left below the summit crags, then angle right over blocks and scree to the 3000-m (9843-ft) **summit**. Total elevation gain: 780 m (2558 ft) from Chester Lake, 1090 m (3575 ft) from the trailhead. Total distance: 8.2 km (5.1 mi) from the trailhead. A few of the panorama highlights are Mt. Assiniboine (west), Mt. Joffre (south), the Opal Range (southeast), Mt. Kidd (north-northeast), and Mt. Galatea (nearby northwest).

Headwall Lakes

From the 2710-m (8889-ft) col on the ridgecrest leading to The Fortress, it's possible to drop east, then south down-canyon, looping back to the Chester Lake trailhead via Headwall Lakes. The day's total mileage— 15 km (9.3 mi)—makes the journey sound easier than it is. The col is extremely steep; both the ascent and descent are demanding. Most of the 4 km (2.5 mi) from Chester Lake to upper Headwall Lake is on untracked, rocky terrain. Navigation, however, should pose no problem if you have a topo map in hand, or you're an experienced cross-country rambler.

TRIP 12

Headwall Lakes

LOCATION	Peter Lougheed Provincial Park, Hwy 742
ROUND TRIP	14 km (8.7 mi) to upper lake
ELEVATION GAIN	430 m (1410 ft)
KEY ELEVATIONS	trailhead 1910 m (6265 ft)
	upper lake 2340 m (7675 ft)
HIKING TIME	5 to 6 hours
DIFFICULTY	moderate
MAPS	page 72; Gem Trek Kananaskis Lakes
	Spray Lakes Reservoir 82 J/14

Opinion

Hiking whittles away at people, chipping them down to their essence. That's why true hikers, those for whom hiking is a bright, strong thread in the fabric of their lives, are authentic, without pretense or facade. Almost never will you meet a hiker who's a monster of self-regard. Maybe that's why Canmorites are so amiable. Many can start hiking at their doorsteps. And some of the Rockies' most rewarding trails are nearby. Like this one, to Headwall Lakes.

It begins at the same trailhead that serves Chester Lake. The trip to Chester, just one canyon north, is easier, shorter, more popular, and therefore siphons off most of the crowd. Headwall Lakes canyon, however, is equally beautiful. It's just a little longer, a bit more challenging, and feels wilder. But the Three Lakes Valley extension of the Chester hike also fits that description. So, you've a decision to make. Go to Chester if you're feeling social, in the mood for meadows. Go to Headwall if you're drawn to austerity and want to see waterfalls.

Your first 45 minutes hiking to Headwall Lakes will be on former logging roads reincarnated as hiking and ski trails. Though less than lovely, they allow brisk striding and an occasional mountain view. Then you'll follow an undeveloped trail along a creek to a cascade crashing down the first headwall. An abrupt ascent then vaults you into alplands. The view explodes all the way to the Great Divide. After a rest at lower Headwall Lake, climb past the cascade adorning the next headwall to arrive at the upper lake.

Before booting it home, consider your options. The head of the canyon above upper Headwall Lake is not a dead end. It's possible to scramble to a col and, from there, either assault The Fortress or loop back to the trailhead via Chester Lake.

Looping over the col, without detouring to The Fortress, your total day's mileage will be 15 km (9.3 mi). It makes the journey sound easier than it is. The col is extremely steep; both the ascent and descent are demanding. Most of the 4 km (2.5 mi) from upper Headwall Lake to Chester Lake is on untracked,

Ascending from lower to upper Headwall Lake.
Great Divide in background.

rocky terrain. Navigation, however, should pose no problem if you have a topo map in hand, or you're an experienced cross-country rambler. Reading Chester Lake (Trip 11) will help you fully appreciate what the loop entails.

Fact

By Vehicle

Follow the directions for Chester Lake (Trip 11). Chester and Headwall lakes share the same trailhead, at 1910 m (6265 ft).

On Foot

From the northeast corner of the parking lot (above the toilets and info kiosk), follow the unpaved road northeast. Pass a gate in 40 m/yd. Quickly reach a fork. The broad, gravel road (left / north) crosses bridged Chester Creek and leads to Chester Lake. For Headwall Lakes, turn right (east) onto the narrower, overgrown road marked with a blue cross-country ski-trail sign. It snakes through forest before heading generally south-southeast. Peaks across the valley are occasionally visible.

In about 15 minutes, at 1.4 km (0.9 mi), 1966 m (6450 ft), cross a regrowing clearcut and reach a fork. There's a map-sign here. Left (northeast) ascends sharply and is marked with an orange ski-trail sign. Go right (east), following the blue ski-trail sign.

At 1.9 km (1.1 mi) intersect the road marked with a yellow ski-trail sign. Right descends west. Go left (southeast). The gentle ascent continues.

A tight curve left (northeast) rises to a junction at 2.6 km (1.6 mi), 2021 m (6630 ft), in another regrowing clearcut. Your destination, Headwall Creek canyon, is visible ahead (northeast). Mt Chester is north-northeast. The road marked with an orange ski-trail sign ascends left (north). Descend right (northeast) on the road marked with a yellow ski-trail sign.

After a short, easy ascent, drop to a **bridge over Headwall Creek**, at 3.2 km (2 mi), 2037 m (6680 ft), about 45 minutes from the trailhead.

Cross the bridge and bear left. Shortly upstream, above the southeast bank, the road curves right (south) and ascends steeply. In a couple minutes, the road levels at 3.7 km (2.3 mi). Look left for a **cairn** indicating where to abandon the road and turn east onto a trail.

Ascend through rooty, disenchanted forest. Your general direction of travel is soon north-northeast. At 2073 m (6800 ft), about an hour from the trailhead, enter the subalpine zone near boisterous Headwall Creek. The peak-lined valley is visible ahead. Left (north) is 3054-m (10,017-ft) Mt. Chester. Right (northeast) is 3035-m (9958-ft) Mt. James Walker.

In another 15 minutes, the trail goes left, along the creek, at the base of a **rockslide**. It heads toward the cascade on the first headwall, then climbs very steeply right (east). Zigzag up steps and ledges. Curve north.

Crest the **first headwall** at 6.8 km (4.2 mi), 2296 m (7530 ft), about two hours from the trailhead. The first of the two Headwall Lakes is just ahead. Sharp limestone karst is underfoot. Visible behind you (southwest) are glacier-laden, 3050-m (10,000-ft) peaks on the Great Divide.

At 2260 m (7413 ft) round the east shore of **lower Headwall Lake**. A rough, steep path climbs right of the cascade on the second headwall. Though there's no exposure, the ascent demands sure footing and might require you to grapple with roots and rocks. Crest the second headwall and arrive at **upper Headwall Lake** about 15 minutes after leaving the lower lake. Elevation: 2340 m (7675 ft). Total distance: 7 km (4.3 mi).

To scramble up The Fortress, or to loop back to the trailhead via Chester Lake (Trip 11), proceed up-canyon. Start by rounding the east shore of upper Headwall Lake. Ascend steadily. The terrain gradually tilts skyward. Scramble up the scree. Aim for the left gap in the low point northwest. Keep toiling until you reach the 2710-m (8889-ft) **col** on the ridgecrest leading to The Fortress. You've gained 370 m (1214 ft) in 1.9 km (1.2 mi) since leaving upper Headwall Lake.

From the col, **The Fortress** is right (north-northeast), 290 m (951 ft) higher and 1.6 km (1 mi) farther. If that's your goal, follow the directions in Trip 11.

Your other option is **Chester Lake**, 490 m (1607 ft) below you and 2.1 km (1.3 mi) distant. To loop back to the trailhead that way, begin the sharp descent west. Upon reaching the jumbled canyon floor, bear left (southwest). Pass upper Chester Creek at 2400 m (7872 ft). It's above ground for only 50 m (55 yd). Then pick up the path dropping to Chester Lake (visible below). The rest of the way to the trailhead is well defined and popular. If you need directions, follow those for Trip 11 in reverse.

TRIP 13
James Walker Creek

LOCATION	Peter Lougheed Provincial Park, Hwy 742
ROUND TRIP	17 km (10.5 mi)
ELEVATION GAIN	510 m (1673 ft)
KEY ELEVATIONS	trailhead 1875 m (6150 ft)
	upper basin tarn 2385 m (7823 ft)
HIKING TIME	7 to 9 hours
DIFFICULTY	moderate
MAP	Gem Trek Kananaskis Lakes

Opinion

This isn't a trail. It's a psycho path. Oh, the trailhead looks normal enough. It even affords views as impressive as those you typically must hike to attain. But a few minutes into the journey you'll discover the psychotic nature of the path itself.

The first half is an old, abandoned logging road, one in a network of manmade scars snaking all over this slope. The roads were eventually reclaimed by the provincial park for cross-country skiing and signed with colour-coded trail symbols. But, due to lack of funds, that use was abandoned too. So you'll initially be hiking on an overgrown road marked with derelict signs that in summer look absurd. Then, where the road ends, you'll proceed not on a trail but rather a bootbeaten route: distinct, easy to follow, but narrow throughout, often rough, steep near the end, possibly muddy and slick, for hardy hikers only.

So the path's psychosis is due to the same cruelties—abuse and neglect—that induce psychopathic behaviour in humans. And, just as psychologically aberrant people sometimes exhibit startling brilliance, so does this psycho path: it leads to a pair of scenically splendid, wonderfully lonely, tarn-dotted alpine basins, both of which you can savour on a dayhike.

These are the headwater basins of James Walker Creek. About two hours from the trailhead, you'll spurt out of the forest into the rolling, parklike expanse beneath the basins' confluence. From there on, you can romp with abandon: across rock slabs, over rock outcrops, among scattered larches, through grass and heather, around the tarns. You'll enjoy constant views. The 3000-m (9800-ft) peaks walling in the basins are impressive when glimpsed from Hwy 40 but are spectacular up close. And you'll likely roam in delicious solitude, because the deranged approach deters crowds.

Though similar, each basin is distinctive enough that you should poke your nose into both. It takes about eight hours. The basin mouths are soft, welcoming, alpine havens, while the upper reaches are austere, forbidding

James Walker Creek headwaters basin

lunarscapes. Your energy and curiosity, as well as the sun's proximity to the horizon, will determine how far you probe them. If you have time for only one, go left (north-northwest) into the basin beneath Mt. James Walker's long, south ridge.

Be keenly aware of bears. Though an encounter here is no more likely than elsewhere in the Canadian Rockies, it could have more serious consequences. That's because the basins' confluence is prime grizzly habitat. We saw an alarming amount of bear tear (ground cover disturbed by feeding bears). Yet the area is small and has only one narrow point at which people or bruins can enter or exit. So, after surmounting the headwall and entering the subalpine zone, if you spot a bear, turn around immediately and leave—quickly but quietly. Otherwise you'll corner the bear. It would perceive you as an imminent threat and would likely launch an aggressive defense.

Fact

By Vehicle

From downtown **Canmore**, follow signs leading uphill to the Canmore Nordic Centre. Reset your trip odometer to 0 at the Nordic Centre turnoff. Continue ascending on Smith-Dorrien / Spray Trail (Hwy 742). Pavement soon ends. After crossing Whiteman's Gap, proceed generally southeast 47.6 km (29.5 mi).

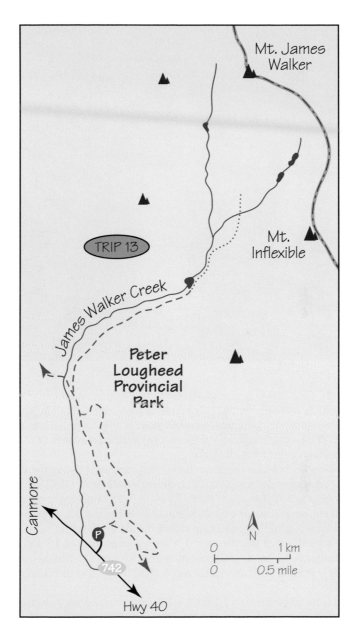

From the **junction of Hwy 40 and Kananaskis Lakes Trail** (50 km / 31 mi south of Trans-Canada Hwy 1, or 17 km / 10.5 mi north of Highwood Pass), turn southwest onto Kananaskis Lakes Trail. Reset your trip odometer to 0. At 2.2 km (1.4 mi) turn right (northwest) onto unpaved Smith-Dorrien / Spray Trail (Hwy 742) and drive to 16.6 km (10.3 mi).

From either approach, turn northeast into the Sawmill day-use-area parking lot. Elevation: 1875 m (6150 ft).

James Walker Creek, north fork

On Foot

The trail is initially an old, abandoned logging road. It's signed with colour-coded symbols for cross-country skiing, but that use has also been abandoned. The road/trail starts at the north-northeast corner of the parking lot. Follow it uphill to a nearby **gate.**

Fifteen paces beyond the gate, fork left (northeast) onto the road/trail that, 20 m/yd farther, is posted with an **orange-yellow** ski-trail symbol. (The Gem Trek map labels this road/trail "R/Y/G.") Hiking at a moderate pace, you'll pass no junctions for about the next 20 minutes. Though you'll have occasional views, you'll be hiking in forest for about the next two hours.

After a gentle but steady ascent, reach a **junction** at 1.7 km (1.1 mi). Go left (north) on the road/trail posted with a yellow ski-trail symbol. Right (southeast) is posted with an orange ski-trail symbol, but the Gem Trek map labels it "R."

Five minutes farther, at 2 km (1.3 mi), reach another **junction.** James Walker Creek is audible, but not visible, in the canyon below. Go right (north) and ascend. Left (north-northwest) descends to the creek.

About ten minutes farther, the road/trail gradually curves northeast into **James Walker Creek canyon.** Left (north-northwest), across the canyon, is a forested slope with an inviting swath of grass. Ahead (north), a rocky outlier of Mt. James Walker beckons you to the scenic alplands above. The road/trail soon dwindles to a rough, narrow **route.** Expect to encounter fallen trees.

At 4.2 km (2.5 mi), 2128 m (6980 ft), arrive at a shallow **tarn** that might be dry. The Gem Trek map depicts it as a substantial lakelet. But one September, after a rainy summer, we found it was merely a mud flat cleaved by a creek. At least the clearing is a reprieve from the forest. Beyond, 30 minutes of vigourous hiking on a steep, rough route will propel you into the alpine zone.

Round the tarn's right (east) shore. Proceed to the northeast end of the clearing, where the tarn's **inlet creek** emerges from forest. Re-enter the forest here. Head upstream, on the right bank, following a bootbeaten route. Negotiate a fallen tree. Hop to a tiny peninsula between arms of the creek. Your general direction of travel will be northeast.

The route soon steepens. It's rugged, possibly muddy and slippery. A couple places might briefly require hands-on clambering. But the way forward is distinct, easy to follow. You'll be ascending beside the beautiful **gorge** cut by upper James Walker Creek. Several plunge pools are visible left, below the route.

About 20 minutes after leaving the tarn, reach a **rockslide** beneath a cliffband. Go left (northwest), following cairns along the base of the rock-slide. The route dips into a rocky gully, then re-enters forest, ascending right. Pass a spring cascading from the limestone cliff. The creek is now far below, left of the route. Continue ascending to surmount the headwall. Enter the **subalpine zone** at 6.7 km (4.2 mi), 2300 m (7544 ft).

From here on, you'll be traveling cross-country, past treeline. So it's wise to stop, turn around, and fix in your mind where you exited the trees. After exploring the **upper basins**, you'll have to return to this precise spot and find the descent route. It'll be much easier if you know what to look for.

Ahead, vistas unfold. North is 3035-m (9958-ft) Mt. James Walker (JW). Right (west-southwest) is 3000-m (9843-ft) Mt. Inflexible. Those two giants define your options. A gradual ascent left (north-northwest) leads to the basin beneath JW's long, south ridge. A steeper ascent right (east, then northeast) leads to the basin beneath Inflexible's north ridge.

In either direction, you'll hike over rock slabs and out-crops, and across patches of grass and heather strewn with stunted larches. If time allows, probe both basins. Start by going left (north). In about 20 minutes, reach a lovely tarn and its outlet stream at 8.5 km (5.3 mi), 2385 m (7823 ft). From there, contour southeast, then ascend northeast to enter the second basin in about 25 min-utes. Continue upward to attain a knoll-top view. This basin's first tarn is shortly beyond the knoll. The tarns in both basins are smaller than indicated on the Gem Trek map.

The rough trail ascending to James Walker Creek basin

TRIP 14

Black Prince Cirque

LOCATION	Peter Lougheed Provincial Park, Hwy 742
ROUND TRIP	10 km (6.2 mi)
ELEVATION GAIN	590 m (1934 ft)
KEY ELEVATIONS	trailhead 1732 m (5680 ft), moraine 2322 m (7620 ft)
HIKING TIME	4 to 5 hours
DIFFICULTY	challenging
MAPS	Gem Trek Kananaskis Lakes
	Kananaskis Lakes 82 J/11

Opinion

Black Prince evokes images of medieval castles and chivalrous knights. The name originated with Prince Edward of England, a fierce, 14th Century warrior who wore striking black armor. It was revived as the name of a World War I battleship. In memory of the ship, the name was bestowed on a striking Canadian Rockies peak: 2932-m (9617-ft) Mt. Black Prince.

Channeling the warrior's indomitable spirit will help you assail the headwall guarding Black Prince cirque and the tiny lakes hidden within. It's a brief but arduous ascent over jumbled rocks, through avalanche debris, and beside a precipitous cascade. After easing into the cirque, you must catapult over a steep moraine to reach the lakes. The cirque isn't grand; it's just a wild little niche. The lakes aren't impressive; they're just exclamation points. Go simply to joust with the mountains.

It's a short, half-day adventure. Challenge and solitude are limited to the second half of the trip. The first half is city-park easy: an interpretive trail accommodating toddlers and waddlers. You can bring the whole clan on this 2.1-km (1.3-mi) stroll to Warspite Lake. Keep in mind, it's shallow and can dry up by fall, or even during an arid summer. But when full pool, the lake is a lovely sight beneath Mt. Black Prince. The bouldery shore is dual purpose: playground or rest area.

Smith-Dorrien Valley, where the hike begins, was beset by loggers and miners in the early 1880s. The jaws of industry were clamped on the area until 1978, when it was protected as a provincial park. So this trail, for about the first 15 minutes, is actually a former logging road. A brochure (available at the trailhead) references numbered signposts en route to the lake, providing a self-guided natural history tour. It's a gallant attempt to wring interest and education from a mundane, re-growing clearcut.

Warspite Lake is in lower Black Prince cirque. Black Prince Lakes are in upper Black Prince cirque. So what's a cirque? It's a glacier-gouged, bowl-shaped valley. But the glacier that carved the cirques was a smaller, shallower tributary of the more massive glacier that deeply scoured Smith-

Black Prince Cirque and Mt. Warspite

Dorrien Valley. When the ice retreated, the cirque floors were left hanging high above the valley floor. That's why the upper cirque is also what's called a *hanging valley*.

Fact

By Vehicle

From downtown **Canmore**, follow signs leading uphill to the Canmore Nordic Centre. Reset your trip odometer to 0 at the Nordic Centre turnoff. Continue ascending on Smith-Dorrien / Spray Trail (Hwy 742). Pavement soon ends. After crossing Whiteman's Gap, proceed generally southeast. At 53.2 km (33 mi), turn right (south) into the trailhead parking lot at Mt. Black Prince day use area. Elevation: 1732 m (5680 ft).

From the **junction of Hwy 40 and Kananaskis Lakes Trail** (50 km / 31 mi south of Trans-Canada Hwy 1, or 17 km / 10.5 mi north of Highwood Pass), turn southwest onto Kananaskis Lakes Trail. Reset your trip odometer to 0. At 2.2 km (1.4 mi) turn right (northwest) onto unpaved Smith-Dorrien / Spray Trail (Hwy 742). At 10.5 km (6.5 mi) turn left (south) into the trailhead parking lot at Mt. Black Prince day use area. Elevation: 1732 m (5680 ft).

On Foot

Follow the interpretive trail southwest though willows and trees beside Smith-Dorrien Creek. In one minute, cross a bridge to the southwest bank.

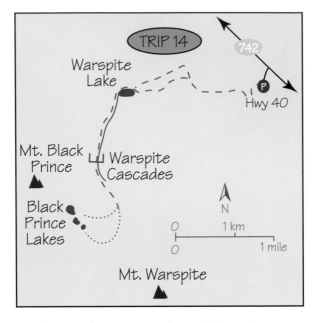

The trail goes left (east), downstream, through forest. It soon curves into an old **logging road** heading northwest. A moderate ascent ensues.

Within 15 minutes, at 1840 m (6035 ft), bear right (west) onto **trail**. There's a bench here, as well as the #4 sign. Mt. Kent is visible northeast, across the valley. Soon descend and enter trees. At 1.4 km (0.9 mi), 1793 m (5880 ft), reach a fork. The Warspite Lake **loop splits** here. Go right.

About half an hour from the trailhead, enter a bouldery clearing at the mouth of lower Black Prince cirque. Visible south-southwest is the headwall you'll ascend to the upper cirque. At 2.1 km (1.3 mi), 1830 m (6002 ft), reach the #9 sign near the east end of **Warspite Lake**. Immediately turn right onto the pine-needle covered path rounding the northeast shore.

The path continues around the north and west shores. After crossing a tiny inlet creek, the trail ends. Proceed along the **west shore**—over rocks, then grass. Cairns lead to a second, larger **inlet stream**. Stay on the right (west) bank and follow the re-emerging trail south, upstream, back into forest.

About 1¼ hours from the trailhead, enter a small meadow. Head toward the willows and cascade visible above the forest. In another five minutes, ascend a **rock pile**. Go around its left edge. Cairns, if still in place, will guide you off the rocks left of two tall dead larches.

Proceed into trees, then up and out through a band of skinny, tall krummholz, onto an **avalanche path** run-out. Ascend southwest over avalanche debris. Stay left of a big gully. Follow the bootbeaten path. Near the top of the gully, the path traverses south toward the **Warspite Cascades**.

The route climbs a wickedly steep 76 m (250 ft) before relaxing above the cascades at 2120 m (6954 ft). Having crested the lip of the upper cirque, the path levels in a **grassy basin** scattered with boulders. Strong hikers will be here 1¾ hours after leaving the trailhead.

Warspite Cascades

Continue southeast several minutes into the basin. Visible ahead (south-southeast) is 2850-m (9348-ft) Mt. Warspite. It forms the east and south walls of the cirque. West is 2932-m (9617-ft) Mt. Black Prince. It forms the cirque's west and northwest walls. Though the cirque invites and rewards deeper wandering, your destination, Black Prince Lakes, doesn't require it.

When the path fades, bear right (west). Work your way up the comfortably steep **grass-and-boulder slope**. Avoid steeper terrain on either side. Stay left of the treed wall, right of the rough boulder field. From where the path ended in the basin, fifteen minutes of vigourous, upward effort will earn you a commanding vantage atop a **moraine**, at 2322 m (7620 ft). The **Black Prince Lakes** are visible immediately below the moraine's west side. You've hiked 5 km (3.1 mi) from the trailhead.

TRIP 15
Mt. Allan

LOCATION	Bow Valley Wildland Provincial Park, Hwy 40
ROUND TRIP	14.4 km (8.9 mi)
ELEVATION GAIN	1314 m (4309 ft)
KEY ELEVATIONS	trailhead 1506 m (4940 ft)
	Olympic Summit 2457 m (8060 ft)
	Mt. Allan 2820 m (9250 ft)
HIKING TIME	7 to 8 hours
DIFFICULTY	challenging due only to elevation gain
MAPS	page 94; Gem Trek Canmore & Kananaskis Village
	Spray Lakes Reservoir 82 J/14

Opinion

Methylsulfonylmethane is a sulphur compound known by the abbreviation MSM. It's easy to remember. Think of it as *Mountain Suffering Minimized*. MSM capsules help prevent joint inflammation. They also support the efforts of another beneficial supplement, glucosamine, which rebuilds damaged joint cartilage. Just thought you'd want to know that before you go charging up the highest trail in the Canadian Rockies.

Few ridgewalks in this or any other range buoy you for so long above treeline. But it's rarely level. You're in for a long, steadily steep, northwest ascent of Mt. Allan's southwest summit ridge, all the way to the 2820-m (9250-ft) peak. You'll follow the Centennial Ridge Trail, built by Calgary's Rocky Mountain Ramblers to commemorate Canada's 1967 Centennial.

The trail rapidly launches you out of the trees. Views are constant and, of course, grow more spectacular as you climb. Mt. Allan snuggles among striking peaks: Mounts Lougheed, Sparrowhawk and Bogart. Also nearby is Mt. Kidd, an arresting, fascinating mountain.

You'll face no exposure on this trip. Indeed, it's a hike, not a scramble. You might have to push through a wall of discouragement, however, when you crest Olympic Summit, roughly the halfway point, and see that Mt. Allan still looks insurmountably distant. Remember: the worst of the climb is behind you, and the scenery explodes ahead. Take joy in the going, not just the goal.

Visit Mt. Allan before autumn, while the grassy summit ridge remains an emerald carpet woven with colourful wildflowers. If you're serious about photography, come before mid-August and get an early-morning start, so you catch the magnificent massif nearby to the west before it's shaded.

When you finally top out, you'll see the trail continues down Mt. Allan's north summit-ridge. It's possible to follow it to a road accessing Trans-Canada Hwy 1 at Dead Man's Flats. So why not a one-way traverse of the entire mountain? Because the north-side trail soon plunges into forest.

Ascending Mt. Allan, across from Mt. Kidd

Better to savour the hard-won alpine zone longer by returning the way you came. Mt. Kidd, dominating the southern horizon, will rustle your soul. The northern horizon, visible only briefly, is not so stirring.

Except for a couple minor cliffbands—quickly, easily overcome—the trail poses no obstacle but steepness. That's enough. After shrugging off the last trees, you'll climb a ballistic 640 m (2100 ft) in less than 2 km (1.2 mi). To put that in perspective, strong hikers consider 305 m (1000 ft) in 1.6 (1 mi) demanding. So enlist your arms and shoulders in the effort, not just your legs. Use trekking poles. The benefits, explained on page 283, include significantly reduced descent-impact on your knees.

What? No trekking poles? Until you get a pair, don't rely on ibuprofen as a solution for joint pain. All it does is mask symptoms, which is like gagging your body so it can't communicate. If overused, ibuprofen will damage your liver. Learning about salubrious, natural supplements and adding them to your regimen can help heal some of the common maladies that cause persistent joint pain.

Fact

Before your trip

Be aware that the trail to Mt Allan is closed annually, April 1 through June 21, when bighorn sheep are lambing on the ridges.

By Vehicle
Follow directions for Trip 16 to the trailhead parking lot at Ribbon Creek day use area. Elevation: 1506 m (4940 ft).

On Foot
For the first 35 minutes, the grade is moderate while you wind through a maze of trails and old logging roads. The junctions are initially frequent. Most are signed, but stay alert and follow these directions carefully until the ascent begins in earnest and the hiking is more straightforward.

0 km (0 mi)
Start near the northeast corner of the parking lot, between the toilets and the kiosk. Head north-northwest on the gravel road signed HIDDEN TRAIL.

0.3 km (0.2 mi)
Turn left (west) onto Coal Mine trail amid spruce and aspen.

1 km (0.6 km)
Reach a three-way junction at 1570 m (5150 ft). Bear left (northwest) to ascend the Centennial Ridge Trail—still an old road, but narrower.

2 km (1.2 mi)
Reach a four-way junction at 1634 m (5360 ft). Cross overgrown Coal Mine road and proceed straight (west-northwest). Mt. Allan's long summit ridge is visible ahead.

- Ascend 73 m (240 ft) in the next 8 minutes. Reach a road and turn right.
- Just 10 m/yd farther, turn left. Ascend the slope back onto a signed trail.
- One minute farther, cross the road again. Continue ascending. Another minute farther, reach an overgrown road. Follow it left (southwest).

At 1759 m (5770 ft), about 35 minutes from the trailhead, the **road narrows to trail** and ascends right (southwest). A viewpoint left overlooks Kananaskis Village. The trail then switchbacks. Your general direction of travel will be northwest all the way to the summit of Mt. Allan.

After hiking about an hour, you'll be on **open, grassy slopes** at 1890 m (6200 ft). The grade steepens. In another 15 to 25 minutes, at 2015 m (6610 ft), visible ahead (northwest) is Mt. Allan's long summit ridge, which you'll be ascending. Mt. Kidd (south, immediately across Ribbon Creek valley) appears increasingly magnificent as you climb. Soon you can peer southwest, up Ribbon Creek valley. The grade eases briefly at 2160 m (6585 ft), then steepens again.

After negotiating a **cliffband**, the trail leads north, on the northeast side of the ridge, above Nakiska ski runs. Mt. Lorette is visible northeast. Linked to it by a long ridge is Mt. McGillivray (north-northeast).

Ascend a smooth slope to reach the east end of **Olympic Summit** at 4.2 km (2.6 mi), 2457 m (8060 ft). Pass a weather-data gizmo. Elevation gain is minimal for the next 1.2 km (0.7 mi) as you curve west over the rounded summit.

Mt. Lougheed, from Mt. Allan ridgecrest

The long ridge sweeping right (northeast) from Mt. Allan to Mt. Collembola is visible north. Left (west) is 3121-m (10,237-ft) Mt. Sparrowhawk, its summit small and beaky. North of it is multi-peaked, 3108-m (10,194-ft) Mt. Lougheed. Southwest, across Ribbon Creek's north fork canyon, is Ribbon Peak. Northwest of it is the cirque harbouring the Memorial Lakes (Trip 16). Even the third (upper) lake is discernible, beneath 3145-m (10,315-ft) Mt. Bogart. Southeast, across Hwy 40, is Evans Thomas Creek valley. North of it (east-southeast) is Mt. McDougall. Immediately north of that is Old Baldy Mtn (Trip 44).

At a bump on the west edge of Olympic Summit, drop northwest along the ridgecrest. The trail is punctuated here with posts bearing red blazes. The descent is brief. Resume a gentle ascent. Pass lichen-covered conglomerate outcrops. At 5.4 km (3.3 mi) reach the 25-m (82-ft) **rock pinnacles**. The cairned trail continues just beneath the left (west) edge of the crest. Proceed through the pinnacles for about ten minutes before ascending steeply northwest.

After a rough, rocky descent, the trail traverses the scree slope left (west) of the crest. Regain the crest for the final steep pitch. Avoid the sheep trail traversing the right (east) side of the summit block; it skirts your goal.

Top out on **Mt. Allan** at 7.2 km (4.5 mi), 2820 m (9250 ft). Though the scenery has been grand all along, the panorama, now complete, is sufficiently superior to justify your perseverance. The four peaks of Mt. Lougheed are very close (west and northwest).

The trail continues, descending the north summit-ridge. It soon re-enters forest and eventually reaches a road accessing Trans-Canada Hwy 1 at Dead Man's Flats.

TRIP 16
Memorial Lakes

LOCATION	Bow Valley Wildland Provincial Park, Hwy 40
ROUND TRIP	16 km (10 mi) to upper lake
ELEVATION GAIN	759 m (2490 ft) to upper lake
KEY ELEVATIONS	trailhead 1506 m (4940 ft)
	middle lake 2105 m (6904 ft)
	upper lake 2265 m (7429 ft)
HIKING TIME	6 to 7 hours for upper lake
DIFFICULTY	challenging
MAPS	Gem Trek Canmore and Kananaskis Village

Opinion

Hiking can be as much meditation as it is play. For some of us, it's a devotional practice. We hike not just to a worldly destination but into a metaphysical realm of calm, clarity, and oneness.

In pursuit of that loftier goal, aim for upper Memorial Lake. You'll find the tranquility that allows for a deeper experience, because the trail is too obscure and challenging to attract a crowd. And the climax is beautiful. The upper lake adorns an austere, alpine cirque—headwaters of Ribbon Creek's north fork—beneath massive peaks.

The trip begins at Ribbon Creek day-use area, beside the boisterous creek. From here, a broad, former road popular with mountainbikers ascends mercifully. It shadows the creek for about 8 km (5 mi) to Ribbon Falls. Early on, it twice crosses the creek on sturdy bridges and passes a creekside picnic table. This initial stretch—walkable May through November—is a soothing, 45-minute, out-and-back amble, ideal for anyone soft as meringue.

You're tough as beef jerky? Veer off the road onto an unsigned, primitive trail: brushy, rocky, rooty, narrow. At times, it's just a scratch in the earth. And it tilts increasingly skyward, following Ribbon Creek's rowdy north fork. The first Memorial Lake is a bush-bound puddle—a disappointment, though it does afford a tantalizing view of the high country. Only a scurfy route continues. Expect a steep, moderately-difficult rock romp to the turquoise middle lake in a classically beautiful, subalpine bowl. But even there, you might feel overworked and under compensated. Push on. Just above is the upper lake, guarded by a short, precipitous scramble on gritty, unstable terrain.

If you're fit and capable, you'll enjoy grappling with this final obstacle and surmount it quickly. You can then celebrate your accomplishment with a lakeshore victory lap. Admire the surrounding alplands. Gaze up at the lake's guardian peaks. Peer down at the first lake far below. Perhaps savour a few precious moments of calm, clarity and oneness.

Scrambling above middle Memorial Lake

Fact

By Vehicle

From the Trans-Canada (Hwy 1), drive south 23 km (14.3 mi) on Hwy 40. Or, from the junction of Hwy 40 and Kananaskis Lakes Trail, drive north 27 km (16.7 mi) on Hwy 40. From either approach, turn west following signs for Kananaskis Village. Reset your trip odometer to 0. Immediately cross a bridge over the Kananaskis River. At 0.8 km (0.5 mi) turn left. At 1 km (0.6 mi) turn right. Pass the hostel, then a covered picnic shelter, both on the right. At 1.6 km (1 mi) reach the Ribbon Creek day-use area and trailhead parking lot. Continue to the far (west) end, at 1506 m (4940 ft).

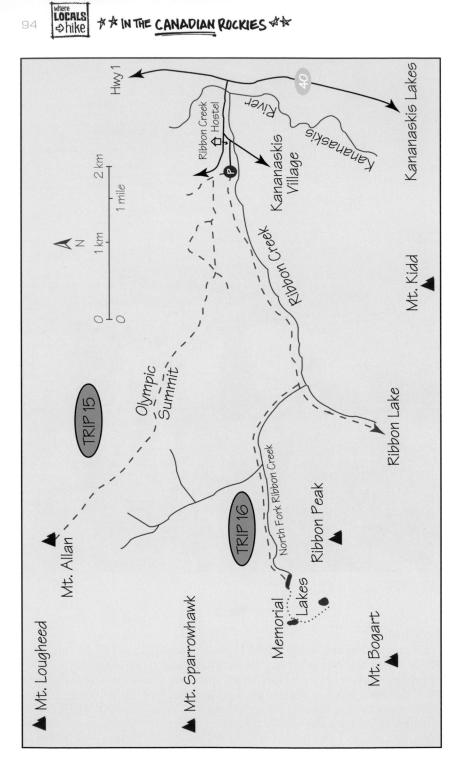

On Foot

The Ribbon Creek trail, a former road, departs the far (west) end of the parking lot. After two bridged creek crossings, pass a picnic table and begin a gradual ascent. Reach a signed junction at 2.5 km (1.6 mi), 1595 m (5230 ft). The Kovach ski trail drops left to a bridge. Continue straight.

Where the road levels again and the forest opens, look for a **cairned trail** (right / northwest). It's at 3.7 km (2.3 mi), about 40 minutes along. The road parallels Ribbon Creek southwest to Ribbon Falls. For Memorial Lakes, follow the trail into Ribbon Creek's **north-fork drainage**.

The trail plows through small trees, climbs above the north fork's northeast bank, and soon forks. Left is easier. A few minutes farther, stay high, on the better trail. Ahead, cross a steep, eroded slope.

At 1726 m (5660 ft), about 1¼ hours along, the trail levels briefly along the creek bank, then ascends right. Cross a footlog spanning a **tributary**. Proceed west.

At 1890 m (6200 ft), about 1¾ hours along, the trail is comfortably broad and level, heading west. A left spur detours to a showy **cascade** where the north fork plummets through a rocky gorge.

Resume on the trail, ascending steeply, skirting the right (north) edge of the gorge. Above the cascade, enjoy a level respite along the creek bank. Turn left, hop a **tributary**, and hike south-southwest.

Middle Memorial Lake

The **first Memorial Lake** is at 6.8 km (4.2 mi), 1955 m (6412 ft). Strong hikers arrive here in about two hours. It's just a pond in a willow-choked bowl with muddy banks, but formidable mountains surround it.

Left (southeast) is 2880-m (9446-ft) Ribbon Peak. On the horizon (south-southwest) is 3144-m (10,312-ft) Mt. Bogart. Nearby (west-southwest) is Bogart Tower. Far right (northwest) is 3121-m (10,237-ft) Mt. Sparrowhawk. A multistage cascade drops beneath Bogart Tower to the far (south) side of the first lake.

Begin an athletic 30-minute clamber to the middle lake. The trail, diminishing to route, rounds the first lake's west end. Rough but discernible, it leads through willows. Hop the inlet stream.

Above the stream's south bank, turn right (west). Ascend along the base of Bogart Tower. Cairns guide you up a rockslide. Reach a cairned boulder at the edge of a small, treed bench, beneath another rockslide.

Ascend steeply left (generally southwest). Follow a bootbeaten path above the rockslide, angling left beneath an overhanging rock shelf then curving right above it. At 7.4 km (4.6 mi), 2105 m (6904 ft), overlook **middle Memorial Lake** (right / north) from its south shore.

Only strong, experienced scramblers should continue. If you're capable, the way forward is obvious. From the middle lake, ascend south. The route steepens and narrows dramatically. Soon bear left and scramble (yes, hands-on) through a vertical gully. A few minutes above, the grade eases but remains steep.

A path leads southwest through a meadowy draw. It levels, then ascends the right side of a tiny basin. At 8 km (5 mi), 2265 m (7429 ft), overlook **upper Memorial Lake** (east).

The lake occupies an alpine cirque beneath Ribbon Peak (east-south-east) and Mt. Bogart (south-southwest). The namesake memorial—a heart-rending **cenotaph** honouring the 13 victims of a tragic, 1986 aviation disaster—is atop a knoll above the northeast shore.

Memorial above upper lake's northeast shore

TRIP 17
Galatea Lakes / Guinn's Pass

LOCATION	Spray Valley Provincial Park, Hwy 40
ROUND TRIP	17 km (10.5 mi) to upper Galatea Lake
	16 km (10 mi) to Guinn's Pass
ELEVATION GAIN	670 m (2198 ft) to upper Galatea Lake
	870 m (2854 ft) to Guinn's Pass
KEY ELEVATIONS	trailhead 1550 m (5084 ft)
	lower Galatea Lake 2180 m (7150 ft)
	Guinn's Pass 2420 m (7940 ft)
HIKING TIME	5½ hours for Galatea Lakes
	7 hours for Guinn's Pass
DIFFICULTY	moderate to Galatea Lakes
	challenging to Guinn's Pass
MAPS	Gem Trek Canmore and Kananaskis Village
	Spray Lakes Reservoir 82 J/14

Opinion

If you're lucky enough to be in the mountains, you're lucky enough. If the range you're in is the Canadian Rockies, you're fortunate indeed. And if it's Guinn's Pass you're standing atop, well, you're positively blessed. This marvelous vantage is encircled by peaks as rousing as any that K-Country has tossed at the sky.

Guinn's is often overlooked. Perhaps because the ascent is seriously steep. Or because people fixate on reaching the popular Galatea Lakes. For whatever reason, most blow right by the turnoff to Guinn's. Sure, the lakes basin is beautiful. But it's our responsibility to acid rain on the parade: Galatea is the area's consolation prize. You want an experience branded into your brain? Go to Guinn's.

The trail to Galatea and Guinn's starts by crossing a bridge over the Kananaskis River. It then romps up Galatea Creek canyon, where you'll partake of K-Country's most delightful creekside hiking. The signed Guinn's Pass fork peels off just before Lillian Lake.

Lillian is not a desirable destination. Thickly girdled by trees, she's merely the maid answering the door for the lovely ladies of the house—the Galatea Lakes. And it's an impressive house: an alpine basin clutched by immense peaks. But when weighing the comparative merits of Galatea Lakes and Guinn's Pass, consider that an outlier of Mt. Kidd—a short, easy walk-up from Guinn's—overlooks these lakes, plus a lot more.

Guinn's Pass will test your mettle. Just gazing up at the trail's skyward trajectory might weaken your knees. Switchbacks are minimal. The lower reaches are bouldery. It's thirsty work on a hot day, and you'll find no water at the pass. So don't rely on the trailside trickle. Bring all the water you'll need.

But the challenge of the ascent compensates even before your victory dance at the pass. Winsome wildflowers sprout with surprising alacrity in this steep, rocky terrain. And the anticipation aroused on such an intense climb can be as delicious as the climax. Savour it. The traverse of green, alpine slopes, just before the trail tops out, is exhilarating.

Highlights of the stupendous Guinn's Pass view include Mt. Galatea, The Fortress, Mt. Bogart (Trip 16), the inviting alplands beneath Buller and North Buller passes (Trip 7), and the nearby, towering, sheer wall of an unnamed peak. Push on, a few minutes higher and farther to the upper edge of the pass, and you'll survey all of the sumptuous Ribbon Lake basin and mighty Mt. Kidd.

Okay, options. If you cross Guinn's Pass, you can make this a loop or a one-way trip, either backpacking or dayhiking. You'll probably choose not to, however. There's just no point in hauling a full pack over Guinn's to see what's well within dayhiking range if you're strong and start early. Even traveling light and fast, the one-way and loop extensions are, upon further analysis, unattractive.

Looping past Ribbon Lake, down Ribbon Creek, back to Hwy 40, requires only a short, easy shuttle. And Ribbon Lake is wonderful. But standing on the shore is less impressive than the Guinn's Pass aerial view. (See photo on page 103.) And from Ribbon Falls out, nearly half the loop, you'll plod an old road (popular with mountainbikers) through forest. We didn't include that section as a dayhike in the book, because it's not premier.

Hiking one-way to Hwy 742, through either of the Buller Passes, would be excellent if it didn't necessitate a tediously long shuttle. Enjoying the Bullers as a dayhike circuit, as described in Trip 7, is easier and will therefore increase your likelihood of completing the exciting, scenic detour above North Buller Pass.

So, instead of proceeding over Guinn's Pass, continue upward. Summit the aforementioned Mt. Kidd outlier. If you still have time and energy after descending back to the Galatea Creek trail, spurt up to Galatea Lakes. By then it should be late afternoon and the crowd will have dispersed.

Fact

By Vehicle

From Trans-Canada Hwy 1, drive south 32.7 km (20.3 mi) on Hwy 40. Or, from the junction of Hwy 40 and Kananaskis Lakes Trail, drive north 17.2 km (10.7 mi) on Hwy 40. From either approach, turn southwest into the Galatea trailhead parking lot, at 1550 m (5084 ft).

On Foot

Descend the wide path departing the northwest corner of the parking lot, near the info kiosk. In two minutes, cross a suspension bridge over the Kananaskis River. Mt. Kidd's stark, swirling cliffs are visible north-northwest. The trail briefly heads southwest, then crosses a **bridge over Galatea Creek** at 0.5 km (0.3 mi), 1524 m (5000 ft).

Galatea Creek

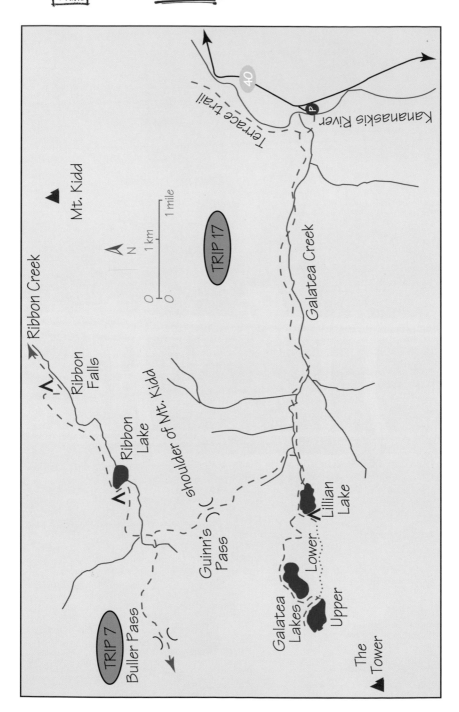

Ribbon Creek

Mt. Kidd

Ribbon Falls

Ribbon Lake

shoulder of Mt. Kidd

Guinn's Pass

Galatea Lakes

Lower

Lillian Lake

Upper

The Tower

Buller Pass

TRIP 7

TRIP 17

Galatea Creek

Kananaskis River

Terrace trail

40

P

N

0   1 km
0   1 mile

Ascending from Lower Galatea Lake to upper lake

On the creek's north bank is a **T-junction**. Turn left (southwest) on the Galatea Creek trail. From here, all the way to lower Galatea Lake, it ascends generally west. It closely follows the rambunctious creek as far as Lillian Lake. Turning right at the T-junction would put you on the Terrace trail. It goes generally north-northeast through forest, beneath the east slope of Mt. Kidd, reaching Kananaskis Village in 7 km (4.3 mi).

While gently undulating through forest, the Galatea Creek trail crosses the creek seven times on sturdy bridges within the next 2.6 km (1.6 mi). About 30 minutes from the trailhead, ascend a **rockslide** at 1680 m (5510 ft) on the canyon's north wall and attain views. The south-facing cliffs of Mt. Kidd are above you. The Wedge is visible east-southeast, across Hwy 40. Slightly farther, overlook the deep inner gorge and a short waterfall.

At the sixth bridge since the T-junction, **log benches** on the north bank offer comfort to the weary. Elevation: 1769 m (5800 ft). You're now about an hour from the trailhead, entering Galatea Creek's northwest-fork drainage. In a few minutes, traverse a lush avalanche path, then a grassy, flowery slope. Soon, at 1860 m (6100 ft), a more earnest ascent begins. You can look forward to a few level respites about ten minutes after the trail steepens.

At 5.5 km (3.4 mi), 1960 m (6430 ft), reach a **signed junction**. Moderately fast hikers will be here 1½ hours after leaving the trailhead. Straight (west) leads to Lillian and Galatea lakes. Right (north) leads to Guinn's Pass.

Galatea Lakes

In 0.6 km (0.4 mi) reach the east end of **Lillian Lake**, at 2030 m (6658 ft). The trail rounds the north shore, then forks at the lake's northwest corner. Left (southwest) enters the **campground**. For Galatea Lakes bear right (northwest) and resume ascending through forest.

Attain a view of Lillian Lake below and Galatea Creek canyon beyond in about 15 minutes. Steep scree ensues. Within another 15 minutes, overlook **Lower Galatea Lake** from 2180 m (7150 ft), just above its northeast shore. The trail continues around the north shore, descending gradually across talus. After curving south around the west shore at the water's edge, the trail ascends to the low ridge—2220 m (7282 ft)—overlooking **Upper Galatea Lake** (west). Total distance from the trailhead: 8.5 km (5.3 mi).

Departing Upper Galatea Lake, you can of course retrace your steps all the way to the trailhead. But if you prefer to vary the return to Lillian Lake, you can do so on a rough, sketchy, ultimately very steep route. From the low ridge above Upper Galatea, the route contours east across the talus slope high above Lower Galatea's south shore. It then plunges along the forest margin, continues generally east, and ends near the outhouse at Lillian Lake campground. It's possible to descend from Upper Galatea to Lillian in about 30 minutes this way. Most hikers, however, should follow the route only onto the talus slope above Lower Galatea's south shore, appreciate this perspective of the basin, then return the way they came.

Guinn's Pass

From the signed junction on the Galatea Creek trail, Guinn's Pass is 2.5 km (1.6 mi) farther and 457 m (1500 ft) higher. Turn right (north). Briefly descend to cross bridged Galatea Creek. Fill water bottles here. Just five minutes farther, Guinn's Pass is visible ahead (north-northwest).

Upper Galatea Lake

The narrow trail ascends moderately above a grassy slope burgeoning with flowers mid-July to early August. You might see white spirea, yellow columbines, lavender harebells, nodding onion (light pink bells), orange false dandelions, purple scorpionweed, cobalt monkshood, lavender fleabane, willow-herb, baby-blue alpine-forget-me-nots, plus red, orange and fuchsia versions of the seemingly omnipresent Indian paintbrush.

Continue upward through a steepening dirt-and-talus gully. Pockets of flowers brighten the stark rock. Two-thirds of the way to the pass, where water dribbles through the talus, look for another display of purple flowers: fleabane, willowherb, and penstemon. Though rocky, the ground is reasonably stable underfoot, except for

Ribbon Lake, from Guinn's Pass

one five-minute section of shifting, slabby rock. Watch for columbine and alpine-forget-me-not sheltered beneath small, trailside boulders.

Nearing the pass, hop to the west side of a creeklet. The trail is now dirt. It sweeps across flower-dense slopes of heather and grass. Mt. Kidd's long, smooth scree slopes are east-northeast, across the draw. Strong hikers will arrive at 2420-m (7940-ft) **Guinn's Pass** one hour after turning off the Galatea Creek trail. Total distance from the trailhead: 8 km (5 mi). Immediately west-southwest of the pass is a stupefying presence: the towering, sheer, 700-m (2296-ft) wall of a massive, unnamed, 3052-m (10,015-ft) peak. Right (north-east) of the pass, grassy slopes give way to scree cascading from Mt. Kidd's southwest outlier. Peaks visible behind you while ascending are now in better view: 3185-m (10,447-ft) Mt. Galatea is south-southwest, the 3000-m (9840-ft) Fortress is southeast, and the serrated Opal Range is southeast across Hwy 40. (Explore the Opals by hiking to King Creek Ridge, Piper Pass, or Paradise Pass: Trips 19, 27, and 38.) The north side of Guinn's Pass overlooks the upper basin of Ribbon Lake. North-northwest is 3144-m (10,315-ft) Mt. Bogart.

Before dropping your pack and collapsing, proceed a few minutes farther northeast. Ascend toward the **ridgecrest**. Then go left (west-northwest) descending slightly to the edge of the crest. Here, Ribbon Lake is entirely within view, far below. Mt. Bogart looms beyond the lake. Forested Ribbon Creek valley descends northeast. Mt. Kidd forms the valley's south wall. Mt. Allan (Trip 15) is in the distance, north-northeast. Looking northwest, into the grassy, upper basin above Ribbon Lake, you can see Buller Pass. Just north of it, between two knobs, is North Buller Pass. Trip 7 describes both passes and the traverse linking them. Underfoot, look for pink moss campion, mountain buttercup (taut, bright-yellow bunches), and white asters.

Above Guinn's Pass

For a superior prospect, ascend the ridgecrest east about 20 minutes. Follow scraps of bootbeaten path. After gaining 160 m (545 ft) in 0.8 km (0.5 mi), top out on the 2585-m (8480-ft) **southwest outlier of Mt. Kidd**. Lillian Lake is visible southwest, beneath an outlier of The Tower. In the basin above and west of Lillian, you can see both Galatea lakes, closer to the 3117-m (10,224-ft) Tower. Distant southwest, you can identify the distinctively long, northwest ridge of Mt. Birdwood (Trip 9). From Mt. Kidd's southwest outlier, brave, adept scramblers proceed along the crest—northeast, west, then northeast again—to summit 2959-m (9705-ft) Mt. Kidd. But the outlier will be the day's crowning achievement for most hikers.

Beyond Guinn's Pass

If pursuing the one-way or loop extensions described but not recommended in the *Opinion* section, the following directions will be helpful.

From Guinn's Pass, the trail descends steep talus north-northwest. It skirts the flank of Mt. Kidd, then drops through subalpine forest and meadow to a junction in **Ribbon Lake's upper basin**. At this point, you're 0.5 km (0.3 mi) beyond the pass.

A right turn at the junction leads to **Ribbon Lake** and, a bit farther, **Ribbon Falls**. The trail then descends northeast through Ribbon Creek valley, reaching Ribbon Creek trailhead in 12.1 km (7.5 mi). Total loop distance (up Galatea Creek, over Guinn's Pass, out Ribbon Creek) is 20.6 km (12.8 mi), not counting a one-hour round-trip detour to the outlier above the pass.

Left at the junction ascends open slopes generally west, cresting **Buller Pass** in 2 km (1.2 mi). The trail then follows Buller Creek downstream to Buller Mtn trailhead, on Hwy 742. The trailhead is 9 km (5.6 mi) from the junction and 0.6 km (0.4 mi) west of the lake. Ribbon Lake's upper basin. Total one-way distance (up Galatea Creek, over Guinn's Pass, out Buller Pass) is 17.5 km (10.9 mi).

Here's further detail on the Ribbon option. From the junction in Ribbon Lake's upper basin, right goes north. Soon cross to the north side of Ribbon Creek. Descend through forest. The trail bends right (east), traversing willowy meadow to reach **Ribbon Lake campground** 1.5 km (0.9 mi) from the junction and 0.6 km (0.4 mi) west of the lake. You'll find 20 tent pads, a cooking shelter, metal fire pits, metal food-cache, food-hanging cable, and an outhouse here. After rounding Ribbon Lake's north shore, the trail heads northeast beneath Mt. Bogart. Reach Ribbon Falls headwall 2 km (1.2 mi) from the lake. Downclimb with the aid of a handrail and fixed chain. From the falls, it's 8.1 km (5 mi) northeast to the trailhead at Ribbon Creek day use area, just west of Hwy 40. This stretch is easy but uneventful—a broad track through forest, following Ribbon Creek downstream. For *By Vehicle* directions to Ribbon Creek trailhead, read Mt. Allan (Trip 15).

TRIP 18
Rummel Lake

LOCATION	Peter Lougheed Provincial Park, Hwy 742
ROUND TRIP	8.6 km (5.3 mi) to Rummel Lake
	plus 5 km (3 mi) to Rummel Pass
ELEVATION GAIN	355 m (1164 ft) to the lake
	plus 185 m (607 ft) to the pass
KEY ELEVATIONS	trailhead 1865 m (6117 ft)
	Rummel Lake 2220 m (7281 ft)
	Rummel Pass 2405 m (7888 ft)
HIKING TIME	3 to 4 hours for the lake
	plus 1 to 1½ hours for the pass
DIFFICULTY	easy
MAPS	Gem Trek Kananaskis Lakes
	Gem Trek Canmore and Kananaskis Village

Opinion

Ask Calgarians what they like best about their city, and not one in ten will say "the Rockies." It's like asking Parisians the same question and never hearing "the food."

It's not that Calgarians simply forget what's really important to them. It's that most are only dimly aware they live beside one of the world's great ranges, many rarely visit the mountains, and a substantial number have never (!) set foot on a trail.

That's okay. It's their choice. But it's shocking. And we'd all be better off if it were otherwise. Because hiking makes people healthier, happier, saner, calmer, more aware and appreciative of nature, and better able to deal with the stress and complexity of city life.

Hiking makes people better people.

And in Calgary, of all places, hiking should be celebrated by the masses. Here, you can drive to a Canadian Rockies trailhead in less time than most of us spend checking our email each day.

One of those trails leads to Rummel Lake, a little-known, easy-to-reach, scenic destination that's rarely crowded, usually tranquil, and likely to afford solitude.

Nearby Chester Lake (Trip 11), which is no more impressive than Rummel and arguably less so, has a palatial trailhead parking lot to accommodate a year-round parade of admirers.

Rummel has no parking lot. There's just a small, unsigned pullout across the road. So the trail inauspiciously departs the dusty shoulder of Hwy 742. Then it rises unceremoniously through a cutblock.

Rummel Lake

But the cutblock is regrowing vigourously. The view it grants of Spray Lakes Reservoir and the Sundance Range is stirring. And the trail soon enters forest, then delivers you to the grass-fringed lake at the base of soaring Mt. Galatea. The setting epitomizes the golden mean: exciting yet calming.

Plus, if you can resist the park-like lakeshore's curiously strong gravitational pull, or muster the will to resume hiking after you've succumbed, you can proceed to Rummel Pass. A few minutes above the lake, the trail transcends treeline and rolls through an alpine expanse worthy of Jasper National Park. After passing several lakelets, you'll crest the pass and find Lost Lake below the far side.

Fact

By Vehicle

From downtown **Canmore**, follow signs leading uphill to the Canmore Nordic Centre. Reset your trip odometer to 0 at the Nordic Centre turnoff. Continue ascending on Smith-Dorrien / Spray Trail (Hwy 742). Pavement soon ends. After crossing Whiteman's Gap, proceed generally southeast to 34 km (21.1 mi).

From the **junction of Hwy 40 and Kananaskis Lakes Trail** (50 km / 31 mi south of Trans-Canada Hwy 1, or 17 km / 10.5 mi north of Highwood Pass), turn southwest onto Kananaskis Lakes Trail. Reset your trip odometer to 0. At 2.2 km (1.4 mi) turn right (northwest) onto unpaved Smith-Dorrien / Spray Trail (Hwy 742). Proceed generally northwest to 30.2 km (18.7 mi).

From either approach, just south of Rummel Creek, turn west onto Mt. Shark Road, signed for Engadine Lodge. Park in the first pullout (left / south). The unsigned trail starts across the highway, east-northeast from Mt. Shark Road, at 1865 m (6117 ft).

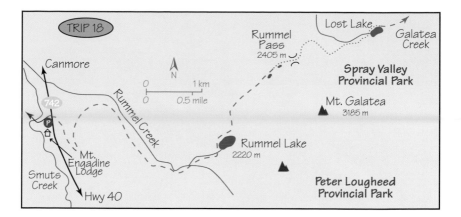

On Foot

The trail initially leads southeast. Pass a sign reminding dog owners to leash their pets.

Heading south-southeast, parallel the highway through a bushy **cutblock** for ten minutes. The young, robust trees are 20 to 25 ft (6 to 7.6 m) high. Still in the cutblock, curve left and ascend northeast.

At 20 minutes, Spray Lakes Reservoir is visible left (northwest). Mt. Birdwood is the prominent peak right (south-southwest). At nearly 30 minutes, 2065 m (6773 ft), the trail leads east-southeast into a **mature forest** of spruce and fir.

About 40 minutes along, the forest is more open and bearberry is profuse. At one hour, the trail grazes Rummel Creek at 2150 m (7052 ft). Follow the trail upstream (east). Ignore the bridge to the left (northeast) bank. Stay on the right (south) bank for the more interesting approach.

Where the bank briefly steepens and crowds the creek, the trail traverses it, deteriorating to a rough, narrow route. Comfortable trail resumes just beyond. Pass above the right (south) side of a **cascade**. The trail continues northeast along the base of a small rockslide, toward Mt. Galatea. Soon push through brush and rockhop to the creek's left (north-northwest) bank.

Subalpine zone between Rummel Lake and Rummel Pass

Ascending through the cutblock to Rummel Creek

Reach the southwest shore of **Rummel Lake**, beside the outlet, at 4.3 km (2.7 mi), 2220 m (7281 ft), about 1¼ hours from the trailhead. Rising abruptly from the southeast shore is 3185-m (10,447-ft) Mt. Galatea. Grass and alpine larch ring the lake.

For Rummel Pass, follow the main trail left (north-northeast), away from the lake. After a five-minute ascent left (north), break into the **alpine zone**. The trail curves right (northeast). The groundcover includes tiny, white, mountain avens. Mounts Birdwood and Smuts are visible behind you (southwest).

Cross an expanse of rocks and ascend a dryfall to arrive at a shallow **lakelet** (possibly dry) at 2350 m (7708 ft). Continue northeast, passing another **lakelet** five minutes farther. On its left (north) side is a cairned route leading east-northeast toward the pass.

Ascend across chunky talus. Follow cairns through a depression. After hiking 2.5 km (1.6 mi) from the southwest end of Rummel Lake, crest 2405-m (7888-ft) **Rummel Pass**. Total distance from the trailhead: 13.6 km (8.4 mi).

Lost Lake is visible down-valley (east-northeast). From the pass, the route descends left (northeast) across scree. It passes Lost Lake in 2.2 km (1.4 mi), then continues northeast through forest another 3.2 km (2 mi) to intersect Galatea Creek trail (Trip 17) 2 mi (3.2 km) east of Lillian Lake.

TRIP 19
King Creek Ridge

LOCATION	Peter Lougheed Provincial Park, Hwy 40
LOOP	7 km (4.3 mi)
ELEVATION GAIN	729 m (2390 ft)
KEY ELEVATIONS	trailhead 1692 m (5550 ft)
	second summit 2421 m (7940 ft)
HIKING TIME	4 to 5 hours
DIFFICULTY	challenging
MAPS	Gem Trek Kananaskis Lakes
	Kananaskis Lakes 82 J/11

Opinion

Zen Buddhists refer to our incessant, mental chatter as "monkey mind." It's needless, futile worrying, for the most part. It keeps us anxiously fixated on the past or future, preventing us from living fully in the present moment. They quell monkey mind by meditating. You can also do it by hiking. To still the mind, move the body. Vigourously. On steep, rough terrain. Like King Creek Ridge.

Though the distance is short, it's excruciatingly steep, so it demands intense effort. You'll scuttle up to and along the crest, ease down the other side, then loop back through a deep, narrow canyon cut by King Creek. You can, of course, simply hike up and down the west face of the ridge, but the loop feels like a journey rather than a mere workout, so it earns you a much greater sense of accomplishment.

Either way, your chief reward will be a nonpareil view of the distinctive Opal Range. Imagine a mountain wall created by layer upon layer of gigantic, skyward-pointing arrowheads. That's the Opals. They're an arresting sight from Hwy 40. But once you crest the ridge, they'll vacuum up every speck of your attention. Your travail below will suddenly seem worthwhile.

After romping along the crest, enjoying frequent views despite the trees, you'll plummet off the east side, into the canyon beneath the Opals. This slope, too, is relentlessly steep. But because it's trail-less, vegetation helps provide footing, making it slightly less precarious than the gravity-swept trail ascending the west side.

Once you tag onto the path descending the east-side canyon, you can relax and enjoy a deliciously remote atmosphere that belies your proximity to the highway. You're unlikely to see other bipeds here, but you might spot bighorn sheep clinging to the crags. Make noise to warn the odd grizzly of your presence.

Upon reaching King Creek, you'll exit via a sheer-walled slot that briefly creates the illusion that you're in southern Utah. The trail repeatedly

The Opal Range, from King Creek Ridge

crosses the creek. Easy rockhopping forces you to interact with and more fully appreciate the lively water. It's a fun, carefree finale to an otherwise taxing hike.

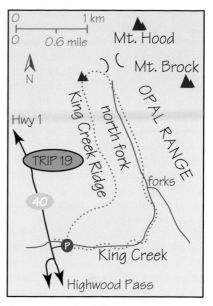

Fact

By Vehicle

From Trans-Canada Hwy 1, drive south 49.9 km (30.9 mi) on Hwy 40. Or, from Highwood Pass, drive north 17 km (10.5 mi) on Hwy 40. From either approach, turn east into the signed King Creek day use area trailhead parking lot, at 1692 m (5550 ft). It's 100 m (110 yd) north of where Kananaskis Lakes Trail intersects Hwy 40.

On Foot

Ignore the signed trail departing the east end of the parking lot. It probes King Creek canyon. You'll loop back that way. Your initial goal is to begin ascending the slope north of the parking lot, across the creek.

If the creek's shallow, rockhop it. Otherwise walk out to the highway. Immediately before the stop sign, leave the pavement by turning right (north) onto the bootbeaten path crossing the grassy slope below the guardrail. It drops then rises, curving upstream to a level bench well above the creek's north bank. Ahead you'll see two diverging paths. Go right (east) and descend toward the creek. Just before the final drop to the bank, look left (east). **Flagging** and a **cairn** mark where a **distinct trail** rockets up the treed slope.

About two minutes up, the path traverses north and the grade eases. Clink and clank across a **rockslide**. About eight minutes up, at 1782 m (5846 ft), reach a fork. Left (north) is crudely blocked by rocks. Go right (east) and ascend sharply again. About twelve minutes up, break out of the trees momentarily. Stonecrop (yellow) is profuse here. Arrive at a **cairn** on a level, narrow, open **bench**.

Scramblers might choose to abandon the trail at this cairn and proceed cross-country, generally east-northeast, directly to the ridgecrest. If you're comfortable forging your own route, you'll actually find more secure traction on the rocky, vegetated slope than you will on the dirt trail.

Hikers preferring to stay on the trail should proceed north from the cairn, along the forest edge. Drop into a **draw**, rise out of it, then switchback right (east), climbing very steeply again. The trail leads farther north than might seem necessary, but in doing so it skirts small rock bands, avoids most of the forest, and grants an ever-improving view of Lower Kananaskis Lake.

About 30 minutes up, at 1939 m (6360 ft), the trail climbs through a grassy **clearing**. About 42 minutes up, at 2073 m (6800 ft), the trail forks. Left (north) is crudely blocked by small tree trunks. Go right. Soon enter forest.

Fork right one more time, shortly before cresting **King Creek Ridge** at 2192 m (7190 ft). Fast hikers will arrive here about 55 minutes after departing the creek. If you intend to return the way you came, note where the trail exits the ridge, so you can find it easily. After tearing your eyes from the striking Opal Range (east), you'll see Mt. Wintour (south), and the Mangin Glacier on Mt. Joffre (southwest, beyond Upper Kananaskis Lake).

Ready to continue hiking? Go left (north). Paths on both sides of the crest lead to the **first summit** at 2332 m (7650 ft). Watch for bighorn sheep on outcroppings below (east). About 20 minutes along the crest, the second summit is visible ahead.

The path drops, then ascends grass, reaching the **second summit** at 3 km (1.9 mi), 2421 m (7940 ft). Across the canyon, 2904-m (9525-ft) Mt. Hood (northeast) and 2902-m (9520-ft) Mt. Brock (east) punctuate the Opals. Northwest, across Hwy 40, you can identify the dirt road winding up to Fortress Ski Area and Fortress Ridge (Trip 18). Ahead (north) the ridgecrest dips, then rises to a third, more precarious summit.

The **descent route** into the canyon is the gully right (east) of the dip. This gouged scar funnels down between rock outcroppings. Initially bailing off the ridge is a challenge. Erosion has left slippery dirt here and little else. Traverse slowly back and forth, seeking purchase on the margins of the gully. Small rock ledges offer traction beneath the outcroppings.

Where you pop out of the gully and step down on a meter-high rock, look left for a cairn on the rock ledge. Contour left. Cross a narrow strip of rock. Briefly proceed north on a narrow path—below a short rock wall (left), above the edge of trees (right). Then descend the **grassy slope** right (east). The grade gradually eases. Keep working your way down. Remember to scan for bighorn sheep, and to make bear-warning calls. From the ridgecrest, it takes about 15 minutes to reach the faint path near the canyon bottom.

You're now in the **north fork of King Creek canyon**, at about 2160 m (7085 ft). The saddle linking the ridge with the Opals is left (north) just above you. Look right (south). You can see where the canyon's north and south forks split from the main canyon, which runs east / west. That's your next goal. At a moderate pace, you'll be there in about an hour. The following paragraph offers more detail than you might want or need. Simply descend the willow-choked drainage. There's a discernible path most of the way.

Soon reach a nearly flat area. Continue down-canyon. Stay above the right (west) bank of the streambed, through grass and red-lanced shrubs. Where the path dumps you in the rocky streambed, with taller trees to the right, look left for an opening in the head-high willows. Burrow through for about a minute. The path resumes above the left (east) bank of the streambed. About five minutes farther, enter a stand of mature spruce. Keep descending the path. It favours the canyon's left (east) side, though it does cross and re-cross the streambed, as well as tributary ravines. A few cairns offer guidance.

King Creek Canyon

Reach the **main King Creek canyon**, where the north and south forks split, at 1825 m (5986 ft). Turn right (southwest). Rockhop to the creek's left (south) bank. The trail leads downstream, curving west. You'll arrive at the trailhead—1.6 km (1 mi) distant—in about 40 minutes.

The canyon is narrow, with sheer walls. Flooding runoff has left numerous logjams in the creek. Watch for dippers: tiny birds that do a knee-bending dance before plunging into running water to snatch food. Cross the creek several times, wherever necessary to keep following the trail. It leads to the paved trailhead parking lot, above the creek's south bank.

TRIP 20
Mt. Indefatigable

LOCATION	Peter Lougheed Provincial Park
	between Upper and Lower Kananaskis lakes
ROUND TRIP	7.6 km (4.7 mi) to summit ridge
ELEVATION GAIN	920 m (3018 ft)
KEY ELEVATIONS	trailhead 1725 m (5658 ft), NE outlier 2485 m (8150 ft)
	summit ridge 2645 m (8676 ft)
HIKING TIME	3½ to 4½ hours
DIFFICULTY	moderate
MAPS	Gem Trek Kananaskis Lakes
	Kananaskis Lakes 82 J/11

Opinion

Mt. In-duh-FAT-igabull. Mt. In-duh-fuh-TEEG-a-bull. Mt. Unpronounceable. Or simply *Mt. Fatty.* Call it what you will. Just don't miss this astounding hike. And don't succumb to fatigue until you reach the culminating alpine ridgecrest just south of Fatty's summit—a majestic vantage high above Upper and Lower Kananaskis lakes. It's worth enduring the labouriously vertical trail simply to survey these sprawling mountain lakes from such a grand height. But the scenic reward extends above and beyond the lakes, to burly peaks in every direction.

For those unable to surmount treeline and attain Fatty's summit ridge, there are consolation prizes: two fine viewpoints. The first is about a third of the way up. The second is two-thirds of the way up, at trail's end. But strong hikers should proceed west to the premier K-Country vantage. The route to the ridgecrest is steep and rocky, but it's not quite a scramble and can be dispatched in half an hour. Even a Hufflepuff can do it in 45 minutes.

Another option beyond trail's end is the generally northwest ascent through a meadowy basin to Fatty's northeast outlier. Though slightly farther than Fatty's summit ridge, the outlier is a less strenuous goal. It's also less scenic. The basin's wildflower display, however, can be kaleidoscopic. Purple fleabane, red paintbrush, white Sitka valerian, yellow glacier lilies, and white mountain avens abound in early summer.

But hang on. Before fixating on Fatty as your destination, be aware that the trail is unsigned and unmaintained, gradually deteriorated to a mere route. It also passes through critical grizzly-bear habitat, where sows with cubs typically linger for weeks. If you go, remain vigilantly alert. Make noise frequently. If you see a bear, or fresh scat indicating a bear is present, abort your trip. Hike elsewhere. Visit Fatty another time.

Ascending Fatty's northeast outlier, Upper Kananaskis Lake in background

Fact

By Vehicle

From Trans-Canada Hwy 1, drive south 50 km (31 mi) on Hwy 40. Or, from Highwood Pass, drive north 17 km (10.5 mi) on Hwy 40. From either approach, turn southwest onto Kananaskis Lakes Trail. Reset your trip odometer to 0.

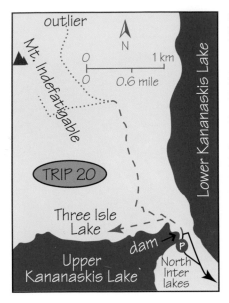

0 km (0 mi)
Starting southwest on Kananaskis Lakes Trail.

2.2 km (1.4 mi)
Proceed straight where Smith-Dorrien / Spray Trail (Hwy 742) forks right.

9.8 km (6.1 mi)
Proceed straight where right leads to Lower Kananaskis Lake and Boulton Creek campground.

12.6 km (7.8 mi)
Proceed straight where left leads to the trailhead parking lot on the southeast shore of Upper Kananaskis Lake.

14.8 km (9.2 mi)
Bear left, uphill. Straight leads to Panorama. Right leads to Interlakes campground.

15.2 km (9.4 mi)
Reach the trailhead parking lot at North Interlakes day use area. It's on the northeast shore of Upper Kananaskis Lake. Elevation: 1725 m (5658 ft).

On Foot
From the trailhead kiosk at the north end of the parking lot, walk northwest atop the dam. Soon cross the **spillway bridge**. Turn left (west) onto an old road. Reach an **unsigned junction** just beyond, at 0.3 km (0.2 mi). The old road continues west, above the lake's north shore. It leads to Trips 21, 22, 23 and 24. Turn right here onto the Mt. Indefatigable trail, initially blocked by boulders.

The trail undulates generally northwest in subalpine forest. Climbing through rock bands, several paths diverge but rejoin above. A severe ascent north (dirt and scree) leads to a rocky **promontory** at 1.3 km (0.8 mi), 1980 m (6495 ft). It overlooks Upper and Lower Kananaskis lakes. Also visible are Mt. Sarrail (south-southwest) and Mt. Lyautey (southwest).

The rocky route continues ascending steeply north, above the east-facing limestone escarpment that rises from Lower Kananaskis Lake. The view is panoramic. The Opal Range is northeast, the Elk Range southeast. Larch trees begin to appear.

Nearly an hour up, at 2207 m (7240 ft), pass a minor, left (west) spur. Proceed straight (north). One minute farther, the narrow, rooty path forking left (west) leads to Fatty's summit ridge. But before going that way, continue a few minutes farther north to the **trail's end viewpoint** at 2.5 km (1.6 mi),

Above Upper Kananaskis Lake, on Fatty's lower slopes

2210 m (7250 ft). The serrated Opal Range dominates the northeast horizon. For directions to Fatty's northeast outlier, skip below.

Now back at the fork: Fatty's summit ridge is west, 1.3 km (0.8 mi) farther and 415 m (1362 ft) higher. Follow the narrow route uphill through spruce, larch and heather. Where it levels, bear left on a narrower route. Proceed through a glade, then up a broad, grassy slope. The route veers right, granting a view of Fatty's northeast outlier, then left across grass and patches of shale. Where the ridge becomes steeper and rockier, the route splits in a shallow depression. An angling ascent, right to left, leads to a cairn on the **ridgecrest** at 2645 m (8676 ft). Total distance from the trailhead: 3.8 km (2.4 mi).

You can continue right (north-northwest) from the cairn, but the view does not improve significantly. Beyond the communications gizmo, you must negotiate a couple hundred meters of knife-edge if you're intent on reaching Fatty's 2670-m (8760-ft) summit.

Ah, the view. Upper Kananaskis Lake is south, far below. Southwest of it is smaller Hidden Lake. Beyond that is Mt. Sarrail (left) and Aster Lake basin—the descent route from Northover Ridge (Trip 24). Reigning over the peaks, glaciers and snowfields in that direction is Mt. Joffre. West is the valley leading to Three Isle Lake. Northwest, below you, is Invincible Creek canyon, which drains Invincible Lake (Trip 21). Northeast, beyond Lower Kananaskis Lake and Hwy 40, is the Opal Range. West-southwest is Pocaterra Ridge (Trip 30) in the Elk Range. Southwest are the Elk passes (Trip 26).

Basin beneath Fatty's northeast outlier

Northeast Outlier

From the trail's end viewpoint, at 2.5 km (1.6 mi), 2210 m (7250 ft), you'll ascend 280 m (918 ft) in 1.5 km (0.9 mi) to reach Fatty's northeast outlier in about 45 minutes.

Proceed north. Four strides ahead, ignore a minor path. During the next eight minutes, bear right at two forks. Your general direction of travel is northwest. (On the way back, go left on the path with orange flagging.)

Ten minutes beyond trail's end, enter a wet, verdant **basin**. Right (west) is a drainage plummeting to Lower Kananaskis Lake. Round the right (northeast) side of a seasonal **pond** and hop across its narrow outlet stream. Ascend northwest on grassy, flowery slopes beside stands of larch.

Curve north for the final approach. Soon top out at 2485 m (8150 ft) on the **northeast outlier**. Total distance from the trailhead: 4 km (2.5 mi). Total elevation gain: 760 m (2493 ft).

King Creek Ridge (Trip 19) is north-northeast, beneath the Opals. The Smith-Dorrien road is north-northwest. Mt. Indefatigable's true summit is southwest. Separating you from the true summit is a col. Vary your return by descending that way.

Glacier lily

TRIP 21
Invincible Lake

LOCATION	Peter Lougheed Provincial Park, northwest of Upper Kananaskis Lake
ROUND TRIP	14 km (8.7 mi)
ELEVATION GAIN	635 m (2082 ft)
KEY ELEVATIONS	trailhead 1725 m (5658 ft) high point 2375 m (7790 ft), lake 2255 m (7396 ft)
HIKING TIME	7 to 8 hours
DIFFICULTY	challenging
MAPS	page 128; Gem Trek Kananaskis Lakes Kananaskis Lakes 82 J/11

Opinion

On a rough road in Bhutan, a sign warns of worse conditions ahead and suggests what to do. "Treacherous road," it says. "Bash on regardless."

That's the human condition, isn't it? Bash on regardless. Which is why an off-trail hike, such as this one to Invincible Lake, is an apt metaphor for life. It's a physical reminder that faith and determination are necessary to overcome the inevitable difficulties.

En route to Invincible Lake, the difficulties are not treacherous. And, given the assurances of a guidebook, faith comes easily. But you'll still feel you're bashing on regardless.

You'll start by hiking the old road maintained as trail around the north shore of Upper Kananaskis Lake, just as you would for Three Isle Lake (Trip 23). Then you'll veer onto the road's rougher, unmaintained, upper reaches. Soon you'll abandon the road and commit to a steep, arduous, cross-country ascent on an eerily beautiful slope swept by fire long ago. The terrain is bristling with silver snags. The grass is lush. Fuschia fireweed is profuse. Deadfall is a frequent obstacle. The views are inspiring. Your goal is skyward: a ridgecrest that looks discouragingly distant.

Though the navigation is not puzzling, to enjoy this trip you'll need either off-trail experience or a keen desire to begin extending your hiking range. The ascent ends on a ridgecrest overlooking Invincible Lake sequestered in a lonely basin and guarded by titans: Mounts Indefatigable, Invincible, and Warspite. Decision time: call it a day, or proceed to the lake?

You can turn back at the ridge pleased with your reward: a rousing panorama that includes Upper Kananaskis Lake, the Great Divide, and the mountains extending into Elk Lakes Provincial Park. Or you can continue the exploration all the way to Invincible Lake. That necessitates descending via game trail, then briefly ascending cross-country yet again. Though day-hiking to the lake is feasible, backpacking is preferable. The trail-less approach all but guarantees you'll enjoy a solitudinous night in the wilds. And camping enables you to wander farther the next morning, into Invincible Creek's meadowy north-fork basin.

Fact

By Vehicle

Follow directions for Mt. Indefatigable (Trip 20) to the trailhead parking lot at North Interlakes day use area. It's on the northeast shore of Upper Kananaskis Lake. Elevation: 1725 m (5658 ft).

On Foot

From the trailhead kiosk at the north end of the parking lot, walk northwest atop the dam. Soon cross the bridge over the spillway. Turn left (west) onto an old road. Reach a **signed junction** just beyond, at 0.3 km (0.2 mi). The trail forking right ascends Mt. Indefatigable (Trip 20). Continue west on the old road above Kananaskis Lake's north shore. Soon bear right at the map-sign.

At 0.8 km (0.5 mi) and 2.2 km (1.4 mi), where left forks drop to the lakeshore trail, bear right and stay high on the rocky, old road. The lake is visible below. Also attain a view left (south-southwest), beyond the lake, up Aster Creek canyon (Trip 24), formed by 3174-m (10,414-ft) Mt. Sarrail on its east side and 3082-m (10,112-ft) Mt. Lyautey on its west.

Cross the Palliser rockslide. After curving northwest, the road descends. About an hour from the trailhead, reach a bridge over **Invincible Creek** at 3.8 km (2.3 mi), 1750 m (5740 ft). Mountainbikers must stop here. The trail to Three Isle Lake (Trip 23), Northover Ridge (Trip 24) and North Kananaskis Pass (Trip 22) continues across the bridge. Turn right for Invincible Lake.

About 25 m/yd upstream from the bridge, the old road continues on the far (west) bank. Rockhop across and proceed northwest on the gently ascending road. If the creek is too deep, cross the bridge, go right (upstream), regain the road and follow it left (northwest). The forest is slowly reclaiming the road. It's choked with young trees and cluttered with deadfall. Note the following landmarks so you know precisely where to begin the cross-country ascent.

The road bends left (west). About 15 minutes beyond Invincible Creek, an enormous **log jam** on the right testifies to nature's might. Two minutes farther, at a small **clearing**, Mt. Lyautey is visible again southwest. Mt. Putnik is west-southwest. One minute past the clearing, at 1857 m (6090 ft), reach a **cairn**. Depart the road here by turning right. Ascend the steep sand-and-dirt bank into open forest. This departure point is immediately before the road curves right and dips.

You're now hiking trail-less terrain. Ascend north on the steep, snag-strewn slope. Follow the crest of the **rib** running all the way to the ridgecrest. The view west-southwest is up Three Isle Creek valley. At 2240 m (7347 ft), continue upward beside small rock outcrops and a ribbon of trees. Fireweed and asters festoon the grass. Keep heading north.

Invincible Lake and Spray Mountains

Top out on the **ridgecrest** at about 2375 m (7790 ft), slightly right (east) of and just above a treed gap. Turn left, pass a cairn, drop into the gap, and ascend the crest west-northwest to attain a better **vantage point**. Within five minutes, overlook Invincible Lake northwest. The great cliffs of an unnamed ridge rise above scree left (west) of the lake. Mt. Nomad, the small, conical peak right (east) of the lake, is north. Sculpted Mt. Invincible is northeast. Mt. Indefatigable is east. Upper Kananaskis Lake is southeast. Hidden Lake is south-southeast. The farther you ascend the crest, the better the view.

To reach Invincible Lake, follow the elk trail starting on the northeast side of the gap. It rounds a knob and descends into larch forest on the north side of the ridge. After crossing shale and scree, the path fades in grass near the bottom of the draw. Rockhop to the north bank of Invincible Creek (the lake's outlet stream), then begin a gentle ascent west-northwest on grassy slopes. Curve northwest across a rockslide. The terrain steepens on the final approach. Reach **Invincible Lake** at 7 km (4.3 mi), 2255 m (7396 ft). Cross the low ridge north of the lake to explore Invincible Creek's meadowy north-fork basin below 2850-m (9348-ft) Mt. Warspite.

TRIP 22
North Kananaskis Pass

LOCATION	Peter Lougheed Provincial Park, northwest of Upper Kananaskis Lake
ROUND TRIP	34.4 km (21.3 mi)
ELEVATION GAIN	660 m (2165 ft)
KEY ELEVATIONS	trailhead 1725 m (5658 ft)
	Lawson Lake 2220 m (2782 ft), pass 2365 m (7757 ft)
HIKING TIME	10 hours to 2 days
DIFFICULTY	moderate
MAPS	Gem Trek Kananaskis Lakes
	Kananaskis Lakes 82 J/11

Opinion

Trendy restaurants, blaring concerts, terrifying movies, and recreational drugs are inadequate substitutes for the adventure missing from modern life. The more you strip away *modern* from *life*, the more adventurous it gets. And here's a beautiful hike where you can easily do that for a couple days.

North Kananaskis Pass is one of several premier K-Country destinations that share the same trailhead and initial approach. Before planning a journey here, read Three Isle Lake (Trip 23). It will broaden your understanding of the area and explain the many dayhiking and backpacking options available.

If you're fit and focused, North K Pass is hikeable in a day. But it's more rewarding to wag a full pack and camp at least one night at Turbine Canyon, just below the pass. Stay two nights if you also want to venture north, toward Mt. Jellicoe and Haig Glacier.

Bound for North K Pass, you'll begin on an old, rocky road that suffices as a trail. A few striking vistas will inspire you to keep chugging around the north shore of Upper Kananaskis Lake. At Invincible Creek, continue on a soft path winding through lovely forest. After Forks campground, follow the Upper Kananaskis River, then gear down for a long ascent.

Views expand while you assail an avalanche slope. Escape the trees and enjoy a long, nearly level traverse through rock gardens, subalpine meadows, and a princely stand of larches. Peaks roar to life around you. Pass a tarn, a small but sensational canyon, and two alpine lakes before coasting into the pass—a wonderfully scenic, rolling alpine ridge on the Great Divide.

The mountains crowding the pass are impressively forbidding, but a verdant slope beckons you down the far side. Decline the invitation. Yes, the Gem Trek map indicates a route proceeding to South K Pass (Trip 23) via LeRoy Creek valley and Beatty Lake. And yes, it conceivably allows you to hike a circuit linking these two marvelous passes. But don't take that dotted line casually. It entails routefinding, bushwhacking, an elevation loss of 620 m (2034 ft), and a gain of 555 m (1820 ft).

Lawson Lake, Mt. Maude (left), Mt. Jellicoe (right)

Fact

Before your trip

If you're staying overnight, bring a stove. Open fires are prohibited at Turbine Canyon.

By Vehicle

Follow directions for Mt. Indefatigable (Trip 20) to the trailhead parking lot at North Interlakes day use area. It's on the northeast shore of Upper Kananaskis Lake. Elevation: 1725 m (5658 ft).

On Foot

Follow directions for Three Isle Lake (Trip 23) to **Forks junction and campground** at 7.2 km (4.5 mi), 1785 m (5855 ft). Left (west) leads to Three Isle Lake and South Kananaskis Pass, as well as Northover Ridge (Trip 24). Bear right and proceed north-northwest for Lawson Lake, Turbine Canyon, and North Kananaskis Pass.

Forks campground is in forest, above the Kananaskis River. In addition to 15 tent pads, it has outhouses, four tables, benches around a fire pit, plus a metal food cache. The optimal site is #15, at the northwest end of the campground, between the creek and the trail.

The trail parallels the **Upper Kananaskis River** gorge for about the next 20 minutes, heading upstream above the west bank. Your general direction

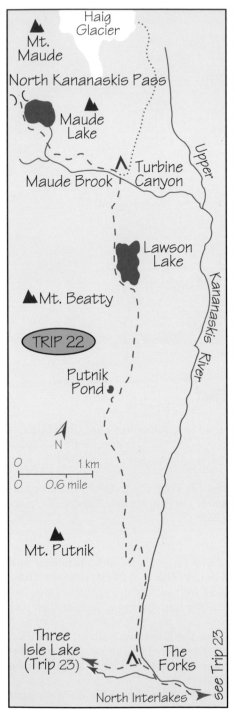

of travel will remain north-north-west all the way to Turbine Canyon.

At 8.5 km (5.3 mi), just after a cascade flowing off Mt. Putnik (left), begin ascending steeply. The trail soon switchbacks up an **avalanche slope**, through head-high willows and alders. Attain views south to 3081-m (10,112-ft) Mt. Lyautey. Nearly an hour from the Forks, re-enter forest near 2150 m (7050 ft), where larches signal that treeline is near. Cross a bridged stream beneath the massive walls of a cirque on your left (west), between Mounts Putnik (south) and Beatty (northwest). Continue switchbacking.

At 11.5 km (7.1 mi) the trail emerges from forest onto a small saddle on a larch-covered ridge overlooking **Putnik's Pond**. The Spray Mtns, including Mt. Black Prince, are northeast. Descend into the valley to begin a long, nearly level traverse—through rock gardens, subalpine meadows, and an impressive larch forest—on a 2240-m (7347-ft) bench beneath Mt. Beatty's east slope. Visible ahead (just left of north) is 3247-m (10,650-ft) Mt. Jellicoe. North-northwest are 3043-m (9981-ft) Mt. Maude and Haig Glacier.

Reach **Lawson Lake** at 13.2 km (8.2 mi), 2220 m (7282 ft). Part of Beatty Glacier is visible west. Northwest beyond the lake, the twin summits of Mt. Maude are a spectacular sight. The trail curves left, then continues north-northwest, up the lake's west shore. Near the north end of the lake, at 14.7 km (9.1 mi), a sign indicates a ranger cabin to the left.

At 15 km (9.3 mi), cross a bridge over Maude Brook and

Maude Lake and Mt. Maude

reach **Turbine Canyon campground**. Fast hikers will arrive here 3½ hours after departing the trailhead. It has 12 tent pads, a separate eating area, bear-proof food storage, an outhouse, and a view of Beatty Glacier (southwest). Just downstream is Turbine Canyon—a narrow, snaking chasm in which Maude Brook plummets 330 m (1082 ft) eastward into Upper Kananaskis River canyon.

Left (west) at the campground leads to North Kananaskis Pass. The trail climbs gradually through meadows and stunted trees. Crest a rocky, alpine ridge at 16.5 km (10.2 mi), 2370 m (7774 ft)—the trip's highpoint. Then drop to **Maude Lake** beneath the steep, desolate, north slope of Mt. Maude. Round the west shore to arrive at 2365-m (7757-ft) **North Kananaskis Pass**. You've hiked 17.2 km (10.7 mi) from the trailhead.

The pass straddles the boundary distinguishing Alberta's Peter Lougheed Provincial Park from B.C.'s Height of the Rockies Provincial Park. The north arm of Mt. Beatty drops to the south edge of the pass. Visible northwest, across Leroy Creek valley, are Mounts LeRoy (left) and Monro (right). Southwest, across the Palliser River valley, are Mounts Prince Henry (right), Prince Edward (middle), and Prince Albert (left) in the Royal Group. An uninviting, severely steep, rough trail dives off the west side of the pass and curves southwest, following LeRoy Creek downstream to the Palliser River.

TRIP 23

Three Isle Lake / South Kananaskis Pass

LOCATION	Peter Lougheed Provincial Park, west of Upper Kananaskis Lake
ROUND TRIP	20.8 km (12.9 mi) to lake, 24.8 km (15.4 mi) to pass
ELEVATION GAIN	475 m (1558 ft) to lake, 610 m (2000 ft) to pass
KEY ELEVATIONS	trailhead 1725 m (5658 ft), lake 2160 m (7085 ft) pass 2305 m (7560 ft)
HIKING TIME	8 hours to 2 days
DIFFICULTY	moderate
MAPS	Gem Trek Kananaskis Lakes Kananaskis Lakes 82 J/11

Opinion

Drive a paved road, shamble a few steps from your car, and magnificence greets you: vast Upper Kananaskis Lake haloed by lofty mountains. So why leave it and plod into the wilderness beyond? For the same reason you don't just gaze at your lover. You make love, meld, become one.

Hiking propels you from sightseeing to experience; from spectator to participant; from taking a snapshot with your eyes, to putting yourself in the picture. Here, the picture is multi-faceted. Like a painting by Hieronymus Bosch, it contains worlds within worlds. You must choose among them.

Shortly beyond Upper Kananaskis Lake, you have the choice of detouring to Invincible Lake (Trip 21). At Upper Kananaskis River, the choice is North Kananaskis Pass (Trip 22), or Three Isle Lake? At the lake, the choice is Northover Ridge (Trip 24), or South Kananaskis Pass? At South Kananaskis Pass, you have the choice of continuing to Beatty Lake. On Northover Ridge, you have the choice of proceeding to Aster Lake and looping back to Upper Kananaskis Lake. The following synopses will help you decide.

Think of the Invincible Lake hike as distinctly separate, though it shares the same initial approach as the other options. It merits an overnight backpack trip but can be dayhiked. The rugged route requires navigational skill, so it promises solitude.

The trip to North K Pass is beautiful and lenient. It's hikeable in a day from the trailhead, if you're strong and determined, but you'll be rewarded for lugging a full pack and spending a night out.

Three Isle Lake is simply a landmark en route to superior scenery and greater adventure. The lake is pretty when full-pool, but expect to see a broad, muddy shoreline lending a ring-around-the-tub appearance. If you go, keep going at least to South K Pass, where you'll overlook the entire

Three Isle Lake and South Kananaskis Pass, from ascent to Northover Ridge (Trip 24)

lake basin and gain a revelatory view across enticing meadowlands toward venerable Mt. Beatty. Time permitting, heed the meadowy invitation, forge onward to Beatty Lake and glimpse the Royal Group. Dayhiking to Beatty demands vigour and resolve. Burdened with a backpack, however, surmounting the headwall that guards Three Isle Lake is a chore.

To visit both North and South K passes, consider backpacking the utterly easy 7.2 km (4.5 mi) to Forks campground. Start early. After setting up camp, dayhike to South K Pass and possibly Beatty Lake. On day two, light out for North K Pass, scoot back to camp, then head home. Most people, preferring a leisurely pace, will make this a three-day trip by hiking only as far as the campground on day one.

Now hear this. The real reason to hike to Three Isle Lake is because it's on the way to Northover Ridge. Nowhere in K-Country, perhaps nowhere in the entire Canadian Rockies, is there a more sensational hike than the Northover loop. If you're a gladiator capable of marching with Caesar, you can pull it off in a single, ambitiously long, arduously challenging, gloriously fulfilling day. Backpacking Northover in two or three days is equally splendid, though less of a crowning achievement. But Northover is strictly for confident scramblers and proficient cross-country navigators.

If the Northover loop exceeds your ability or desire, try a one-way trip: attain the supremely scenic ridge, then turn back before descending to Aster Lake. It's possible to do this as a long dayhike from Upper Kananaskis Lake trailhead, but much easier if you start at Three Isle Lake campground.

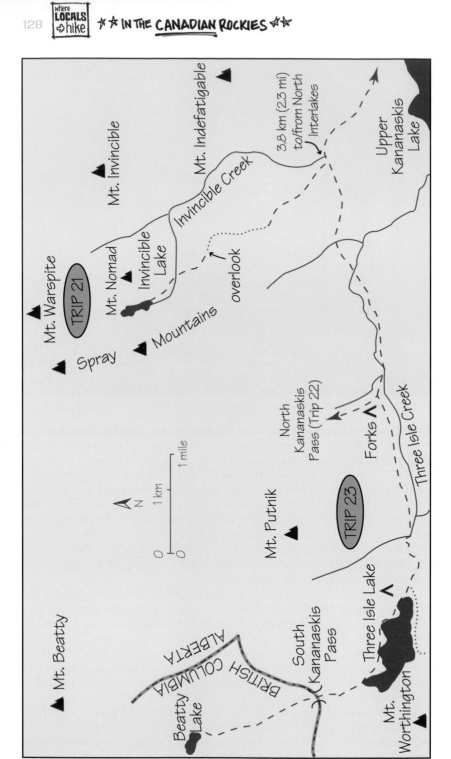

Mt. Beatty

Beatty Lake

BRITISH COLUMBIA
ALBERTA

South Kananaskis Pass

Three Isle Lake

Mt. Worthington

Mt. Putnik

North Kananaskis Pass (Trip 22)

TRIP 23

Forks

Three Isle Creek

N

0 — 1 km
0 — 1 mile

Mt. Warspite

Spray

Mountains

TRIP 21

Mt. Nomad

Invincible Lake

overlook

Mt. Invincible

Invincible Creek

Mt. Indefatigable

3.8 km (2.3 mi) to/from North Interlakes

Upper Kananaskis Lake

Ascending the headwall to Three Isle Lake

Camping at Three Isle also gives you the option of dayhiking to Northover one day, and South K Pass on your day out.

Finally, here's a brief summary of the hike to Three Isle Lake. It follows a rocky road littered with stones that jackhammer your joints. Occasional impressive vistas help keep you motivated. A soft path then winds through lovely, mature forest. After Forks campground, views of surrounding mountains expand while you ascend out of the trees. Assault an avalanche slope. Toil over a very steep headwall. Then catch your breath during a short, gentle descent to the lake.

Fact

Before your trip

If you're staying overnight at Three Isle Lake, bring a stove. Open fires are prohibited.

By Vehicle

Follow directions for Mt. Indefatigable (Trip 20) to the trailhead parking lot at North Interlakes day use area. It's on the northeast shore of Upper Kananaskis Lake. Elevation: 1725 m (5658 ft).

On Foot

From the trailhead kiosk at the north end of the parking lot, walk northwest atop the dam. Soon cross the bridge over the spillway. Turn left (west) onto an old road. Reach a **signed junction** just beyond, at 0.3 km (0.2 mi). The trail forking right ascends Mt. Indefatigable. Continue west on the old road above Upper Kananaskis Lake's north shore. Soon bear right at the mapsign.

At 0.8 km (0.5 mi) and 2.2 km (1.4 mi), where left forks drop to the lakeshore trail, bear right and stay high on the rocky, old road. The lake is visible below. Also attain a view left (south-southwest), beyond the lake, up Aster Creek canyon. Scrutinize it if you intend to complete the entire Northover Ridge loop (Trip 24), because the route descends the left (southeast) wall of that canyon, from high above the falls. This is your only chance to assess the route conditions. If the left wall of the canyon is snow covered, descending could be treacherous. You want to know that now—not near the end of the loop, when turning back would require you to spend the night out and repeat the entire arduous hike in reverse.

Resuming your trip to Three Isle Lake, cross the Palliser rockslide. After curving northwest, the road descends, reaching a bridge over **Invincible Creek** at 3.8 km (2.3 mi). Mountainbikers must stop here. Right leads to Invincible Lake (Trip 21). For Three Isle Lake, cross the bridge and follow the dirt trail generally west through ancient forest. Among the spruce is a stand of 400-year-old lodgepole pine.

At 5.8 km (3.6 mi), 1780 m (5838 ft), cross a bridge over the cascading **Kananaskis River**. Proceed generally west. The headwall you'll ascend to reach the lake is soon visible ahead. In quick succession, cross several bridged streams, all flowing into the river. The trail skirts a rockslide at the base of Mt. Lyautey (left / south).

Shortly after crossing the bridged river again, enter **Forks campground** at 7.2 km (4.5 mi), 1785 m (5855 ft). It's in forest, just above Kananaskis River. You'll find 15 tent pads, outhouses, tables, benches around two communal fire pits, plus a metal food-cache. There's a junction here. Right leads north-northwest to Lawson Lake, Turbine Canyon, and North Kananaskis Pass (Trip 22). Go left (west) for Three Isle Lake and South Kananaskis Pass. The lake is 3.2 km (2 mi) farther. Right (northwest) is Mt. Putnik.

About ten minutes past Forks campground, the trail begins climbing. The grade is increasingly steep. Soon cross an avalanche slope overgrown with willow and alder. Attain views down-valley to Mt. Indefatigable (eastnortheast). At 1980 m (6495 ft), about an hour from Forks campground, begin a skyward ascent of the headwall—a strenuous 15-minute task for strong dayhikers. Stairs assist you over awkward rock bands. Arrive **atop the headwall** at 10 km (6.2 mi), 2200 m (7216 ft).

Proceeding west-northwest, descend 30 m (100 ft) in the next 200 m (220 yd) to a signed junction. Left keeps descending to reach the east shore of **Three Isle Lake** at 10.4 km (6.4 mi), 2160 m (7085 ft). Right enters Three Isle Lake campground (16 tent pads well above the lake, metal food cache) and continues to South Kananaskis Pass.

After delivering you to the lake, the trail leads west, around the south shore. South Kananaskis Pass is visible northwest, beyond the lake. A left spur climbs to a ranger cabin above the south shore. At the lake's southwest corner, shortly past the spur, the route to **Northover Ridge** (Trip 24) curves left (south) up-valley. The ridge is then visible ahead on the skyline.

For South Kananaskis Pass, follow the trail generally northwest from Three Isle Lake campground. It rounds the lake's north shore. Mt. Putnik is right (northeast) above you. Mt. Worthington is left (southwest) beyond the lake. Near the lake's northwest corner, Northover Ridge is visible south. The trail then turns right, heading generally north, ascending moderately through subalpine forest. Surpass treeline and reach **South Kananaskis Pass** at 12.4 km (7.7 mi), 2305 m (7560 ft), on the Great Divide. There's a large cairn here and a sign HEIGHT OF THE ROCKIES WILDERNESS AREA. WELCOME TO B.C. Meadows extend north toward pyramidal, 3000-m (9840-ft) Mt. Beatty.

The trail continues north-northwest from the pass. It descends 120 m (394 ft) in 2 km (1.2 mi) to **Beatty Lake** at 2185 m (7167 ft). Total distance: 14.4 km (8.9 mi). The lake is enclosed by forest and a cliff. Ascend grassy slopes east to gaze southeast, across Palliser River Valley to the Royal Group.

The Royal Group, from Northover Ridge (Trip 24)

TRIP 24
Northover Ridge / Aster Lake

LOCATION	Peter Lougheed Provincial Park, west of Upper Kananaskis Lake
LOOP	33.7 km (20.9 mi)
ELEVATION GAIN	1180 m (3870 ft)
KEY ELEVATIONS	trailhead 1725 m (5658 ft)
	Three Isle Lake 2160 m (7085 ft)
	high point 2830 m (9282 ft)
	Aster Lake 2305 m (7560 ft)
HIKING TIME	11-hour dayhike, or 2-3 day backpack
DIFFICULTY	challenging
MAPS	Gem Trek Kananaskis Lakes
	Kananaskis Lakes 82 J/11

Opinion

Earth is speeding through space at 107,320 kph (66,700 mph). Good thing this galactic vehicle of ours has spoilers. The Himalayas. The Andes. The Alps. The Sierra Nevada. The Rockies. Surely these skyscraping protuberances slow the planet and keep it from spinning out of control. No? Well, maybe not. But on this adventure, into the heart of one of the world's great mountain ranges, it's easy to imagine.

The approach to Northover is via Three Isle Lake (Trip 23). The description of that hike is a helpful preface to this one. Read the *Opinion* section, particularly the last three paragraphs. Go ahead. Do it now. We'll wait here for you.

You're back? Okay. As we were saying, the Northover loop affords an ecstatic sense of exploration. Between Three Isle and Aster lakes, you'll be deep in the wilderness. On trail-less terrain. Labouring up steep scree. Following a sustained high-elevation route. Surrounded by peaks grinding their teeth on passing clouds. Peering into deep, remote, bear-haven valleys. Below Aster Lake, you'll descend an alarmingly steep route into an exciting, severe canyon. Then, if Hidden Lake is full-pool, you might have to thwack 'n thrash around its forested shore to reach Upper Kananaskis Lake and the groomed path that leads back to the trailhead.

So, this thrill ride's price of admission is competence born of backcountry experience. To safely attempt the Northover loop, you must be a strong hiker, able to navigate cross-country. No matter how confident you are, bring a topo map and compass—for enjoyment as well as insurance. If you intend to flash the entire loop in a single day, be prepared to bivouac. Essentials include surplus food, extra layers of warm clothing, and a headlamp.

You're acrophobic? Whoa. For you, Northover would be a mistake. The ridge itself is 2.7 km (1.7 mi) long. A significant stretch is shoulder width

The narrowest section of Northover Ridge

Mt. Joffre, from Northover Ridge

and outer-space airy. This amplifies the thrill if you're sure-footed and unafraid of heights. Otherwise it will reduce you to quivering Jello. The Aster Creek canyon descent route is equally exposed, but unstable, even narrower, and therefore more perilous. If you're rattled by the ridge, you'll be petrified at the prospect of edging along the canyon's heart-stopping cliffs.

Truly hardy hikers: fear not. For you, the challenges described above are reasonable and make the journey more rewarding. And some of the way is as easy as it is sublime. Once the ridge broadens, and foot placement is no longer your focus, you'll simply be walking in the sky, enjoying operatic vistas. You'll see why the Royal Group deserves its august name. You'll see 3450-m (11,319-ft) Mt. Joffre shouldering the Mangin Glacier. You'll see a lonely, lovely, tarn-dappled sanctuary (photo on page 3) beneath Warrior Mtn. After dismounting the ridge, you'll drop into the sprawling basin harbouring Aster Lake. You'll stride through meadows while skirting the lake's shore. It was here that a well-traveled American friend of ours summed up the Northover experience in just three words: "Who needs Alaska?"

Delay your Northover assault until August. By then, the snow should have melted off most of the route, making it safer. It's critical that Aster Creek canyon be free of snow, or the risk of slipping off that precarious descent route will be deadly serious. The second paragraph under *On Foot* in Trip 23 describes where you can view the descent route and assess conditions. If it looks snow-covered, don't go. Also call the park office (403-591-6322) and ask to speak to a ranger who has current information about the route.

Above Aster Lake basin

If you backpack, it's logical to camp at Three Isle Lake your first night out. You can then be atop Northover Ridge before noon on day two, in time for optimal photographs of the Royal Group. If you make this a three-day trip, camp at Aster Lake the second night. Approaching the lake basin in the afternoon is best for photography, because you'll have an aerial view, plus the lake and Mt. Sarrail will be bathed in low-angle light.

Fact

Before your trip

If you're staying overnight, bring a stove. Open fires are prohibited. Also be aware that you must ford Aster Creek. Though shallow, it's broad, frigid and rocky. River sandals or neoprene socks will spare you a few minutes of pain, if you don't mind hauling them the whole way. Bring an extra bandana to dry your feet before rebooting.

By Vehicle

Follow directions for Mt. Indefatigable (Trip 20) to the trailhead parking lot at North Interlakes day use area. It's on the northeast shore of Upper Kananaskis Lake. Elevation: 1725 m (5658 ft).

Although not strictly necessary, you should arrange a shuttle. You'll be glad you did at the end of this trip. Follow directions for Rawson Lake (Trip 25) to leave a vehicle in the trailhead parking lot at Upper Kananaskis Lake day

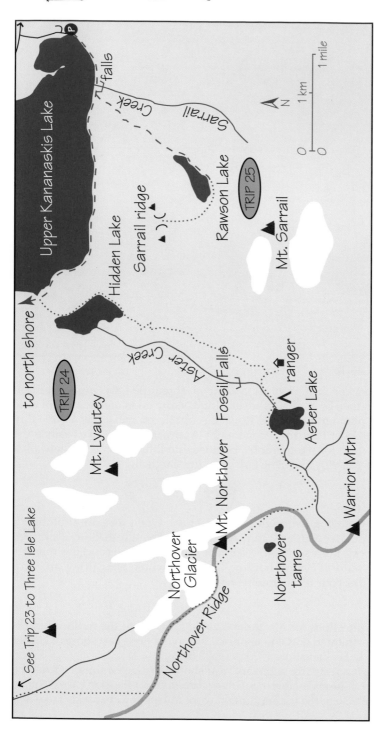

Upper Kananaskis Lake

to north shore

See Trip 23 to Three Isle Lake

TRIP 24

Mt. Lyautey

Northover Glacier

Mt. Northover

Northover Ridge

Northover tarns

Warrior Mtn

Aster Lake

ranger

Fossil Falls

Aster Creek

Hidden Lake

Sarrail ridge

Rawson Lake

Mt. Sarrail

TRIP 25

Sarrail Creek

falls

N

0   1 km
0   1 mile

Northover Ridge loop descends Mt. Sarrail's lower slopes to reach Hidden and Upper Kanananskis lakes.

use area, on the southeast shore. This will spare you a 3.2-km (2-mi) hitchhike or road-walk to link the trailheads and complete the loop.

On Foot

Follow directions for Three Isle Lake (Trip 23). Above the headwall, at the signed junction where right enters Three Isle Lake campground, bear left. Descend to reach the east shore of **Three Isle Lake** at 10.4 km (6.4 mi), 2160 m (7085 ft). Your total elevation gain so far is 475 m (1558 ft).

Follow the trail west, around the south shore. Pass a left spur that climbs to a ranger cabin above the south shore. At the lake's southwest corner, shortly past the spur, the route to Northover Ridge curves left (south) up-valley. The ridge is then visible ahead on the skyline. Right (west) is 2838-m (9311-ft) Mt. Worthington. South Kananaskis Pass is north-northwest, beyond the lake.

The terrain is now open and level. Your general direction of travel will remain south, all the way to the ridgecrest. Visible on the valley's right rear wall is the steep scree slope you must surmount to reach a pass on the crest.

Initially follow a path along the left (east) side of the **valley**. It soon disappears on the rocky flats. Continue, aiming for the scree slope and the pass above it. Before hopping across the stream, top-up your water bottles. Though you might find a snowmelt puddle on the ridge, don't count on it. The next reliable water source is the Northover tarns, below the far end of the ridge, a couple hours distant.

Near the back of the valley, begin ascending the right side of a rocky drainage. Enjoy a reprieve on a **tussocky bench** at 2410 m (7905 ft). The view north is dramatic: over Three Isle Lake basin to South Kananaskis Pass and beyond to Mt. Beatty and neighbouring peaks.

From the bench, keep working your way toward the scree slope and the pass above it. Approaching the scree, you'll see a path bootbeaten into the slope. Tag onto it and toil upward. Atop the 2630-m (8626-ft) **pass**, drop your pack, relax, and congratulate yourself for attaining the **crest of Northover Ridge**. Defender Mtn is on the west side of the pass. Here at the northwest end of the ridge, however, you're still well below the high point. You've hiked 3.8 km (2.4 mi), or about 1½ hours, from Three Isle Lake's east shore. Your total distance is 14.2 km (8.8 mi).

Turn left at the pass and trudge up the talusy ridgecrest southeast. Though it looks dauntingly steep, it's easier than the slope you vanquished below the pass. The ascent route, bootbeaten into loose rock, favours the right (southwest) side. At 2760 m (9053 ft) regain the crest for good. Ups and downs are now minimal. But the crest briefly narrows to a slender **arete**. At one point, you must step from one dinner-plate-size stone to the next, with the earth falling away dramatically on either side. Acrophobes might come unglued here. Surefooted hikers cruise on unconcerned. The crest then broadens, affording easy, carefree, spectacularly scenic hiking. Proceed east-southeast. Keep following the crest.

Dominating the mountainous panorama is the Royal Group (west-northwest) across the deep, forested, Palliser River valley. The massif comprises eight peaks and shoulders a couple glaciers. Visible west, beyond the Rockies, is the Purcell Range in the Kootenays. Mt. Joffre and the Mangin Glacier are southeast. Mt Lyautey is east. These are but a few highlights. Your map will reveal all.

The route closely follows the ridgecrest, which divides Alberta from B.C. Allow time to sit and gaze. The scenery ahead is wonderfully vast and wild, but you're now at the scenic climax of the trip. Looking south, Joffre Creek valley is 1150 m (3772 ft) below you. Above it, south-southwest, is the little-visited Shangri-La of Limestone Lakes basin.

After passing the top edge of Northover Glacier, reach the **Northover Ridge high point**: 2830 m (9282 ft). It's just west-northwest of 3003-m (9850-ft) Mt. Northover. Descend talus slopes, then ascend along the southwest side of the ridge. Looking north-northwest, beyond Northover Glacier, you can again see South Kananaskis Pass. Visible north of the pass is Beatty Glacier, on Mt. Beatty's right (east) side.

The route heads east briefly, toward Mt. Northover, then southeast, dismounting the ridge, plunging into the small basin harbouring the two **Northover tarns**. It's a long, steep, rocky descent, possibly snow covered. After losing about 160 m (535 ft), pick up a path bootbeaten into the scree. It curves south, traversing just left (east) of the tarns, passing about 50 m (164 ft) above the smaller, higher one. South of the basin is 2973-m (9754-ft) Warrior Mtn.

After passing the tarns, the bootbeaten path ascends south to a prominent, 2585-m (8480-ft) **gap**. There's an Alberta provincial-park boundary sign here, announcing your re-entry into Alberta from B.C. Proceed through

Aster Creek ford

the gap. Then descend south, following a faint path on the left (east) wall of the rocky **gorge**. It curves east, dropping toward Aster Lake basin. The lake is visible ahead. Beyond it (east) is 3174-m (10,414-ft) Mt. Sarrail. Pause here to survey the next leg of the journey. Identify the outhouse on the southeast bank of Aster Creek—the lake's outlet. That's your immediate goal. Get there by rounding the lake's north shore. Ignore the south-shore route indicated on the Gem Trek map and you'll avoid splashing through the braided, icy, glacier melt-water streams that feed the lake.

Where scree gives way to dryas, the path disappears. Keep descending the steep, heather-and-dryas slope. Head northeast, curving north. Aim for the delta created by the creek flowing from the left (northwest) drainage. Push through the brush in the delta. Find a place to rockhop across the stream. Then bear right (east). Your total distance is now 20.6 km (12.8 mi). You've hiked 10.2 km (6.3 mi) from the east end of Three Isle Lake.

Pick up scraps of path along the creek's north bank while you hike generally east to **Aster Lake**. Elevation: 2305 m (7560 ft). A more defined path rounds the north shore. Reach the mouth of the outlet—**Aster Creek**—at 22 km (13.6 mi). Ford to the southeast bank. Then go left (northeast) to the outhouse. Trail resumes here, above where the creek cascades into a rocky gorge. A few minutes farther, pass Aster Lake Campground. It has five tent pads and a metal food-cache.

Descend a rocky declivity beside the rampaging falls. The trail zigzags, dropping steeply beside Fossil Falls gorge. Enter trees. Proceed through a grassy gully beneath a water-worn escarpment. Turn right (southeast) following the distinct trail. Soon turn left (northeast) and hop over a stream. The trail goes up and down beneath a cliff, over and around rock ribs. Stay on the main trail; needless ones have been blocked.

About 25 minutes beyond Aster Lake, pass a right spur leading to a **ranger cabin** tucked into Foch Creek basin. Then pass Foch Pond. Your general direction of travel is now northeast and will remain so until Hidden Lake. Soon leave the trees behind and gain an aerial view of Hidden and Upper Kananaskis lakes. Steel yourself for an arduous descent of the formidable **canyon** ahead.

The trail careens down the canyon's east wall—the lower scree slopes of Mt. Sarrail's west face. The terrain is very steep. The trail is obvious, but narrow. Early on, several sections are exposed, meaning the trail is immediately above a vertical drop. A fall could be fatal. Stay alert. Be aware of every step.

At 2076 m (6810 ft) cross a stream in a vertical gully beneath a short cliff. Descend another 122 m (400 ft) and you're on safer ground. There's a lot more talus to negotiate, but the canyon wall is now reclining. At 1900 m (6232 ft), about 1½ hours from Aster Lake, the trail is dirt. Re-enter forest for the final 15-minutes down to Hidden Lake.

Reach the south shore of **Hidden Lake** at 26.5 km (16.4 mi), 1775 m (5822 ft). Mt. Indefatigable is visible north. Follow the rough trail around the right (east) shore—about a 20-minute task. (If it's been a rainy summer, the water level could be high, forcing you to bash through the trees, slowing your progress.) Just beyond the lake's north end, pick up a trail leading northeast into the forest. Within ten minutes, at 28.5 km (17.7 mi), 1718 m (5635 ft), intersect the broad, virtually level trail encircling **Upper Kananaskis Lake**. Turn right (southeast), ignoring any sign suggesting otherwise.

Rounding the south shore, the trail curves east. Only during the final 1 km (0.6 mi) is the lake significantly visible. From where you intersected the lake trail, it takes about 1⅓ hours to reach the trailhead parking lot at Upper Kananaskis Lake day use area, on the southeast shore. Your total distance is now 33.7 km (20.9 mi). If you arranged a vehicle shuttle, as suggested in the *By Vehicle* section, you'll have wheels waiting for you here. Otherwise you must hitchhike or road-walk about 3 km (1.9 mi) generally north-northwest to where you began this trip: the trailhead parking lot at North Interlakes day use area.

Lichen

TRIP 25
Rawson Lake / Sarrail Ridge

LOCATION	Peter Lougheed Provincial Park, south of Upper Kananaskis Lake
ROUND TRIP	7.8 km (4.8 mi) to lake, 11.3 km (7 mi) to ridge
ELEVATION GAIN	300 m (984 ft) to lake, plus 355 m (1164 ft) to ridge
KEY ELEVATIONS	trailhead 1725 m (5658 ft), lake 2025 m (6642 ft) ridge 2380 m (7806 ft)
HIKING TIME	2 to 3 hours for lake, 4½ to 5½ hours for ridge
DIFFICULTY	easy to lake, challenging to ridge
MAPS	page 136; Gem Trek Kananaskis Country Kananaskis Lakes 82 J/11

Opinion

"I'm not in shape for hiking." "I don't have any boots." "I've got out-of-town guests." Rawson Lake trashes these worn-out excuses. You can start getting in shape here, on a measured ascent. Wear your runners; the trail to Rawson is broad and smooth. Bring your guests, let the Canadian Rockies relieve you as host for an afternoon.

Your burden lighter now that you left all that rationalizing behind, you'll stride briskly along a level trail following the shore of mountain-ringed Upper Kananaskis Lake. Then you'll turn into the forest and switch-back upward on a city-park quality path. The elevation gain is significant, but the grade is moderate.

Expect to encounter a steady flow of hikers on summer weekends because this is a short trip starting at a favoured day-use area. Some people don't even intend to hike. They just start walking, see the Rawson Lake sign, and say "Why not?" But despite the lake's popularity, if you proceed along its rocky, southeast shore, you'll likely find a quiet spot where you can meditate on the serene beauty of this cirque clasped in the awesome arms of Mt. Sarrail.

Rawson's too tame to satisfy your appetite for adventure? Keep going. From the southwest shore, storm the steep slope to Sarrail Ridge. It over-looks Upper and Lower Kananaskis lakes, affords an excellent view of Haig Glacier, and boosts you high enough to see over Mt. Sarrail's shoulder to Mt. Foch—an astounding sight. Though you can try the ascent in late June, it might be early July before this southeast-facing slope is hikeable without an ice axe.

It's a hot, summer day? After returning from Rawson Lake, stop just before reaching your vehicle. Drop your pack on the gravel beach below the trailhead. Kick off your footwear, strip to your shorts and halter-top, and plunge into glacier-cold Upper Kananaskis Lake. Your initial gasping shock will soon ease, leaving you relaxed and refreshed. Ahhh.

Looking down the Sarrail Ridge ascent route, above Rawson Lake

Fact

By Vehicle

From Trans-Canada Hwy 1, drive south 50 km (31 mi) on Hwy 40. Or, from Highwood Pass, drive north 17 km (10.5 mi) on Hwy 40. From either approach, turn southwest onto Kananaskis Lakes Trail. Reset your trip odometer to 0.

0 km (0 mi)
Starting southwest on Kananaskis Lakes Trail.

2.2 km (1.4 mi)
Proceed straight where Smith-Dorrien / Spray Trail (Hwy 742) forks right.

9.8 km (6.1 mi)
Proceed straight where right leads to Lower Kananaskis Lake and Boulton Creek campground.

12.6 km (7.8 mi)
Turn left. Straight leads to the trailhead parking lot on the northeast shore of Upper Kananaskis Lake.

12.9 km (8 km)
Bear left. Right is a boat ramp.

13 km (8.1 mi)
Bear right. Left is a parking lot for boat trailers.

13.2 km (8.2 mi)
Arrive at Upper Kananaskis Lake day use area, on the southeast shore. Turn left (south) onto dirt. Right is a paved parking lot and public phone. Both sides have picnic tables above the lake.

13.4 km (8.3 mi)
Park at the far south end of this unpaved lot, near the trailhead sign for Kananaskis and Rawson lakes. Elevation: 1725 m (5658 ft).

On Foot

The wide trail leads southwest around the shore of Upper Kananaskis Lake. Breaks in the forest grant views. Curve west. Mt. Indefatigable (Trip 20) is visible north-northwest, across the lake. At 1.2 km (0.75 mi), just west of the bridge over **Sarrail Creek falls**, fork left at the sign for Rawson Lake.

The trail climbs via moderate switchbacks through a mature forest of Engelmann spruce and subalpine fir. Your general direction of travel will remain southwest to the lake. About 20 minutes up, the ascent eases for the final 1 km (0.6 mi). Stretches of boardwalk start 0.5 km (0.3 mi) before the lake. Reach the northeast shore of **Rawson Lake**, near the outlet stream, at 3.5 km (2.3 mi), 2025 m (6642 ft). Fast hikers will be here in less than an hour. An outhouse is 100 m (110 yd) farther.

Rawson Lake and Mt. Sarrail

The wall just beyond the far (southwest) end of the lake belongs to 3174-m (10,411-ft) Mt. Sarrail. The mountain's flanks clench the lake. Follow the path at least another 300 m (328 yd) southwest, along the southeast shore. The view improves, and you'll find comfortable places to sit and enjoy it. A sign indicates the **end of official trail** and warns that grizzly-bear sightings are common. There's a rock-slab bench here.

A bootbeaten route continues below cliffs and scree slopes, around the **southwest shore**, to an inlet stream created by early-summer snowmelt. Sarrail Ridge looms 355-m (1164-ft) above, north-northwest. Scan the lush slope for feeding bears. If you see one, turn around. Leave quietly without disturbing it. If you proceed, be observant. Make noise to warn unseen bears of your presence.

Hop the inlet stream. Follow the path through krummholz, over the knoll. Pick your way across a rocky, bushy area. Bootbeaten path resumes between the stream gully (left, possibly snow-filled) and the forest edge (right). Ascend north-northwest.

The path leads to a rocky pour-off at the head of the **gully**. Veer right. Scramble out of the gully, up the dirt slope. The path resumes in the grass above. Turn left and follow it north-northwest, up the green **draw** bordered by krummholz. It's very steep, but solid footholds allow you to keep stair-stepping upward to the ridgecrest between Mt. Sarrail's sheer face and a small, rocky tower. Top out on 2380-m (7806-ft) **Sarrail Ridge** about 45 minutes after leaving the lake.

Upper and Lower Kananaskis lakes are visible below (north and northeast). Haig Glacier is northwest, up the Kananaskis River Valley, between Mounts Maude (left) and Jellicoe (right). South-southeast, just past dual-peaked Mt. Sarrail, is 3180-m (10,434-ft) Mt. Foch.

TRIP 26

Elk Lakes / Petain Basin

LOCATION	Peter Lougheed and Elk Lakes provincial parks
ROUND TRIP	16.4 km (10.2 mi) to Upper Elk Lake
	29.4 km (18.2 mi) to Petain Basin
ELEVATION CHANGE	185-m (608-ft) gain / 140-m (460-ft) loss to lake
	plus 521-m (1710-ft) gain to basin
KEY ELEVATIONS	trailhead 1720 m (5642 ft)
	Upper Elk Lake 1765 m (5790 ft)
	basin 2287 m (7500 ft)
HIKING TIME	6 hours for lake, overnight for basin
DIFFICULTY	easy to lake, challenging to basin
MAPS	Gem Trek Kananaskis Lakes
	Kananaskis Lakes 82 J/11

Opinion

Nature isn't a destination. It's not merely a place you enjoy visiting occasionally. Nature is the energy manifested in all of life, including you. So when you're awed by nature at its most pure and grand, such as when hiking through wildly beautiful Petain Basin, remember: you and it share the same life force. This visceral awareness can help sustain you—long after your trek into B.C.'s Elk Lakes Provincial Park—during those inevitable times when nature is less powerfully evident.

Just don't be discouraged by the journey's inauspicious start: an old road plowing into dense, viewless forest. The hiking is soon surprisingly engaging. And the access described here, from the north, spares you the tedious, southern approach, which entails a 1¾-hour drive from Sparwood, mostly on an unpaved Forest Service road. The trail should be sufficiently snow-free from late May through October as far as Upper Elk Lake. Within that comparatively wide window, you have many appealing options for dayhiking or backpacking.

Just 5.2 km (3.2 mi) from the trailhead is a steep, 1.3-km (0.8-mi) spur climbing to Frozen Lake. Gripped in a spectacular cirque on the northeast face of Mount Fox, the lake is shaded from afternoon sun and therefore resembles a daiquiri much of the year. Expect the route to be partly snow-covered but discernible by mid-June, snow-free by mid-July. Whether day-hiking or backpacking, definitely detour to Frozen Lake on your way back from Upper Elk Lake.

If you're dayhiking here in early June, plan to turn around at Upper Elk Lake, where you can eat lunch at the water's edge beneath the sheer south face of Mount Fox. By mid-July, strong dayhikers might go beyond Upper Elk, crossing impetuous Petain Creek and ascending to a flowery meadow

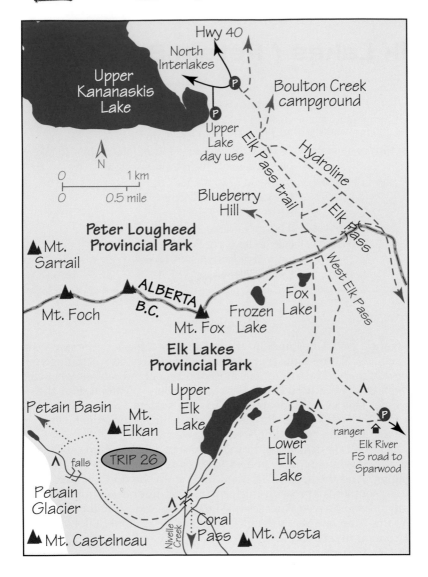

Hwy 40

North
Interlakes

P

Boulton Creek
campground

Upper
Kananaskis
Lake

P

Upper
Lake
day use

Elk Pass trail

Hydroline

N

0   1 km

0   0.5 mile

Elk Pass

Blueberry
Hill

Peter Lougheed
Provincial Park

West Elk Pass

▲ Mt.
Sarrail

ALBERTA
B.C.

Fox
Lake

▲ Mt. Foch

Frozen Lake

Mt. Fox Lake

Elk Lakes
Provincial Park

Upper
Elk
Lake

Petain Basin

Mt.
▲ Elkan

Lower
Elk
Lake

∧
ranger

P
🏠
Elk River
FS road to
Sparwood

∧ falls

TRIP 26

Petain
Glacier

▲ Mt. Castelneau

Niveille Creek

∧∨∨
Coral
∨ Pass ▲ Mt. Aosta

beneath impressive Petain Falls. But you're cheating yourself to go that far and not make the final vault into Petain Basin. To accomplish that goal and relish it requires a two-night backpack trip: late July through early October.

If you're backpacking, you can choose from three campgrounds: Lower Elk Lake, Petain Creek, or Petain Basin. All are appealing. Lower Elk Lake, however, is a bit out of the way. Petain Creek is the logical choice. Petain Basin is the most scenic. But before deciding where to plunk your temporary home, consider the 410-m (1345-ft) headwall guarding the basin. It's seemingly vertical, exceedingly rough. You don't just hike it; you assault it. (See photo on inside back cover.) Carrying only a daypack, it's a challenge.

Lower Elk Lake

Bearing the weight of a full backpack, it's a chore. Most hikers will be glad they camped two nights below—either at the lake or beside the creek—and enjoyed a lightly-laden, one-day venture into the basin.

After clambering over the headwall, you'll enter an alpine Eden. Once again you'll be striding freely—over rock slabs, across meadows—but only if you aren't knocked off your feet by the beauty of it all. Petain Glacier is just one of the enthralling sights. The temptation to lounge is the only obstacle between you and the basin's upper reaches, at 2440 m (8000 ft).

Fact

Before your trip

Be aware that camping is prohibited at Frozen Lake. Mountain bikes are allowed only as far as West Elk Pass, at 4.8 km (3 mi), because they're not permitted in Elk Lakes Provincial Park.

By Vehicle

From Trans-Canada Hwy 1, drive south 50 km (31 mi) on Hwy 40. Or, from Highwood Pass, drive north 17 km (10.5 mi) on Hwy 40. From either approach, turn southwest onto Kananaskis Lakes Trail. Reset your trip odometer to 0 and proceed generally south. At 12 km (7.4 mi) turn left into the signed Elk Pass trailhead parking lot, at 1720 m (5642 ft).

Petain Creek

On Foot

Immediately right (south) of the outhouse is a gated gravel road. Follow it east-southeast. In about seven minutes, near the first rise, ignore the ski trail forking left (north). Proceed straight. In about 15 minutes, the road passes beneath power lines and grants a view north-northwest over Lower Kananaskis Lake to Mt. Indefatigable (Trip 20). The road then curves right and descends. Several minutes farther, ignore a smaller road veering left.

About 30 minutes from the trailhead, cross a bridge over **Fox Creek** at 2 km (1.2 mi), 1785 m (5855 ft). On the far (east) bank are three options. Left (north-northeast) ascends to the hydroline. The trail ahead (southeast) is blocked by a berm. Go right (south) on the diminishing road marked by a hiker sign. Just 15 minutes farther cross two more bridges over Fox Creek.

About an hour from the trailhead, reach a three-way junction at 3.8 km (2.4 mi), 1880 m (6166 ft). Mt. Fox is visible southwest. Behind it (west) is Mt. Sarrail. Ignore the distinct road ascending left (southeast) and what appears to be an overgrown road right (west). Proceed straight (south-southwest) over a low shoulder, on a trail marked by a hiker sign.

About 50 m/yd farther, the trail merges with an old road. Follow it left and quickly reach a junction at 4.3 km (2.7 mi), near a picnic table, immediately northeast of a bridge. Don't cross the bridge; the trail beyond ascends southwest, then curves northwest to Blueberry Hill. Instead, proceed straight (south-southeast) on the level, overgrown road, past a brushy clearing (right) with a stream meandering through it.

Within five minutes, reach another junction. The road proceeds straight (east). Turn right (south) onto a trail marked by a hiker sign. Drop in and out of a drainage. A bit farther, at 4.8 km (3 mi), 1905 m (6250 ft), reach a signed junction in **West Elk Pass**, where you'll leave Peter Lougheed Park and enter Elk Lakes Park.

At the pass, left (southeast) descends the Elkan Creek drainage 4.2 km (2.6 mi) to the north terminus of Elk River Forest Service Road, which is 1.6 km (1 mi) east of the backcountry campground on Lower Elk Lake. Don't go that way, even if you intend to camp at Lower Elk. Instead, turn right (southwest), following the sign for Upper Elk Lake via Fox Lake.

In a couple minutes, reach a signed fork at 5.2 km (3.2 mi). Right (southwest) leads to Frozen Lake. Skip below for details. Go left (south) for Fox and Upper Elk lakes.

Proceeding south toward Upper Elk Lake, soon reach a lengthy boardwalk traversing marshy terrain. Just beyond, at 5.6 km (3.5 mi), a short, right spur leads to **Fox Lake**. From the shore, at 1940 m (6363 ft), you can peer up at where Mount Fox clutches Frozen Lake. Departing Fox Lake, the trail is fairly level for about 15 minutes before starting the long descent to Upper Elk Lake.

About ten minutes into the descent, attain a view of Lower Elk Lake and Mt. Aosta. A bit farther, the trail drops sharply through an avalanche swathe granting a broader view of Upper Elk Valley. After briefly resuming in forest, the trail plunges across a rockslide affording a view southwest of Upper Elk Lake and Castelneau Glacier beyond. The Petain Basin route ascends beneath that glacier.

At the bottom of the rockslide, reach the northeast end of **Upper Elk Lake**. Cross the bridged outlet stream to reach a T-junction on the south bank. You've hiked 8.2 km (5.1 mi) from the trailhead. The elevation here is 1765 m (5790 ft). Left (east-southeast) passes Lower Elk Lake campground in 1 km (0.6 mi), at 1740 m (5707 ft). Go right (southwest) along the upper lake's southeast shore for Petain Basin. The south face of Mount Fox rises abruptly from the north shore.

When the water is high, you'll be stepping across flooded sections of trail. After recent rain, scan the mountain's folded limestone face for spouting cascades. From the lake's south shore, hike about 12 minutes—generally southwest, across gravel beds, then back into forest—to a signed fork. Left follows Nivelle Creek upstream (south) 6 km (3.7 mi) to Coral Pass. Go right (southwest). Two minutes farther is a bridged crossing of **Petain Creek**. The trail continues upstream (southwest), on the west bank. In another eight minutes, reach **Petain Creek campground**. It's between the trail and the creek, at 11 km (6.8 mi).

For Petain Basin, resume southwest. At 12.7 km (7.8 mi), 1835 m (6020 ft) arrive at a signed fork. Left (northwest) is a spur to the base of **Petain Falls**. Even if you don't want to tag the falls, briefly probe the meadow. Mid-July through early August, it explodes with wildflowers: tall, light-blue alpine forget-me-nots, yellow columbine, graceful lavender clematis on long stalks, yellow hedysarum, and white spirea.

Petain Basin

Heading to Petain Basin? At the waterfall fork, bear right (northeast) and ascend. Soon cross a rocky gorge and continue up its left (west) side. Heading generally north, the trail rapidly deteriorates to a route and dramatically steepens. Traction is hard won even when the route is dry. If it's wet, good luck.

Tunnel through krummholz (stunted trees) for about 15 minutes. Negotiate a short, awkward stretch. Enjoy a short reprieve where the ascent eases among bigger trees. Resume labouring skyward. The route soon exits the trees and enters a rocky chute—the upper reaches of the gorge you crossed below. Keep powering higher, over the loose boulders.

Near 2200 m (7216 ft) a cairn indicates where to turn left, out of the chute, onto a path traversing a steep, grassy slope. Wfffeww! The hard part's behind you. Wildflowers are again profuse: deep purple larkspur, lavender sky pilot, purple penstemon, red paintbrush. The hanging Castelneau Glacier is visible south. Mt. McCuaig is on the glacier's southeast edge. Keep following the narrow but well-defined path. Crest the lip of **Petain Basin** at 14.7 km (9.1 mi), 2287 m (7500 ft).

Ascend another 61 m (200 ft) over rock slabs and grass for improved glacier-views. Mt. Nivelle is visible southwest of Castelneau Glacier. Pointy Mt. Castelneau is northeast of it. A bit of Petain Glacier is visible west. Ignore the cairned route descending left (southwest) to upper Petain Creek, unless you're spending the night in the treed campground on the far bank

Upper Petain Basin

(fires prohibited). Instead, go north, cross-country, up gentle, green, slabby ridges, toward the right (east) side of the basin.

The deeper you probe the basin, the more you'll see of broad Petain Glacier. Even 15 minutes makes a big difference. Mt. Petain is west. Keep ascending to see Mount Joffre southwest, rising at the upper edge of the ice. Given sufficient daylight, energy and will, it's possible for hikers to summit 3180-m (10,430-ft) Mt. Foch—the basin's northernmost guardian and the ultimate vantage from which to survey Petain Basin.

Frozen Lake

The signed spur to Frozen Lake initially follows the Alberta / British Columbia boundary. It departs the main trail 0.4 km (0.2 mi) north of the spur to Fox Lake, or 0.4 km (0.2 mi) southwest of the signed junction in West Elk Pass.

Follow the trail west-southwest. Within five minutes, cross a broad, marshy clearing. Upon re-entering forest, a steep, rough ascent ensues. After gaining 90 m (296 ft) in about 20 minutes, ignore a minor, overgrown path crossing your ascent route. Eventually your trail angles southwest, contouring momentarily then tilting skyward again. In about 45 minutes, reach Frozen Lake at 1.3 km (0.8 mi), 2197 m (7205 ft). It's cupped in a cirque on the northeast face of Mount Fox.

TRIP 27
Elbow Lake / Piper Pass

LOCATION	Elbow-Sheep Wildland Provincial Park
	Hwy 40, north of Highwood Pass
ROUND TRIP	19.2 km (11.9 mi) via short approach
ELEVATION GAIN	617 m (2024 ft)
KEY ELEVATIONS	trailhead 1963 m (6440 ft), lake 2105 m (6905 ft)
	pass 2580 m (8462 ft)
HIKING TIME	7 to 8 hours
DIFFICULTY	easy to moderate
MAPS	Gem Trek Kananaskis Lakes
	Kananaskis Lakes 82 J/11, Mt. Rae 82 J/10

Opinion

Despite proof that the earth is round, apparently we kept wishing it were flat. Because we've succeeded in pounding much of our world flat again. You now spend your life staring at flat surfaces: the pages of books, magazines, newspapers, computer screens, TV screens, movie screens. Even car windshields create the impression of watching a film. And all this one-dimensional imagery, though mentally stimulating, requires you to be motionless, with your eyes focused on a fixed distance. But you're a creature designed to move. So here's a hike as multi-dimensional as they come, leading you through forests and meadows, past a lake, along a river and a creek, down a valley, up a canyon, above a tarn, to a lonely, scenic pass among lofty, jagged peaks.

Most people will arrive at Elbow Lake in about 30 minutes. Like all lakes, it holds a seemingly pheromonal attraction for hikers, campers and anglers. You won't be here alone. If all you're seeking is a short walk in the woods, however, you'll find Elbow Lake a splendid destination. Though the lake is below treeline, the open shore allows you to appreciate the mountainous setting.

Continue at least 1.6 km (1 mi) beyond the lake, into Elbow River valley. The hiking is close-your-eyes easy, on a level road-trail, yet the expansive meadowlands are bug-eyes beautiful. The massive shoulders of Elpoca Mtn and Mt. Rae rise on either side. Solitude is likely here, because the crowd stops at the lake.

The view from the Elbow River meadows extends northwest into Piper Creek canyon, which harbours delights not evident to those prying from a distance. That's why all capable hikers should allow a full day, scurry past Elbow Lake, and scamper into the upper canyon. It's a meadowy, alpine haven, carpeted with grass, heather and wildflowers, at the base of the two Tombstone Mtns. Can you eke out a little more oomph? Dash up to Piper

Piper Creek canyon, from Elbow River trail

Pass, gaze at the ragged Opal Range, and peer into the upper reaches of West Fork Little Elbow River valley (Trip 39).

Between Elbow River valley and the mouth of Piper Creek canyon, you have a choice of two routes. We recommend a direct, cross-country shortcut. It entails only a little, light bushwhacking. Elevation gain and loss is minimal. It takes just 35 to 45 minutes. Or you can hike the longer, circuitous, up-and-down route that stays on road and trail. It might take 1½ hours. For the shortcut to be faster, easier and more fun, you must be an experienced pilgrim. You've never navigated by compass? Around you go.

Study the Gem Trek map. You'll see a potential backpack circuit: from Elbow Lake, north into Elbow River valley, northwest through Piper Creek canyon, over Piper Pass, down the West Fork Little Elbow River valley, northeast to Mt. Romulus campground, up the south fork of Little Elbow River, south over Tombstone Pass, down to Tombstone campground in Elbow River valley, then southwest back to Elbow Lake. It fails to earn premier status because so much of it's on former road, and the 10.4 km (6.4 mi) between Romulus and Tombstone campgrounds is popular with mountain-bikers. Nevertheless, if you're keen to stay out a couple nights, and you fancy combining the Elbow Lake / Piper Pass dayhike with its counterpart—West Fork Little Elbow River (Trip 39)—this makes a fine trek. Compared to separately dayhiking Trip 39, the backpacking circuit spares you the 25-km (15.5-mi) round-trip bike ride between the end of Hwy 66 and Romulus campground.

You intend to back-pack this circuit? On day one, hike over Piper Pass. Camp in the West Fork Little Elbow River valley, near where the Paradise Pass (Trip 38) trail departs. On day two, enjoy the wonderful dayhike to Paradise Pass before continuing to Romulus campground. On day three (ideally mid-week, to avoid bike traffic) hike up the south fork of Little Elbow River, detour to Tombstone Lakes, then proceed to Tombstone campground. Continue hiking out past Elbow Lake to the trailhead, and your day-three mileage will be 17.2 km (10.7 mi). The entire circuit, including the Paradise Pass side trip, totals 37.6 km (23.3 mi).

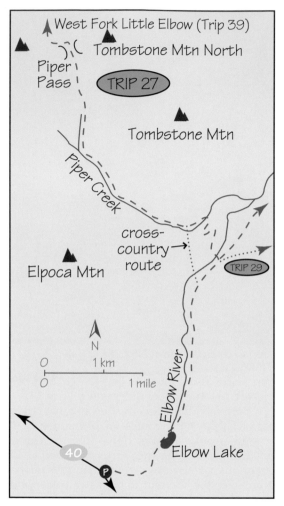

Fact

Before your trip

Be aware that Hwy 40, from Kananaskis Lakes Trail to Highwood Junction, is closed December 1 through June 15.

By Vehicle

From Trans-Canada Hwy 1, drive 62 km (38.4 mi) south on Hwy 40. (Pass the junction with Kananaskis Lakes Trail at 50 km / 31 mi.) Or, from Highwood Pass, drive 5.1 km (3.2 mi) north on Hwy 40. From either approach, turn east into the trailhead parking lot at Elbow Pass day-use area. Elevation: 1963 m (6440 ft).

On Foot

From the middle of the parking lot's east side, ascend the steep, old road through forest. It leads southeast, then curves northeast. After climbing to 2090 m (6855 ft), the road dips. Reach **Elbow Lake** at 1.3 km (0.8 mi), 2105 m (6905 ft). Strong hikers, eagerly pushing on to Piper Pass, will arrive at the

Heading toward Tombstone Mtn, en route to Piper Pass via Piper Creek canyon

lake in 20 minutes. Those sauntering no farther than the lake might take 40 minutes. There's a campground with 15 tent pads behind the south shore.

Follow the road-trail along the left (west) shore. At the lake's north end, cross a bridged creeklet, then bear left. Proceed generally north on the level road-trail, into an expansive **meadow** dominated by willow but also sustaining fuschia moss campion, yellow buttercup, magenta willow-herb, and white western anemone. Ignore the trail veering right. It climbs 405 m (1328 ft) in 2.7 km (1.7 mi) to unimpressive Rae Glacier, which is visible from Piper Pass.

After hiking 4.3 km (2.7 km) from the trailhead, you can see left (northwest) into Piper Creek canyon. Fast hikers will be here roughly an hour after leaving their vehicle, or 35 minutes after leaving the lake's north end. You now have a choice. The recommended *Short Approach* goes cross-country 1.4 km (0.9 mi), directly to the trail ascending the canyon. If you prefer to reach the canyon trail by hiking a more circuitous, up-and-down 3.6 km (2.2 mi) but staying entirely on road and trail, skip to the *Long Approach* below.

Short Approach

When you're directly opposite the mouth of Piper Creek canyon (looking into it northwest), survey the terrain between you and the canyon. Generally, you'll descend, cross the Elbow River, ascend north, descend again, cross Piper Creek, then briefly ascend to pick up the trail at the base of Tombstone Mtn, which forms the canyon's northeast wall. It'll take 35 to 45 minutes. Got the overall picture? Okay, let's go. Here's a detailed route description.

Abandon the road-trail by turning left (north). Follow a descending depression. Rockhop across the **Elbow River** where it breaks into multiple, narrower channels. It's more difficult to cross the single channel farther upstream. Elephant heads (tiny, delicate, with pink stalks) grow in the boggy meadows here; look closely to distinguish the trunks.

From the river's northwest bank, hike north. Ascend 21 m (70 ft). Pick your way through rolling, stunted forest. You'll find passages through the tight trees. Descend 15 m (50 ft) into a gully. You might tag onto a path leading northwest, but follow it only 50 meters (yards) before bearing right and continuing north to Piper Creek. At 5 km (3.1 mi), 2060 m (6757 ft), cross **Piper Creek**. In summer it should be shallow enough here to rockhop over. From the creek's north bank, ascend the hillside through tight alpine fir. Within a few minutes, intersect the **canyon trail**. Athletic hikers will be here about 1 hour and 40 minutes from the trailhead. Mark this spot with a cairn, so you can recognize it when returning. But remember to dismantle the cairn on your way out.

Turn left (west-northwest). The trail climbs steadily beneath the canyon's northeast wall. At 2149 m (7050 ft) cross a dry creek drainage. Ascend northwest. Soon cross a creeklet, then another shortly after. Proceed upstream above Piper Creek cascading through a gorge. At 2226 m (7300 ft), about 30 minutes up the canyon trail, enter **subalpine meadows**. Wildflowers here include alpine forget-me-not, shooting star, Indian paintbrush, and yarrow. The moderate ascent continues generally north.

At 2311 m (7580 ft), about 15 minutes from the meadows, crest the lip of **upper Piper Creek canyon**. Total hiking time: 2½ hours at a vigourous pace. The upper canyon is a meadowy, alpine haven, carpeted with grass, heather and flowers. Looming south is 3030-m (9938-ft) Elpoca Mtn. East is 2997-m (9830-ft) North Tombstone Mtn. Your goal, Piper Pass, is visible ahead (north).

Hike generally north toward the lone, giant boulder at the base of the brown slope. Just beyond the boulder, at 2439 m (8000 ft), begin ascending the very steep trail beaten into the loose talus by boots and hooves. Reach 2580-m (8462-ft) **Piper Pass** about 20 minutes from the giant boulder. Total distance: 9.6 km (6 mi), which is hikeable within 3¼ hours.

Atop Piper Pass, the new view is north-northwest, into the upper reaches of West Fork Little Elbow River valley. The ragged Opal Range forms the West Fork valley's left (west) wall. Left (west-northwest) is 2997-m (9830-ft) Mt. Jerram. Directly below the north side of the pass is a tarn. Visible south-southeast is 3218-m (10,558-ft) Mt. Rae (Trip 29) and its tiny glacier. Another tarn is below the southeast side of the pass.

A faint route veers left (west) from Piper Pass, steeply descending scree and talus on the north slope. For details, read West Fork Little Elbow River (Trip 39), which describes ascending to the pass from north to south.

Returning to the trailhead from Piper Pass, you again have a choice. Either take the cross-country shortcut starting at the cairn you built (remember to dismantle it), or exit the roundabout way staying on trail and road. To go the long way, follow the trail east-southeast around the south slope of Tombstone Mtn. It leads to Piper Creek, which you must ford. The trail then undulates and needlessly zigzags, heading generally southeast. Ford the Elbow River at 2043 m (6700 ft). Continue ascending the trail out of the river gorge to intersect the road-trail you originally hiked from Elbow Lake. Turn right (southwest). Elbow Lake is 3.5 km (2.2 mi) distant—about 45 minutes at a brisk pace. You'll soon be on familiar ground.

Long Approach

From where the cross-country shortcut abandoned the road-trail (directly opposite the mouth of Piper Creek canyon), proceed northeast on the road-trail, slightly downhill, 1 km (0.6 mi), or about ten minutes at a good clip. At 5.3 km (3.6 mi), 2000 m (6560 ft), fork left onto a distinct, cairned and flagged **trail**. It's a couple minutes past an obscure, uncairned trail also forking left.

Before following the trail through a wall of trees, look northwest across the valley. Identify the trail rising on a grassy slope. That's where you'll soon be hiking, between fords of the Elbow River and Piper Creek.

Descend to the **Elbow River** and ford it. Ascend out of the gorge. The trail undulates and needlessly zigzags. It leads to **Piper Creek**, which you must also ford. It then curves northwest beneath Tombstone Mtn and enters the mouth of **Piper Creek canyon**.

After steadily ascending for about ten minutes from the Piper Creek ford, you'll be near where the cross-country shortcut intersects the canyon trail. Continue following the *Short Approach* directions, beginning with the second sentence of the fourth paragraph. Keep in mind that your hiking time will be longer than the stated cumulative estimates. Your total distance to Piper Pass will be 12 km (7.4 mi).

TRIP 28

Tombstone Lakes

LOCATION	Elbow-Sheep Wildland Provincial Park
	Hwy 40, north of Highwood Pass
ROUND TRIP	22.1 km (13.7 mi) including Tombstone Pass
ELEVATION GAIN	545 m (1988 ft)
KEY ELEVATIONS	trailhead 1963 m (6440 ft)
	lower Tombstone Lake 2186 m (7170 ft)
	Tombstone Pass 2238 m (7340 ft)
HIKING TIME	6 to 7½ hours
DIFFICULTY	moderate due only to distance
MAP	Gem Trek Kananaskis Lakes

Opinion

Hikers, almost without exception, drive automobiles to trailheads. Yet it's the automobile, and everything pulled along in its wake, that hikers seek to escape by hiking. We're a conflicted bunch, aren't we? So try to suspend your not-always-logical judgment when you learn that fully 90% of the Tombstone Lakes hike is on a road.

"A road!" you say. "A road?" Yup. But it's a road that might make you recant the hikers' dogma that all roads are abhorrent. Because this is an old road, from which motorized vehicles were banned long ago. It's broad, fairly level and mostly smooth, so instead of fixating on what's underfoot, as trails often force you to do, you can lift your eyes and appreciate the scenery while you stride. And the scenery here is grand.

Elbow Lake, a mere half-hour from the trailhead, is an image suitable for framing. Beyond, you'll hike through upper Elbow River Valley, past the mouth of Piper Creek canyon (Trip 27), and across the north end of Sheep River Valley. Even if you've been to Piper Pass, this approach bears repeating. Much of the area is rolling, sparsely-treed meadowland that's not only beautiful itself but allows nearly constant views of the surrounding peaks: Elpoca Mtn, Mt. Rae, Tombstone Mtn, and Cougar Mtn. They're a visual feast. From Tombstone campground, you'll ascend into forest and turn onto an actual trail for the final approach to Tombstone Lakes. The upper lake, tucked into the bosom of full-breasted Tombstone Mtn, is lovely.

From Tombstone Lakes, you should lengthen and vary your return by detouring through Tombstone Pass, and/or to Rae Lake. Both options significantly boost the day's spectacle quotient. The pass, a sprawling heather-and-grass meadow ringed by larches, affords an impressive, elevated perspective of Mt. Rae and Tombstone Mtn. And Rae Lake is gorgeous, surrounded by subalpine meadow, clutched by mighty Mt. Rae. The Rae Lake detour also includes a brief, enjoyable stretch of hiking on a trail and a less-defined route.

Upper Tombstone Lake

Tagging the Tombstone Lakes, returning via Tombstone Pass, and detouring to Rae Lake is not a Herculean dayhike. The total distance is 25.5 km (15.8 mi). The total elevation gain is 730 m (2395 ft), all of it gradual. Strong hikers who start early will find this a full but not exhausting day. The Rae Lake detour accounts for only 4.4 km (2.7 mi) of the total mileage, so definitely include it. Read Trip 29 for a motivating description. Detour directions are at the bottom of the *On Foot* section below.

The alternative to dayhiking is an easy, two-day backpack trip. Stay at Tombstone campground, in a sheltering stand of trees, near a creeklet. An open bench here offers fire pits and a big view. Though the campground is 3.6 km (2.2 mi) shy of Tombstone Lakes, it spares you from wagging all your gear higher and farther. Here's the plan: hike in, pitch your tent, then loop up to Tombstone Lakes and back through Tombstone Pass. Total mileage for

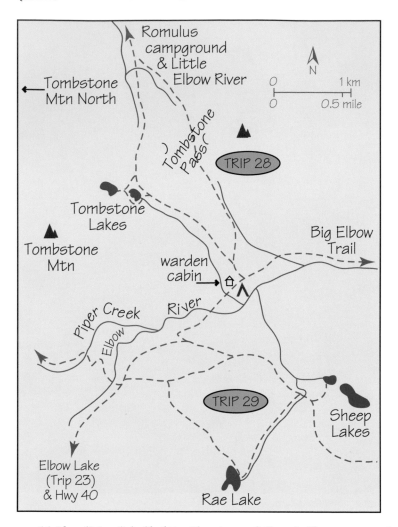

day one: 14.6 km (9.1 mi), half of it without your full pack. The next morning, nip up to Rae Lake on your way back to the trailhead.

Because you'll mostly be hiking on a former road, be prepared to share it momentarily with a few mountain bikers and perhaps some equestrians. Uninterrupted tranquility, however, is still possible on this journey. Bikes are prohibited on the spur trails to Rae and Tombstone lakes, and it's a rare biker who hoofs it farther than is necessary to pee in the roadside bushes.

Fact

Before your trip

Be aware that Hwy 40, from Kananaskis Lakes Trail to Highwood Junction, is closed December 1 through June 15.

Elbow River Valley and Mt. Rae

By Vehicle

From Trans-Canada Hwy 1, drive 62 km (38.4 mi) south on Hwy 40. (Pass the junction with Kananaskis Lakes Trail at 50 km / 31 mi.) Or, from Highwood Pass, drive 5.1 km (3.2 mi) north on Hwy 40. From either approach, turn east into the trailhead parking lot at Elbow Pass day-use area. Elevation: 1963 m (6440 ft).

On Foot

From the middle of the parking lot's east side, ascend the steep, old road through forest. It leads southeast, then curves northeast. After climbing to 2090 m (6855 ft), the road dips. Reach **Elbow Lake** at 1.3 km (0.8 mi), 2105 m (6905 ft). Strong hikers, eagerly pushing onward, will arrive at the lake in 20 minutes. Those sauntering no farther than the lake might take 40 minutes. There's a campground with 15 tent pads behind the south shore.

Follow the road-trail along the left (west) shore. At the lake's north end, cross a bridged creeklet, then bear left. Proceed generally north on the level road-trail, into an expansive **meadow** dominated by willow but also sustaining yellow buttercup, magenta willow-herb, and white western anemone. Ignore the trail veering right. It climbs 405 m (1328 ft) in 2.7 km (1.7 mi) to unimpressive Rae Glacier.

After hiking 4.3 km (2.7 km) from the trailhead, you can see left (northwest) into Piper Creek canyon (Trip 27). Fast hikers will be here roughly an hour after leaving their vehicle, or 35 minutes after leaving the lake's north end. Proceed northeast on the road-trail, which now descends slightly. The **Elbow River** is occasionally visible left.

At 5.3 km (3.6 mi), 2000 m (6560 ft), pass the cairned and flagged left fork leading west-northwest to the Elbow River and Piper Creek canyon. Stay on the road-trail. Fifty paces farther, pass the cairned right fork leading east then southeast to Rae Lake (Trip 29). Again, stay on the road-trail, heading north-northeast. Tombstone Mtn is left (north-northwest). You'll circle behind its east shoulder to reach the Tombstone Lakes.

At 6.5 km (4 mi), 2006 m (6580 ft), reach a T-junction signed with a **Sheep Valley** trail map that exaggerates your distance from the trailhead. The road-trail left descends to cross a bridge (visible below) spanning the Elbow River. Go that way to reach lower Tombstone Lake in 3 km (1.9 mi). The road-trail right runs generally southeast through Sheep Valley, intersecting the trail to Rickert's Pass and Mist Ridge (Trip 35) in 10 km (6.2 mi).

Turn left at the 6.5-km (4-mi) T-junction. Descend a sweeping bend and cross the **Elbow River bridge**. (On your return, you'll see how a brief-but-steep cross-country jaunt will enable you to shortcut this bend.) At 7.1 km (4.4 mi), pass a road forking left to a warden cabin. About five minutes farther, at 7.3 km (4.5 mi), reach **Tombstone campground** on the right.

The tentsites are in a dark stand of trees but within earshot of a creeklet. Nearby is an open bench with fire pits and a fine view of the area. Mt. Rae is south, Elpoca Mtn west-southwest. For Tombstone Lakes, proceed on the road-trail, past the campground. A couple minutes farther, reach a signed junction at 2000 m (6560 ft). Right (northeast) is the Big Elbow trail. For Tombstone Lakes, ascend left (north-northwest) on the **Little Elbow trail**.

Within 15 minutes, after gaining 37 m (120 ft) in 0.4 km (0.25 mi), reach another junction. The Little Elbow trail (still a road) curves right and ascends steeply north over Tombstone Pass. Fork left here onto an actual **trail** leading north-northwest, ascending moderately through forest. Horse travel is destroying this trail. It's severely eroded and braided, and horrendously muddy when wet.

Reach the southeast shore of **lower Tombstone Lake** at 9.2 km (5.7 mi), 2186 m (7170 ft). Trees curtail your view here, so go left, hop the outlet stream, and follow the rooty trail around the west shore. It forks at the lake's northwest corner. Right rounds the north shore. Go left, ascend west-northwest, and in a few minutes cross a small saddle with a view of **upper Tombstone Lake**. The trail ends just below, on the shore of the upper lake. Embraced by 3035-m (9958-ft), dual-peaked Tombstone Mtn, the upper lake is more scenic than its lower sibling.

Upon returning to the northwest corner of the lower lake, you have a choice: (1) Continue retracing your steps all the way to the trailhead. (2) Continue retracing your steps past Tombstone campground, to the signed T-junction above the Elbow River bridge, then extend your dayhike to Rae Lake (Trip 29) as described below. (3) Lengthen and vary your return to Tombstone campground by detouring through Tombstone Pass.

Heading for Tombstone Pass? Don't re-hike the west shore of lower Tombstone Lake. From the lake's northwest corner, turn left and round the **north shore**. A gradual ascent leads to a faint junction. Right descends to where you initially arrived at the lower lake's southeast shore. Go left and resume ascending, generally north through forest, to a larch-fringed meadowy **draw** at 2273 m (7455 ft).

From the draw, descend north 1.5 km (0.9 mi) to intersect the **Little Elbow trail**—a former road. You've now hiked a total of 11.1 km (6.9 mi). The elevation here is 2125 m (6970 ft). Left on the Little Elbow trail leads north 6.8 km (4.2 mi) to Mount Romulus campground. Go right, initially ascending southeast, for Tombstone pass and campground. An unnamed ridge is left (east).

Crest 2238-m (7340-ft) **Tombstone Pass** at 12.5 km (7.8 mi), in a vast, heather-and-grass meadow ringed by larches. To the west, the twin summits of Tombstone Mtn dominate the panorama. The more distant, but still impressive, 3218-m (10,558-ft) Mt. Rae is south. North-northwest is the ridge dividing the Elbow River's west (Trip 39) and south forks. North, in the distance, is 3053-m (10,017-ft) Fisher Peak.

Proceed south-southeast on the road-trail. The descent is gradual at first, allowing you to enjoy the view while striding, but it soon steepens sharply. Stay to one side in case bikers charge down from behind you. Bear left on the road-trail where the Tombstone Lakes trail forks right. Bear right where the signed Big Elbow trail forks left. Soon after, the road levels and passes **Tombstone campground** at 14.6 km (9.1 mi). The trailhead, on Hwy 40, is now 7.3 km (4.5 mi) distant. You know the way.

Detour to Rae Lake

From Tombstone campground, retrace your steps to the signed **T-junction** above the Elbow River bridge. Right (west) is the road-trail leading directly back to the trailhead. To detour to Rae Lake, continue straight on the road-trail leading generally southeast into Sheep Valley. The following distances start at the T-junction.

In 0.6 km (0.4 mi), near the bend of a hairpin turn, pass a cairned trail on the right. It leads west to intersect the Elbow River road-trail across from Piper Creek canyon. Proceed on the road-trail. At 1.8 km (1.1 mi), just before a **culvert**, turn right onto an actual trail. It ascends generally southwest, along the edge of Rae Creek gorge.

Reach **Rae Lake** at 3.2 km (2 mi), 2200 m (7216 ft). Turn left and hop the outlet to extend your detour around Rae Lake's east shore, into the meadow bordering the south shore. Or, to continue as directly as possible, turn right and follow the trail ascending generally northwest, above the northeast shore.

The trail heading northwest gradually climbs out of the lake basin, through lightly forested meadow. It crosses a **shoulder**, then descends—sharply at first but soon gradually—onto a treed slope. The trail diminishes to a route. If you lose it, just keep heading northwest, perhaps on game trails. Though the young forest is thick in places, the going is easy.

After exiting the trees, intersect a trail at 4.9 km (3 mi). This is the trail that departed the Sheep Valley road-trail's hairpin turn. Go left (west-northwest). Descend through a draw and re-enter forest. Intersect the **Elbow River road-trail** at 5.6 km (3.5 mi). Turn left (southwest) to reach the trailhead. You're now on familiar ground.

TRIP 29

Rae Lake

LOCATION	Elbow-Sheep Wildland Provincial Park
	Hwy 40, north of Highwood Pass
ROUND TRIP	17.2 km (10.7 mi)
ELEVATION GAIN	366 m (1200 ft)
KEY ELEVATIONS	trailhead 1963 m (6440 ft), lake 2185 m (7167 ft)
HIKING TIME	5 to 6½ hours
DIFFICULTY	easy
MAPS	page 160; Gem Trek Kananaskis Lakes

Opinion

Behind her back. Behind the scenes. Behind closed doors. Whatever's going on back there, most people are ravenous to find out. But behind that mountain? Only a hiker would care. And the reason they do is that, at some point, they were galvanized by the realization that immensity, purity or intrigue, sometimes all three, will often ambush them around the next bend in the trail. It keeps them hiking in eager anticipation of the discoveries that lie ahead, like those awaiting you on this easy exploration behind Rae Mountain.

No one can say with certainty what *your* discoveries will be here. But they're likely to include these: (1) Elbow Lake is popular not only because it's a mere half-hour from the trailhead but because it's beautiful. And its beauty is unmarred by the sight and sound of others dawdling about the shore. (2) Most people hike no farther than Elbow Lake, yet the going is easy and the scenery stupendous in the upper Elbow River Valley, where rolling, sparsely-treed meadowland allows nearly constant views of Elpoca Mtn, Mt. Rae, Tombstone Mtn, and Cougar Mtn. (3) The obscure route veering off to Rae Lake discourages visitation, so your enjoyment of its impressive setting will likely be enhanced by tranquility.

Rae Lake is Mt. Rae's belly-button ring—a liquid jewel in the navel of this full-figured massif. As big mountains go, she's mysterious. Her shy stance, behind the Elk, Opal and front ranges, does not expose her full glory to passersby. But the glimpse you'll attain here, beneath Rae's north ridge, reveals more than is visible from the popular hike into Ptarmigan Cirque (Trip 31) below Rae's south face. Plus, Rae Lake itself—bordered by sub-alpine meadows, walled in by cliffs—is a climactic sight, unlike Ptarmigan's desolate upper reaches.

For further motivation, read the first three paragraphs of Elbow Lake / Piper Pass (Trip 27). Also read Tombstone Lakes (Trip 28), which describes the advantages of an easy, single-night backpack trip into this area. Finally,

Rae Lake

should you opt to dayhike to Rae Lake, don't be mislead by the mere six hours required to complete the trip. Start early, so you'll have time to loll near the water's edge, circumambulate the shore, or proceed south behind the lake then ascend southeast onto the 2400-m (7872-ft) ridge that forms the cirque's eastern shoulder.

Fact

Before your trip

Be aware that Hwy 40, from Kananaskis Lakes Trail to Highwood Junction, is closed December 1 through June 15.

By Vehicle

From Trans-Canada Hwy 1, drive 62 km (38.4 mi) south on Hwy 40. (Pass the junction with Kananaskis Lakes Trail at 50 km / 31 mi.) Or, from Highwood Pass, drive 5.1 km (3.2 mi) north on Hwy 40. From either approach, turn east into the trailhead parking lot at Elbow Pass day-use area. Elevation: 1963 m (6440 ft).

On Foot

From the middle of the parking lot's east side, ascend the steep, old road through forest. It leads southeast, then curves northeast. Reach **Elbow Lake** at 1.3 km (0.8 mi), 2105 m (6905 ft). Strong hikers will be here in 20 minutes.

Follow the road-trail along the left (west) shore. At the lake's north end, cross a bridged creeklet, then bear left. Proceed generally north on the level road-trail, into an expansive **meadow**. Ignore the trail veering right. It climbs 405 m (1328 ft) in 2.7 km (1.7 mi) to unimpressive Rae Glacier.

After hiking 4.3 km (2.7 km) from the trailhead, you can see left (northwest) into Piper Creek canyon (Trip 27). Proceed northeast on the road-trail. The **Elbow River** is occasionally visible left.

At 5.3 km (3.6 mi), 2000 m (6560 ft), pass the cairned and flagged left fork leading west-northwest to the Elbow River and Piper Creek canyon. Stay on the road-trail, heading north-northeast, but only for another 50 paces. Then abandon the road-trail and turn onto a **cairned right fork**. It leads generally east, then southeast to Rae Lake.

Follow the narrow trail through open forest, then up a **grassy draw**. Just beyond and above the draw, reach an unsigned, easy-to-miss right fork at 6 km (3.7 mi), 2037 m (6680 ft). Straight (east) descends to intersect a road; you'll loop back from there after visiting the lake. For now, go right (southeast).

The trail diminishes to a route as it rises across the northern foot of **Mt. Rae**. Behind you, Tombstone Pass (north) and Tombstone Mtn (northwest) are visible across the valley. Near 2100 m (6888 ft), about ten minutes from the last fork, the route is very faint. If you lose it, just keep heading southeast, perhaps on game trails. Though the young forest is thick in places, the going is easy.

About 30 minutes from the last fork, proceed through blowdown to the base of a low **shoulder**. The route reappears here, angling upward, over the shoulder. Ascend to the subalpine meadow atop the shoulder. Here, the route becomes a more discernible trail leading right (south). But before continuing, briefly detour left (east), off-trail, toward a lone larch, where you can glimpse the Sheep Lakes (east) in the valley below.

Upon returning to the shoulder-top trail, follow it generally south. It dips, then rises into open forest peppered with larch. In a few minutes, you'll be descending southeast through lightly forested meadow, with **Rae Lake** visible below.

Reach the lake's **northeast shore** at 7.7 km (4.8 mi), 2185 m (7167 ft). Beyond the south shore, a meadow extends into the cirque beneath the north ridge of 3218-m (10,558-ft) Mt. Rae. You can reach it by rounding the lake in either direction. Right, via the thickly forested west shore, is longer. So bear left (south-southeast), which is also the most efficient way to continue the circuit.

Soon arrive at Rae Lake's **outlet**, where idiots oblivious to *Leave No Trace* guidelines have denuded the shore by camping on it and building multiple firepits. Hop the outlet to detour around the east shore, into the meadow behind the south shore. Or continue the circuit by turning left immediately before the outlet and descending generally northeast on a scenic trail above the left (northwest) side of **Rae Creek gorge**.

Intersect the **Sheep River Valley road-trail** at 9.1 km (5.6 mi), 2070 m (6788 ft). A few steps to the right, Rae Creek flows through a culvert. Turn left and follow the road-trail northwest. At 10.3 km (6.4 mi), 2034 m (6670 ft),

Wood Lily

near the bend of a **hairpin turn**, abandon the road by turning left (west-southwest) onto a trail marked by a cairn. It leads generally west, through brushy, rolling terrain.

About fifteen minutes farther, at 11.1 km (6.9 mi), pass an unsigned, easy-to-miss left fork—the route you previously followed across the northern foot of Mt. Rae, to Rae Lake. You're now on familiar ground. Proceed straight (west-northwest). Descend through a grassy draw and re-enter forest. Intersect the **Elbow River road-trail** at 11.8 km (7.3 mi). Turn left (south-west) to return past Elbow Lake and reach the trailhead on **Hwy 40** at 17.2 km (10.7 mi).

Calypso orchid

Elephant's head

TRIP 30
Pocaterra Ridge

LOCATION	Peter Lougheed Provincial Park
	Hwy 40, near Highwood Pass
SHUTTLE TRIP	9.3 km (5.8 mi)
ELEVATION CHANGE	550-m (1804-ft) gain / 875-m (2870-ft) loss
KEY ELEVATIONS	trailhead 2206 m (7239 ft)
	high point 2670 m (8758 ft)
HIKING TIME	5 to 8 hours
DIFFICULTY	moderate
MAPS	Gem Trek Kananaskis Lakes
	Mount Rae 82 J/10

Opinion

"Solvitur ambulando," the Romans said. To solve a problem, walk around. Try it. It works. In the city. In the country. But ideally in the wilds, where you must physically and mentally grapple with the terrain. A robust romp is what you want. And here it is.

Lighting out for Pocaterra Ridge, you'll begin at Highwood Pass—the highest point in Canada accessible by public road. So within half an hour, you'll burst into splendid subalpine meadows, in Pocaterra Cirque. A steep slog ensues. You'll clamber briefly, then resume toiling upward. Transcend the first and highest bump, at the south end of the ridgecrest, and away you go. You'll gallop 4 km (2.5 mi), or about two hours, along the mostly alpine crest before dismounting the ridge at its north end.

Exhilarating scenery is constant. Paralleling Pocaterra Ridge, west across a narrow valley, is the spine of the Elk Range. Lower Kananaskis Lake is northwest. Elpoca Mtn, distinguished by steeply-angled sawtooth ridges, is north. Beyond it is Piper Creek canyon (Trip 27) and Tombstone Mtn. Hulking Mt. Rae is east. You can ask more of a ridgewalk, but you'd be greedy. Especially considering this is a convenient one-way trip—a rare indulgence for a hiker. Take advantage of it.

Stride the entire ridge by arranging a vehicle shuttle between the trail-heads at each end. You're limited to a single vehicle? A round trip to the third bump on the crest is certainly worthwhile. Better yet, park at the north trailhead, where the trip ends, then hitchhike the short distance to the south trailhead, where the trip begins. You'll snag a ride quickly, especially on a weekend.

Note that the first bump on the crest is a little scrambly—no problem for accomplished hikers, mildly difficult for the unsteady, perhaps prohibitive for the acrophobic. From there on, it's a comfortable cruise. The only challenge

Pocaterra Ridge. Mt. Tyrwhitt distant right.

will be regaining lost elevation after each of the inevitable dips and drops. Overall, you'll be coasting slightly downhill. Swooping off the north end of the ridge, the trail eventually withers. Expect a brief thrash near the bottom, just before you pop out of the woods onto the highway.

Robo-hikers equipped with booster rockets can add an additional hour of adventure to the day by detouring from Pocaterra Cirque to Grizzly Col. It's a short, engaging ascent. And the view from the col comprises Grizzly Ridge, part of another wild, mountain dance described below.

Fact

Before your trip

Be aware that Hwy 40, from Kananaskis Lakes Trail to Highwood Junction, is closed December 1 through June 15.

By Vehicle

From Trans-Canada Hwy 1—to reach the south (upper) trailhead, where the **hike begins**—drive south 67.4 km (41.8 mi) on Hwy 40. Or, from Highwood Junction (where Hwys 40, 541 and 940 intersect), drive northwest 37.7 km (23.4 mi) on Hwy 40. From either approach, turn west into the Highwood Pass parking lot, at 2206 m (7239 ft).

From Trans-Canada Hwy 1—to reach the north (lower) trailhead, where the **hike ends**—drive south 60.6 km (37.6 mi) on Hwy 40. Or, from the

Highwood Pass parking lot, drive north 6.8 km (4.2 mi) on Hwy 40. From either approach, turn east into Little Highwood Pass day use area, at 1880 m (6166 ft).

On Foot

From the kiosk at the north end of the parking lot, follow the trail northwest through willowy meadows. In five minutes, at 0.4 km (0.25 mi), proceed onto the boardwalk. The trail forking right (northeast) leads to Ptarmigan Cirque (Trip 31).

After passing benches and interpretive signs, turn off the boardwalk. Follow the path right (west-southwest) through trees. In one minute, pass a left spur. Bear right (north). Then curve left, drop into a meadowy draw, intersect another trail, and turn right (northwest).

About ten minutes along, where the highway is visible, begin a moderate ascent left. The trail is rooty and probably muddy. In another ten minutes, ignore the bootbeaten path ascending left. Proceed on the main trail, descending southwest. Soon attain a view southwest into Pocaterra Cirque. Pocaterra Ridge begins on the right (north) side of the cirque.

The trail drops through forest, then crosses an avalanche path adorned with cow's parsnip and fuschia fireweed. It undulates over a rockslide and continues through larches. At 2213 m (7260 ft), beside a **creeklet**, begin ascending again. You've now hiked about 40 minutes from the trailhead. Pass a cairn at the west end of a **tarn**. The trail heads west, on grass at the edge of talus.

Reach a large, level meadow in **Pocaterra Cirque** at 2.9 km (1.8 mi), 2285 m (7490 ft). You're now south-southeast of Little Highwood Pass—the saddle linking Pocaterra Ridge with the spine of the Elk Range. The **trail forks** here at a cairn. Straight (west) continues to the base of Pocaterra Ridge. Left (southwest) ascends to Grizzly Col, where snow lingers long. It's worth nipping up there for the view, even if you don't continue beyond. A round-trip detour from Pocaterra Cirque takes 45 minutes to an hour. Upon returning to the cirque, you can resume to Pocaterra Ridge. Skip below for details about Grizzly Col.

Resuming to Pocaterra Ridge, follow the trail northwest, toward the grassy slope at the base of a rockslide near the head of Pocaterra Cirque. Choose either of two routes to the south end of the ridgecrest: (1) north, directly up the steep talus slope, with rough sections on black-lichen-covered rocks; or (2) northwest, on a moderately ascending path, then north to **Little Highwood Pass** at 2545 m (8348 ft), 4.3 km (2.7 mi). From the pass, turn right (east) for the final, steep, rough ascent to the ridgecrest. The first option is easier, and you'll miss nothing at Little Highwood Pass; it's all visible from the ridge.

From either approach, reach the **south end of Pocaterra Ridge** at 2670 m (8758 ft). This **first bump** is the highest on the ridge. The roughly two-hour ridgewalk along the 4-km (2.5-mi) crest begins here. Follow the bootbeaten path northeast, then north-northwest.

Descend to a 2500-m (8200-ft) saddle, then ascend again. Reach the **second bump** at 2560 m (8400 ft). The Elk Range is left (west) across the canyon. From here on, while hiking the crest, your general direction of

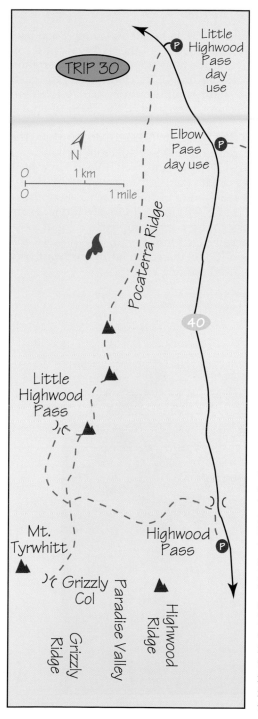

travel will be north-northwest. The ridge dips again, then rises to a **third bump** at 2595 m (8512 ft). Elbow Lake (Trip 27) is visible north-northeast, just beyond and above Hwy 40.

The ridgecrest drops significantly from the third bump. The path is occasionally along the right side of the crest. Rockfall Lake (shallow, possibly dry) is visible left (west) below you. North of it, trees and boulders clutter the canyon.

Reach a lightly treed **gap** on the crest at 2450 m (8036 ft). Here, a route descends right (southeast) initiating a steep, rough, but viable escape to Hwy 40. Proceeding along the ridge, angle right to stay on the northeast side. Pass a faint trail descending left.

Enter a spectacular larch forest at 2380 m (7806 ft). Surmount the **fourth bump**. Visible northwest is Lower Kananaskis Lake. North is 3030-m (9938-ft) Elpoca Mtn. Begin dismounting the ridge.

Continue following the occasionally sketchy path generally north, dropping steeply through open forest, willow, and grass. Your goal, initially visible below, is Little Highwood Pass trailhead parking lot. You'll lose sight of it while descending. Nearing the bottom, bear right. The trail disappears. Rockhop or ford to the north bank of **Pocaterra Creek**. Then thrash onward and upward another few minutes to Hwy 40 and the trailhead immediately north of it. You've hiked 9.3 km (5.8 mi) from Highwood Pass, excluding the Grizzly Col detour.

Grizzly Col

Turn left (southwest) at the cairned fork in Pocaterra Cirque. Soon take your pick of paths ascending generally south-southeast toward the col. Pause at 2440 m (8003 ft), near the base of a talus slope. See the trail angling across the headwall, up to the col? Tag onto it by clambering left (east) up the talus. Then follow the trail right (south-southwest). Crest 2607-m (8550-ft) **Grizzly Col** about half an hour from, and 322 m (1056 ft) above, Pocaterra Cirque.

Towering above the col's west side is 2875-m (9430-ft) Mt. Tyrwhitt. The unnamed valley south of the pass descends to Hwy 40. From the col's east side, Grizzly Ridge extends southeast. Visible north, well beyond Hwy 40, is Piper Creek canyon, flanked by Elpoca Mtn (left) and Tombstone Mtn (right).

A trail continues on the left (east) side of the col. After contouring southeast, it gradually gains 120 m (394 ft) to crest Grizzly Ridge. From there it's possible to proceed cross country and complete a rugged loop. Begin with a sharp descent generally east into Paradise Valley, ascend generally northeast over Highwood Ridge, then drop north-northeast very steeply to the Highwood Pass trailhead parking lot.

Descending Pocaterra Ridge toward Elpoca Mountain

TRIP 31
Ptarmigan Cirque

LOCATION	Peter Lougheed Provincial Park, near Highwood Pass
CIRCUIT	4.5 km (2.8 mi)
ELEVATION GAIN	214 m (702 ft)
KEY ELEVATIONS	trailhead 2206 m (7239 ft), high point 2420 m (7938 ft)
HIKING TIME	1½ to 2 hours
DIFFICULTY	easy
MAPS	Gem Trek Kananaskis Lakes; Mount Rae 82 J/10

Opinion

Like the trailer for a Hollywood movie, this hike lashes you with fleeting glimpses of drama and adventure. The scenery is thrilling—typical of feature-length hikes in the Canadian Rockies—but cursory. You won't relish a full day's experience here, nor will you pay for it. You'll simply be tantalized, in return for minimal time and effort.

Ptarmigan Cirque is gouged between 3218-m (10,555-ft) Mt. Rae and 2912-m (9551-ft) Mt. Arethusa. After a very brief ascent through forest, the trail enters the cirque and contours meadowy slopes below the soaring peaks. The meadow is a wildflower haven that contrasts sharply with the surrounding austere scree and talus. You'll see yellow glacier lilies here in early July. Dozens of species bloom later, including larkspur, yellow heart-leafed arnica, lavender fleabane, western anemone, alpine forget-me-not, and the ubiquitous alpine-red paintbrush. In fall, expect to see crimson alpine vegetation, and grass the colour of mustard.

Any time of year, just driving to the trailhead is marvelously scenic. The hike begins at Highwood Pass, the highest point in Canada accessible by public road. En route you'll survey a vast expanse of K-Country, including colossal peaks along the Continental Divide.

Because it begins so high, this trail rockets you into the alpine much faster than most. You'll be there within 30 minutes, and back to your vehicle within two hours. For a longer outing, first hike to Pocaterra Cirque or Grizzly Col. Both are described in Pocaterra Ridge (Trip 30), which shares the same trailhead as Ptarmigan. After enjoying the morning sun in Pocaterra Cirque, catch the afternoon rays in Ptarmigan Cirque. Another short trail nearby, easily combined with this one in half a day, is Little Arethusa (Trip 32).

Fact

Before your trip

Be aware that Hwy 40, from Kananaskis Lakes Trail to Highwood Junction, is closed December 1 through June 15.

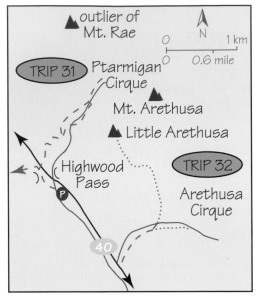

By Vehicle

From Trans-Canada Hwy 1, drive south 67.4 km (41.8 mi) on Hwy 40. Or, from Highwood Junction (where Hwys 40, 541 and 940 intersect), drive northwest 37.7 km (23.4 mi) on Hwy 40. From either approach, turn west into the Highwood Pass trailhead parking lot, at 2206 m (7239 ft).

On Foot

From the kiosk at the north end of the parking lot, follow the trail northwest through willowy meadows. In four minutes, at 0.4 km (0.25 mi), just before a boardwalk, turn right (northeast) at the sign for Ptarmigan Cirque. Cross the **highway**. The trail resumes, heading northeast, ascending moderately into subalpine forest.

In about 20 minutes, a right spur offers a very short detour to a viewpoint where you can gaze south, across the highway, at the swooping slopes of Highwood Ridge. At 1.3 km (0.8 mi), 2335 m (7660 ft), reach a **fork**. Go left (north). Right is signed ONE WAY, DO NOT ENTER. It attests to how busy it can be here on weekends. After touring the cirque, you'll loop back to this point

Five minutes farther, break out of trees into the alpine meadow of **Ptarmigan Cirque**. The trail levels, contouring northeast on grassy slopes.

Bighorn sheep above Highwood Pass

A quick ascent through subalpine forest leads to Ptarmigan Cirque beneath Mt. Rae.

Mt. Arethusa is east-northeast across the drainage. At 2.25 km (1.4 mi), reach the head of the loop, on a rocky **terminal moraine**. This is the trail's high point: 2420 m (7938 ft).

At the moraine, you can opt to leave the trail and proceed straight (northeast), roaming deeper into the desolate cirque. To continue the loop, stay on the trail. It crosses the **creeklet** and curves right.

Watch for hoary marmots on the moraine. They're burrowing rodents: stout-bodied, short-legged, about the size of a cat. Chiefly herbivorous, they have coarse fur, a short bushy tail, and very small ears. Their high-pitched whistle is distinctive, which is why they're also known as whistlers, or whistle pigs.

From the moraine, the trail bends southwest beneath Mt. Arethusa. Begin a gradual descent on a rockslide above the creeklet and meadow. Here, where the highway is hidden from view, it's easy to imagine you're deep in the wilderness.

Hop over the **creeklet** near the mouth of the cirque. Visible southwest, across Highwood Pass, is twin-topped Mt. Tyrwhitt. Just north of it is Poca-terra Cirque (Trip 30). Watch for a left spur leading 25 m/yd to a **bench** shaded by trees and overlooking cascades in a gorge.

Shortly after passing the spur, intersect the trail you originally followed into the cirque. Turn left and descend through forest. You're now on famil-iar ground and will soon reach the highway at Highwood Pass.

TRIP 32
Little Arethusa

LOCATION	Peter Lougheed Provincial Park, near Highwood Pass
ROUND TRIP	5.4 km (3.3 mi)
ELEVATION GAIN	559 m (1832 ft)
KEY ELEVATIONS	trailhead 2170 m (7118 ft), summit 2729 m (8950 ft)
HIKING TIME	3 to 4 hours
DIFFICULTY	moderate
MAPS	page 174; Gem Trek Kananaskis Lakes Mount Rae 82 J/10

Opinion

Arethusa was the Greek goddess of springs and fountains. Perhaps Little Arethusa was her contrarian devil-child, because this outlier is a bone-dry rock pile. The little one's summit, however, is a refreshing destination. It affords a splendid panorama, quickly attained with moderate effort.

Little Arethusa is ideal for neophyte scramblers. Though steep, the ascent is on a broad slope covered with scree. Exposure is nil as far as the first summit. And, should you decide to bail, that's okay. About halfway up are grassy terraces with gratifying views. You'll peer down into Arethusa Cirque, gape at tempestuous Storm Mountain with its distinctive swirling strata, and gaze at Highwood Ridge and the Elk Range.

Attain the first summit and you'll see much more. Beyond the Elk Range is a shark's mouth horizon: row upon row of 3000-m (9840-ft) peaks. For optimal views west across the Continental Divide, ascend before noon. Photographers might want to ascend after 2 p.m., for saturated light on Storm Mtn. Come in autumn and the larches near the mouth of Arethusa Cirque will be electric gold.

En route to Little Arethusa, you'll nip into Arethusa Cirque. Don't bother probing it. Don't even stop there. It's not a worthy objective. Too brushy. Very disappointing compared to nearby, meadowy Ptarmigan Cirque (Trip 31). Besides, you'll survey all of Arethusa Cirque from the shoulder of Little Arethusa.

Fact

Before your trip

Be aware that Hwy 40, from Kananaskis Lakes Trail to Highwood Junction, is closed December 1 through June 15.

Ascending Little Arethusa. Storm Mountain beyond.

By Vehicle

From **Trans-Canada Hwy 1**, drive south 67.4 km (41.8 mi) on Hwy 40. Reset your trip odometer to 0 at the Highwood Pass trailhead parking lot. Proceed south another 1.4 km (0.9 mi).

From **Highwood Junction** (where Hwys 40, 541 and 940 intersect), drive northwest 36 km (22.3 mi) on Hwy 40.

From **either approach**, turn northeast onto the short, unpaved spur entering a clearing immediately south of the guardrail. Park here, just off the highway, at 2170 m (7118 ft).

On Foot

Walk north through the clearing. About 30 m/yd before the creek, turn right (east). A **cairn** indicates where the trail enters the forest. It climbs moderately above the creek's southeast bank, among Englemann spruce and alpine fir. Your general direction of travel is northeast, gradually curving east.

In about 15 minutes, at 0.7 km (0.4 mi), 2268 m (7450 ft), the **trail ends** at the creek. This is the mouth of Arethusa Cirque. Little Arethusa is visible left (north). Hop over the **creek** and proceed straight (east) 15 paces. Then turn left (north) and pick up a **faint route** into the larches. Head toward the slope that rises to a terrace beneath Little Arethusa. Presently, cross another fork of the shallow creek. Proceed north, up its west bank.

The route soon disappears. Follow the path of least resistance amid the larches. Several minutes farther, emerge on the left side of a north-south **gully**. Ascend northwest, above the gully's left side. Take advantage of steps bootbeaten into the steep, grassy slope. Gain the **terrace** at 2384 m (7820 ft). Having hiked about 30 minutes, you're now in the alpine zone, with no trees between you and Little Arethusa.

Ascend north. Stay between rock (left) and a clutch of krummholz (right). Reach another terrace. Then angle left (northwest) up the grassy slope to attain Little Arethusa's **south ridge**, at 2470 m (8100 ft). Decision time. Want to continue climbing on even rougher talus? If not, appreciate the view, then turn back.

Nearby southeast is 3095-m (10,153 ft) Storm Mtn, with its distinctive swirling strata. Directly west is the south end of Pocaterra Ridge (Trip 30). Beyond it is the Elk Range. West-southwest, below the south end of Pocaterra Ridge, is grassy Pocaterra Cirque. Mt. Tyrwhitt rises left of and immediately behind the cirque.

Continue the steep ascent. The loose rock here is just big enough to hamper progress. Patches of smaller, broken rock offer a reprieve. You'll likely follow traces of sheep trail beaten into the talus. At 2.7 km (1.7 mi), 2729 m (8950 ft), step onto the **first summit** of Little Arethusa. The eastern precipice plunges into the northern reaches Arethusa Cirque.

Storm Mtn appears even more impressive. Peaks beyond the Elk Range are now visible. One of the more distinctive is wedge-shaped, 3450-m (11,316-ft) Mt. Joffre, west-southwest. Others in that vicinity are Mt. Petain and Castlenau Peak. The Royal Group is distant west-northwest. Even farther is 3406-m (11,172-ft) Mt. Sir Douglas, northwest.

Immediately north of the first summit is the 2744-m (9000-ft) second summit of Little Arethusa. The two summits are closely linked by a broken, narrow, precipitous ridge. Only competent climbers should attempt this short, dicey stretch. The second summit grants an aerial view of Ptarmigan Cirque (northwest), but the panorama hardly changes. From Little Arethusa's second summit, a razor-sharp ridge continues northeast to nearby 2912-m (9551-ft) Mt. Arethusa.

TRIP 33
Mist Mountain

LOCATION	Elbow-Sheep Wildland Provincial Park, Hwy 40
ROUND TRIP	11 km (6.8 mi)
ELEVATION GAIN	1264 m (4146 ft)
KEY ELEVATIONS	trailhead 1875 m (6150 ft), summit 3139 m (10,297 ft)
HIKING TIME	6 to 7 hours
DIFFICULTY	challenging scramble
MAPS	page 190; Gem Trek Highwood— South Kananaskis Country; Mount Rae 82 J/10

Opinion

Silence. It's rarely cited as a reason to climb a mountain, but it's an increasingly valid one as our world grows louder. Because intrusive, irritating sound can damage more than your hearing. It contributes to rising blood pressure, declining productivity, and higher serum-cholesterol levels. Studies show that incessant noise makes people less caring, less communicative, less reflective; more apt to feel helpless and powerless. Even routine hospital noise impedes healing.

In search of silence, head for Mist Mountain. The arduous ascent deters all but the hardiest of local hikers and scramblers, so you'll likely be alone, subjected only to the sound of your panting, gasping breath, and the clink of your boots on steep, shifting scree. Up top, bathed in serenity, you can watch the Rockies flowing to the horizon like ragged tidal waves.

Just don't underestimate the difficulty of this adventure, or overrate your mountaineering competence, or miscalculate the suffering involved. Mist Mtn sifts the intrepid from the casual. For about an hour—after the scrambling begins in earnest, until you've dropped your pack on the summit ridge—it's pure trudgery. The scree is so loose, the incline so steep, you'll need Sisyphian endurance. Step up, slide back. Step up, slide back. Step up, slide back.

We include it in this book of premier trips because of the challenge and accomplishment it offers as the highest K-Country peak south of Highwood Pass. And because there are two places en route where, should you decide the summit will outstrip your desire or ability, you can stop and still feel glad you came. The first is about an hour up, on an unnamed, grassy, alpine pass. The second is about two hours up, on top of a prominent rock rib, still below the Mist Mtn cirque, but high enough where you'll have sampled the trials and joys of the scramble.

Ascending Mist Mtn

After grappling with Mist Mtn, you'll fully appreciate it upon subsequent sightings. It's visible from Raspberry Ridge (Trip 52), from Mt. Burke (Trip 53), even from Hwy 40 while driving northwest out of Highwood Junction.

True to its name, the mountain seems to summon mist, clouds, rain. So plan this trip for a day when you're assured of a flawless, blue sky. If the weather threatens to turn, hike elsewhere. Minus its panoramic reward, Mist Mtn—silent though it might be—is just a rock quarry, and you're sentenced to hard labour.

Fact

Before your trip

Be aware that Hwy 40, from Kananaskis Lakes Trail to Highwood Junction, is closed December 1 through June 15.

By Vehicle

From **Trans-Canada Hwy 1**, drive south on Hwy 40. Crest 2206-m (7239-ft) Highwood Pass at 67 km (41.5 mi). Reset your trip odometer to 0 here—not at the parking lot, which is 0.4 km (0.25 mi) farther. In another 13 km (8.1 mi) turn left (north) into a large, grassy clearing between the highway and the forest.

Or start at **Highwood Junction**, where Hwys 40, 541 and 940 intersect. (It's 43 km / 26.7 mi southwest of Longview; 31 km / 19.2 mi northwest of where Hwy 532 joins Hwy 940.) Set your trip odometer to 0. Drive northwest on Hwy 40. At **20.2 km (12.5 mi)** pass Mist Creek day use area on the left. At **21.2 km (13.1 mi)** cross the signed bridge over Mist Creek. At **24.8 km (15.4 mi)** turn right (north) into a large, grassy clearing between the highway and the forest.

From **either approach,** park near the west end of the clearing, at 1875 m (6150 ft).

On Foot

Hike north-northeast. A short, gentle ascent leads to the forest edge. Ignore the orange metal post. Follow the remains of an old road north through trees. Boulders block vehicle entrance. In a few minutes reach a **T-junction** at 1890 m (6199 ft). Turn right (east) on the grassy, former highway. Follow it generally east-northeast through thick brush and young trees.

About 15 minutes from the trailhead, look for a **cairned path** crossing the road. Immediately beyond, hikers have placed logs across the road to discourage you from proceeding in that direction. The path ascends left (north) and descends right (south). It's clearly more substantial than the game trails you've passed thus far. Go left, up the hillside, into an opening in the forest. Right descends to the highway but deteriorates into a bushwhack and dumps you at the wrong end of the clearing.

Ascend steeply for twelve minutes. The path levels briefly at 1997 m (6550 ft). About 30 minutes from the trailhead, reach a **fork.** Bear right, curving (northeast). To prevent you from ascending straight (northwest), hikers have blocked that option with rocks and logs.

View west from just below Mist Mtn summit

The right fork descends slightly and contours. Berry bushes thrive here. Within five minutes, at 2024 m (6640 ft), attain the trip's first view. Ahead is the wide, V-shaped, **grassy draw** you'll be ascending. Northwest, above you, are rocky cliffs on Mist Mtn's southeast-curving arm.

Keep hiking north to the obvious, alpine pass. Follow a faint bootbeaten path through the grass. Re-entering trees, the tread is more distinct. Cross willowy slopes. Step over or around wildflowers growing in the little-used path: powder-blue alpine forget-me-nots, and bright-yellow buttercups. Reach the **unnamed pass** at 3 km (1.9 mi), 2301 m (7547 ft), about an hour from the trailhead.

Piercing the pass, continue left (northwest) around a knob, into the next drainage. Contour across loose, very steep talus. After maintaining your elevation, angle upward where you're comfortable doing so. Clamber onto the prominent **rock rib**. It affords the easiest, most enjoyable route up the drainage. Magenta willow herb thrives here. At about 2410 m (7900 ft), hop over the meltwater stream. Above the stream's north bank, ascend west, then northwest on heather and rock.

Pick your way, gradually curving northwest, into the **cirque** embraced by the arms of Mist Mtn. What begins as a moderately ascending boulder romp soon turns grim as you encounter ever-steepening scree. Either keep slogging up the shifting rock, or scramble onto the airier but more solid spine to the left. Whichever you choose, your goal is north. Crest the **summit ridge** at 3050 m (10,000 ft). Conquistadors will be here about 2 hours from the pass, 3 hours from the trailhead.

After a well-earned rest, turn right for the final, short push, generally east. Compared to the steep scree you just vanquished, the crest of the summit ridge is a relief. The angle of ascent eases; the rock is more stable underfoot. Step onto the 3139-m (10,297-ft) **summit of Mist Mtn** after hiking and scrambling a total of 5.5 km (3.4 mi). If you're here within 3½ hours of leaving the trailhead, you deserve a medal for exceptional fitness and determination. You'll see that a previous visitor was honoured with a plaque after he was smote by lightning. It's a sobering admonition to mind the weather during your summit festivities.

The Mist Mtn panorama is vast. Listed here are but a few notable highlights. The Elk Range is southwest and west. See the gleaming white expanse farther west? That's Petain Glacier (Trip 26). Mt. Assiniboine is northwest. Storm Mtn, north-northwest, anchors the other end of the Misty Range. Misty Basin is north, at the head of Mist Creek valley. Mist Ridge (Trip 35) forms the valley's far wall, northeast. The austere Highwood Range is southeast. Three-peaked Odlum Ridge is southeast.

Because you can glissade down the scree in a fraction of the time it took to climb, it's possible to reach your vehicle 2½ hours after departing the summit of Mist Mtn.

TRIP 34
Mt. Lipsett

LOCATION	Elbow-Sheep Wildland Provincial Park
	Hwy 40, southeast of Highwood Pass
ROUND TRIP	12 km (7.4 mi)
ELEVATION GAIN	705 m (2312 ft)
KEY ELEVATIONS	trailhead 1875 m (6150 ft), summit 2580 m (8465 ft)
HIKING TIME	3½ to 5 hours
DIFFICULTY	moderate
MAP	Gem Trek Highwood & Cataract Creek

Opinion

With TVs all but strapped to their heads like feedbags, North Americans gorge nonstop on spectacles, most of which are not real. That's why they lack patience for ordinary life, in which the excellent and the extraordinary are rare, and much is difficult, imperfect, disappointing, or tedious. No wonder most North Americans don't hike. It almost always entails difficulty and tedium. That's certainly true of the Mt. Lipsett approach. But if you stride on, you'll soon relish a genuine spectacle and the fulfillment that comes from having earned it.

Bear in mind, the spectacle atop Mt. Lipsett doesn't compare with the see-forever, 360° vistas afforded by higher summits nearer the Great Divide. Calling Lipsett a "mountain" strains the definition. By Canadian Rockies standards, it's just a big hill. The western half of the panorama extends across the Highwood River headwaters to distant peaks of the Divide. And the eastern half of the panorama is blocked by 3138-m (10,295-ft) Mist Mtn (Trip 33). But the Patagonian immensity and austerity of Mist Mtn is awesome at such close range. And the rest of the view is enriched by the liberating experience of walking Lipsett's lengthy alpine summit ridge without a single pesky tree imposing its will over yours.

The wilderness you'll survey from atop Lipsett is most scenic in late fall, when larches add a splash of gold to the forest, and a dusting of snow highlights the crags above Running Rain Lake (south-southwest). Lipsett is also a good choice in fall because it's a relatively short trip. You can hike it during the warmest part of the day—11 a.m. to 3 p.m.— avoiding the damp chill of early morning and the plummeting cold of evening.

What's tedious about the hike? The initial hour or so is on a sketchy trail, then an overgrown road. They meander inefficiently through forest that is neither beautiful to behold nor generous with views. It's especially dull a second time, on the return. That's why it's preferable to hike Mt. Lipsett as a one-way shuttle trip rather than a round trip.

Emerging from treeline on Mt. Lipsett

By not retracing the meandering, forested ascent, you'll reduce your total distance to 9 km (5.6 mi), and you'll slash the day's tedium by 50%. Hiking one-way, however, requires a cross-country descent from the summit, southwest to Hwy 40. It's extremely steep, and it ends with a 20-minute bushwhack.

Casual hikers will find this a challenge, perhaps an overwhelming one. They shouldn't attempt it. Strong, experienced hikers will find it spices the trip with a pinch of adventure yet poses no serious obstacle. They should yell "Wahoo!" and go for it. Hitchhiking the short distance back to the trailhead can be easy. But if your party has two vehicles, arrange a shuttle as described in the *By Vehicle* directions below.

Fact

Before your trip

Be aware that Hwy 40, from Kananaskis Lakes Trail to Highwood Junction, is closed December 1 through June 14.

By Vehicle

Follow directions for Trip 33 to the Mist Mountain trailhead—a large, grassy clearing between the highway and the forest—at 1875 m (6150 ft).

If you intend to make this a one-way shuttle trip, and your party has two vehicles, park the second one about 9 km (5.6 mi) south of Highwood Pass, or 4 km (2.5 mi) west of the trailhead. That's roughly where your cross-country descent should end.

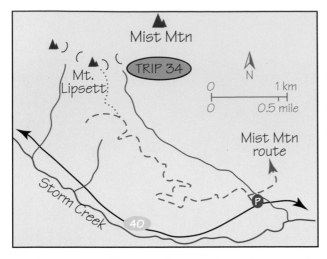

Mist Mtn

Mt. Lipsett

TRIP 34

N

0   1 km

0   0.5 mile

Mist Mtn route

Storm Creek

40

P

On Foot

Start hiking at the west end of the clearing. Ascend north to the forest edge. Look for a **rusted pole** at the northwest corner of the clearing. Follow the sketchy trail that departs near the pole. It leads north into forest.

In about four minutes, reach an overgrown road. Don't turn onto the road. Stay on the trail, continuing directly across the road, ascending northwest. Soon ascend steeply north, just left of a **stream gorge**. A few minutes farther, the trail curves left (west-southwest), away from the gorge.

About 20 minutes from the trailhead, ignore the game path forking left (northwest). The trail is faint here, but stay on it by bearing right and curving north. One minute farther, however, go left (west) onto a gently ascending **old road**.

About 45 minutes from the trailhead, the road-trail makes a **hairpin turn** right (southeast) at 2065 m (6773 ft). Scattered alpine larches here are gold in late September. In thinning forest, attain glimpses across the valley to the rounded ridges of the Elk Range. Mt. Odlum is southwest. Mt. Loomis is south.

Ascend left (west). Views continue. Ten minutes farther, the trail broadens and curves north-northeast. Mist Mtn looms ahead. Mt. Lipsett is visible left (northwest) through trees. About 1½ hours from the trailhead, the trail exits subalpine forest and surges into the **alpine zone**.

Proceed northwest. Enjoy a brief, level respite on a southwest-facing slope. Within 15 minutes, you'll see the trail ahead curving left (northwest). It ends soon in that direction and will only divert you from your goal. So abandon the trail here and continue **cross-country**: straight, ascending moderately, up the fall line.

At 6 km (3.7 mi) ascend just right of the summit and reach the top of 2580-m (8465-ft) **Mt. Lipsett**. The much higher and more dramatic peak a mere 1.2 km (.75 mi) northeast is 3138-m (10,295-m) Mist Mtn. Highwood Pass is northwest. Rugged peaks of the Great Divide are south, beyond the Elk Range.

You now have three options: (1) Retrace your steps to the trailhead. (2) Descend generally southwest, cross-country, to Hwy 40, then either hitchhike or drive your shuttle vehicle back to the trailhead. (3) Descend northwest to a saddle, ascend to Mt. Lipsett's outlier (slightly lower than

Mist Mtn (Trip 33), from Mt. Lipsett

the summit but affording a better vantage of Highwood Pass), then either (a) retrace your steps to the trailhead, or (b) descend generally south, cross-country, to Hwy 40, where you'll either hitchhike or drive your shuttle vehicle back to the trailhead.

Before choosing, look downslope (southwest) from the summit. Are you certain you'll be comfortable on such a steep, trail-less descent to the highway? If you're hesitant, don't be foolish; option one is for you. If you're confident and eager, however, you'll enjoy options two or three, and you'll spare yourself a tediously gradual descent on the trail you just hiked. Option three simply takes about a half hour longer than option two.

Directions for options two and three? They're unnecessary for anyone who's capable, and they might entice those who aren't, so our guidance ends here. If you're up to the challenge, you'll grok the way. That's part of the fun. Below treeline, just maintain your downhill course until you intersect the highway. We found game trails helpful in the dense forest. The approximately 3-km (1.8-mi) descent to the highway (from either the summit or the outlier) takes about 45 minutes. When you hit pavement, the trailhead is left (southeast).

In the unlikely event that you fail to catch a ride back to the trailhead, no worries. It's only a 4-km (2.5-mi) walk, and a pleasantly scenic one at that. Besides, if you don't catch a ride, it's probably because there were few vehicles, which means your walk will be peaceful.

TRIP 35
Mist Ridge

LOCATION	Elbow-Sheep Wildland Provincial Park
	Hwy 40, southeast of Highwood Pass
LOOP	23 km (14.3 mi)
ELEVATION GAIN	1200 m (3936 ft)
KEY ELEVATIONS	trailhead 1774 m (5820 ft)
	north Mist Ridge 2482 m (8140 ft)
	Storm Mtn ridge 2579 m (8460 ft)
HIKING TIME	9 to 11 hours
DIFFICULTY	moderate
MAPS	Gem Trek Highwood—South Kananaskis Country
	Mount Rae 82 J/10

Opinion

Coasting the crest of Mist Ridge, joy will waft you onward. The gentle, alpine terrain is enticingly open. Views are constant. On a fine day, it's as if you're walking as much in the air as on the earth. This soulful buoyancy can make you dismiss corporeal matters as heretical. Friends who joined us here will attest to that. Only while de-booting at day's end did they admit their feet were painfully blistered.

It *is* a long dayhike, especially if you extend it to Storm Mtn ridge—highly recommended. So come shortly after the summer solstice. Get an early-morning start. And bring your headlamp—just in case.

Mist Ridge ranks among K-Country's most thrilling ridge walks. The others are Pocaterra and Northover (Trips 30 and 24). All afford memory-bulging vistas. Pocaterra is way shorter than Mist but has more demanding sections. Northover is even longer than Mist and is severely rigourous. The average hiker will probably prefer Mist.

A big advantage of Mist Ridge is that it's in a rain shadow. When grim weather threatens K-Country, perseverance will most likely be rewarded at Mist. After a normal winter, the ridgecrest should be snow-free in late June. The slopes can be luxuriant in early July. The annual wildflower display is a deva's delight: scorpionweed, fleabane, wild blue flax, plumed aven, alpine forget-me-not, Jacob's ladder, moss campion, rock jasmine.

Mounting the south end of Mist Ridge, where actual ridgewalking begins, takes about two hours. It sounds like a long approach, but it's pleasantly varied. Steepness really isn't an issue on this trip. The crest route has only moderate ups and downs, requires no scrambling, and remains comfortably broad.

As for the view, you'll frequently see Cliff Creek valley off your right shoulder, Mist Creek valley off your left. A stupendous massif wall parallelling the far side of Mist Creek valley is nearly always in sight. This is the Misty

The beginning of Mist Ridge

Range. Mist Mtn (Trip 33) anchors the south end of the range, Storm Mtn the north end. Between them, four canyons drain into Mist Creek valley. The farthest north is tranquil, pastoral Misty Basin, below Storm Mtn ridge. So your eyes will be feasting all day.

Libation for the feast, however, is in short supply. A stream crossing about an hour from the trailhead will be your last opportunity to refill waterbottles until you drop off the ridge, into Mist Creek valley, homeward bound. So haul more water than you think you'll need.

You'll cross several tributary streams in Mist Creek valley. All are reliable water sources. So much for excitement on this leg of the journey. It's just a plod through disenchanted forest of lodgepole pine and Engelmann spruce. Fires raged here long ago. Today, trees again deprive hikers of scenery. A couple meadows offer brief scenic respites, but that's all. Nor will you see Mist Creek. *Missed Creek* is more like it. The trail stays well away. The creek isn't even audible until just before exiting the valley. But you could see a bear. You'll likely see bearberry jam (scat). This is grizzly habitat. Making noise to warn bruins of your presence is the best way to prevent an encounter.

In defense of the Mist Creek valley trail, it does allow a loop. Hiking Mist Ridge one-way, out and back, would be much more strenuous, adding 384 m (1260 ft) of elevation gain. And the Mist Creek valley trail is mercifully level, granting a speedy exit. From Rickert's Pass, where you depart the ridge, it's possible to zoom to the trailhead in 2½ hours.

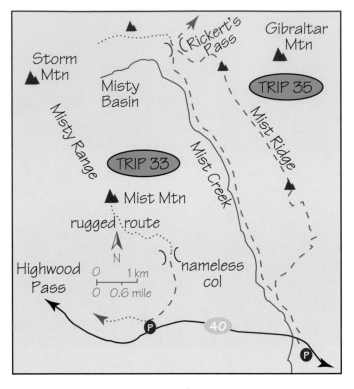

Fact

Before your trip

Be aware that Hwy 40, from Kananaskis Lakes Trail to Highwood Junction, is closed December 1 through June 15.

By Vehicle

From **Trans-Canada Hwy 1**, drive south on Hwy 40. Crest 2206-m (7239-ft) Highwood Pass at 67 km (41.5 mi). Reset your trip odometer to 0 here—not at the parking lot, which is 0.4 km (0.25 mi) farther. Proceed south another 17.5 km (10.9 mi).

From **Highwood Junction** drive northwest 20.2 km (12.5 mi) on Hwy 40. (Highwood Junction is where Hwys 40, 541 and 940 intersect. It's 43 km / 26.7 mi southwest of Longview; 31 km / 19.2 mi northwest of where Hwy 532 joins Hwy 940.)

From **either approach,** turn west into the trailhead parking lot at Mist Creek day use area. Elevation: 1774 m (5820 ft).

On Foot

A signed trail departs the north end of the parking lot. In three minutes reach the highway. Cross it. Bear right (east) on a former road. Soon turn left and proceed up-valley, generally north-northwest, still on old road.

A gradual ascent leads to a **junction** at 1 km (0.6 mi), 1857 m (6090 ft), about 25 minutes from the trailhead. Left (northwest) probes Mist Creek valley. You'll loop back that way from the far end of the ridge. To mount the near end, go right (north) into a tributary drainage. About 45 minutes from the trailhead, attain views: west across the valley, northwest to Mist Mtn, north to the zigzagging road you'll soon follow.

At 2107 m (6910 ft), after hiking about an hour, bear left (east) where a road ascends right (southwest). Descend to 2024 m (6640 ft), rockhop a **stream**, bear left, then immediately curve right. Resume climbing through forest into the subalpine zone. Progress northward via the zigzags you saw earlier. Reach a **saddle** (meadow and krummholz) at 3 km (1.9 mi), 2247 m (7370 ft), about 1½ hours from the trailhead.

Go left briefly before turning right (north) to resume ascending the road. It switchbacks left (southwest) then curves right (northwest), climbing around the south end of Mist Ridge. The road ends in a grassy **gap**. Ignore the game trail ahead. Bear right and pick your own route north-northeast up the alpine slope to the 2432-m (7977-ft) **south summit** of Mist Ridge.

Your general direction of travel all the way to the north summit will be north-northwest. The entire ridgetop route is easy to follow and poses no exposure. Rock outcroppings punctuate the short grass.

The ridge is initially narrow but not awkward. Follow a bootbeaten path, often on the right (east) side of the crest. It's fairly level for about 1 km (0.6 mi). About 2½ hours from the trailhead, Calgary is visible northeast. Beyond the 2430-m (7970-ft) **second summit**, plunge to 2296 m (7530 ft). You'll recoup that elevation loss in moderate steps.

Approaching the north summit, contour at 2482 m (8140 ft), just below the crest, on its left (west) side. Mist Basin is visible west-northwest, beneath Storm Mtn. The route descends the left (west) side of the 2515-m (8250-ft) **north summit**—highest point on Mist Ridge.

Reach a 2427-m (7960-ft) saddle overlooking forested Sheep River Valley (north). After following the route around the south side of a rocky

Lupine

knob, you can survey the route up Storm Mtn ridge (northwest). It's a bootbeaten path roughly 120 m (394 ft) below the pyramidal summit on the right (northeast) end of the ridge.

Whether proceeding up Storm Mtn ridge or heading home, you must drop to **Rickert's Pass**. At 2341-m (7680-ft), it's the lowest point on Mist Ridge. Having hiked 12 km (7.4 mi), reach a junction in the pass. Left (southwest), the Mist Creek valley trail plunges below treeline then follows the valley floor back to the trailhead. Right (northeast), the Rickert's Creek trail descends to intersect the Sheep River trail. Ahead (northwest), a path continues to Storm Mtn ridge.

Northward on the crest of Mist Ridge. Beyond is Gibraltar Mtn.

The Storm Mtn ridge path angles west below the first summit. About 1 km (0.6 mi) from the pass (20 minutes if you can ignite your booster rockets) top out at 2579 m (8460 ft) on the **middle summit of Storm Mtn ridge**. It's the lowest of the three summits, but the view is superb. Burns Creek canyon is north. The creek's source, Burns Lake, is northwest. Above and beyond the lake are Mt. Arethusa and Mt. Rae. Sheep River Valley is northeast. Mist Creek valley is south-southeast. Misty Basin is south. Above and beyond it is Mist Mtn at the south end of the Misty Range. Storm Mtn looms west-southwest.

After retracing the route to Rickert's Pass junction, go right (southwest) on the **Mist Creek valley trail**. Descend short switchbacks into forest. Once the trail levels on the valley floor, your general direction of travel will remain south-southeast for 9 km (5.6 mi). The rate of descent is barely perceptible.

About 25 minutes below the pass, hop over a **stream**—the first dependable water source since below the south end of Mist Ridge. Others are ahead. Shortly beyond, cross a large, willowy meadow. Proceed through uninspiring forest of lodgepole pine and Engelmann spruce. Cross another willowy meadow about 1½ hours from the pass. The last obstacle—a sharp drop into a creek drainage, and a stiff climb out—seems a perverse punishment near the end of such a long day.

Determined striders will arrive at a **junction** two hours after leaving the pass. This is where the loop began. You're now on familiar ground. Bear right to vanquish the final 1 km (0.6 mi) to the trailhead.

TRIP 36
Picklejar Lakes

LOCATION	Elbow-Sheep Wildland Provincial Park
	Hwy 40, southeast of Highwood Pass
ROUND TRIP	9 km (5.6 mi)
ELEVATION GAIN	442 m (1450 ft)
KEY ELEVATIONS	trailhead 1729 m (5670 ft), highpoint 2170 m (7120 ft)
HIKING TIME	3 to 5 hours
DIFFICULTY	moderate (due only to short, steep, final approach)
MAPS	Gem Trek Highwood & Cataract Creek
	South Kananaskis Country

Opinion

Lakes are to hikers what sticks are to dogs. No matter how far God tosses one out there in the woods, we'll chase it down and find it.

Our infatuation with lakes, though obvious, is not easy to explain. Is it because, standing on the shore of a backcountry lake, we can admire the surrounding mountains? Is it because lakes are a diversion, inviting us to swim or fish? Is it simply because lakes serve as destinations by affording a definitive sense of arrival?

There's a deeper reason why we love lakes. It's because they're still. We live complex, frenetic lives. Even the forests we hike through are visually busy. But lakes are islands of stillness. Reaching a lake at trail's end has the effect of a tranquilizer dart. Staring at a lake is profoundly calming.

Our eyes dive into the water. The sight alone refreshes us. It douses the fire of thought. Slakes our thirst for tranquility. Whether they're as clear as the mountain air or an ineffable shade of blue-green, lakes soothe us. And who these days doesn't need a little soothing?

For that reason, the trail to Picklejar Lakes is among the most popular in Kananaskis Country. It quickly leads to four, small lakes stairstepping into a cirque in the desolate Highwood Range. On a sunny day, the Picklejars contrast dramatically with the subalpine greenery and stark gray cliffs surrounding them. The second lake—deep, crystalline, frigid—tempts proud Canadians to demonstrate a cultural conceit: tolerance of cold. A quick dunk might be invigorating, if the weather's hot. You first.

Fact

Before your trip

Be aware that Hwy 40, from Kananaskis Lakes Trail to Highwood Junction, is closed December 1 through June 15.

First Picklejar Lake

By Vehicle

From **Trans-Canada Hwy 1**, drive south on Hwy 40. Just after cresting 2206-m (7239-ft) Highwood Pass, watch for the trailhead parking lot (right / southwest) at 67.4 km (41.8 mi.) Reset your trip odometer to 0 here. Proceed south another 19.7 km (12.2 mi). Do not stop at Picklejar Creek day use area.

From **Highwood Junction**, drive northwest 17.1 km (10.6 mi) on Hwy 40. (Highwood Junction is where Hwys 40, 541 and 940 intersect. It's 43 km / 26.7 mi southwest of Longview; 31 km / 19.2 mi northwest of where Hwy 532 joins Hwy 940.)

From **either approach**, turn west into the trailhead parking lot at Lantern Creek day use area. Elevation: 1729 m (5670 ft).

On Foot

Lantern Creek, not Picklejar Creek, offers the best access to Picklejar Lakes. From the parking lot, walk left (north) along the highway. Just past Lantern Creek, cross to the **right (east) side of the highway**. Pick up the trail curving northeast into aspen and conifers above the creek's northwest bank. Begin a vigourous ascent.

In 20 minutes, reach a viewpoint on a **grassy slope** at 1878 m (6160 ft). Ahead, you can see the trail vaulting to a pass. Continue traversing east. You're high above the creek, which is audible but not visible. The mountains you're entering are among the Highwood Range.

At 1966 m (6450 ft), about 40 minutes from the trailhead, cross a **creeklet** and turn left (north), climbing more grassy slopes. Though the ascent

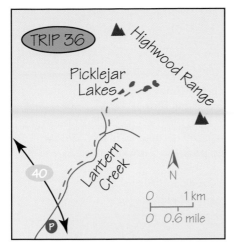

steepens abruptly, there are no switchbacks. Seeking stable footing, hikers have strayed widely. Result: a **broad, denuded swath** affording almost no traction. Toil upward. Descending is even worse.

Having gained a new appreciation for labour-saving, switchbacking trails, crest a 2137-m (7010-ft) **pass**. Strong hikers arrive here one hour after leaving the trailhead. Ahead (north) is a sharp drop into forest. Turn right (east) and resume ascending steeply on a slightly less eroded, grassy slope.

Attain views. West-northwest is Mist Mtn. Northwest is the south end of Mist Ridge. Reach the **highpoint** of the trip: 2170 m (7120 ft). The airy trail, now descending on shale, grants an overview of the first lake. You might also spy a trail in the forested valley below (left / northwest). It leads to Picklejar Creek. Exiting that way is not recommended.

Reach the shallow **first lake** at 4.2 km (2.6 mi), 2160 m (7085 ft). Campsites are across the outlet stream, in trees, above the north shore. Follow the south-shore trail through grass, toward the inlet stream. It briefly climbs, then drops to the smaller **second lake**—five minutes from the first. An arresting, battleship-like peak rises above it. The trail veers right (south) and ascends. Five minutes farther, reach the deep **third lake** at 2183 m (7160 ft). The trail ends here.

Round the third lake on either side. A route skirts the north shore, then ascends through trees and over rock slabs. Another route crosses a rockslide to the south and continues across scree. Whichever you choose, reach the

shallow **fourth lake** at 4.5 km (2.8 mi), 2149 m (7050 ft). A rock-and-grass spur right (south) of the southwest shore offers a view of both the third and fourth lakes. Beyond the fourth lake is a talus bowl topped by banded cliffs.

The fourth Picklejar Lake

TRIP 37
Talus Lake

LOCATION	Hwy 66, southwest of Bragg Creek
ROUND TRIP	20.8 km (12.9 mi) cycling, plus 10 km (6.2 mi) hiking
ELEVATION GAIN	207 m (680 ft) cycling, plus 405 m (1328 ft) hiking
KEY ELEVATIONS	trailhead 1610 m (5280 ft), lake 2223 m (7290 ft)
HIKING TIME	2½ hours cycling, plus 4 to 5 hours hiking
DIFFICULTY	moderate
MAPS	Gem Trek Bragg Creek and Elbow Falls
	Gem Trek Kananaskis Lakes

Opinion

Perhaps modern life is a disaster. That would explain why so many people lack mental and physical vigour. Apathy is a common reaction to disasters. It was widespread among survivors of the Hiroshima bombing. The Japanese called it *burabura*, or *do-nothing sickness*. It can rapidly lead to physical deterioration if not countered. So here's an anti-apathy trip. Not just a hike, but a bike-and-hike. Your goal is a resplendent, teal lake adorning a craggy, austerely handsome Front-Range cirque. It's a hot day? The creeks are running? Plunge into an inviting bedrock pool en route, thus completing your own, vigourous, semi-Iron-Man afternoon: bike, hike, and swim.

The journey begins on the Little Elbow trail—a rocky road initiating a 38-km (23.6-mi) loop popular with mountainbikers. You, however, will pedal only the first stretch, to Mt. Romulus backcountry campground. After stashing your steed, you'll march up an unofficial, infrequently hiked trail. Though not indicated on most maps, the trail is evident on the ground, easy to follow until it approaches the Forks, where you must be mindful.

The Front Range sizzles when summer cooks. Some find the hot, dry atmosphere soothing, especially if inclined to dip in the aforementioned Talus Creek pools about 45 minutes up the trail. Otherwise, save this trip for early summer, cloudy weather, or autumn. Any time of year, you'll be exploring a world of scree, talus, rocks and boulders. After climbing through open forest you won't burst into meadows. A few hardy wildflowers will nevertheless brighten the way: purple asters, shrubby cinquefoil with yellow flowers, and white, exotic-looking, fringed grass-of-Parnassus. Upon reaching Talus Lake, the depth and clarity of the water might tempt you to dive in. Talk about vigourous. Even on a day of record-setting heat, the water will be numbingly cold.

Before coming solely to visit Talus Lake, consider that two other trips in this book—West Fork Little Elbow River (Trip 39), and Paradise Pass (Trip 38)—entail cycling to Mt. Romulus campground. If you can muster three days, bring your tent and establish a basecamp at Romulus. Devote

Talus Lake

day one to Talus Lake, the shortest of the three excursions. On day two, trek all the way to Piper Pass via the West Fork Little Elbow. On day three, hike to Paradise Pass, then saddle up and ride out.

For peace of mind, bring a cable and lock to secure your bike to a tree trunk. You'll likely want to wear a helmet, cycling shorts, gloves, and perhaps cycling shoes. Cache those along with your bike while you're hiking.

Fact
Before your trip

Be aware that Hwy 66, from Elbow Falls to the trailhead, is closed December 1 through May 15.

By Vehicle

Follow the directions for Forgetmenot Ridge (Trip 47) to the end of Hwy 66, about an hour southwest of Calgary. Park just beyond the Elbow River campground entrance, in the small pullout on the right, at 33 km (20.5 mi), 1610 m (5280 ft). If the pullout is full, return to the spacious lot just outside the campground entrance.

By Bike

Your goal is Mt. Romulus backcountry campground, 10.4 km (6.5 mi) southwest of the trailhead. Though you'll be on an old road the entire way,

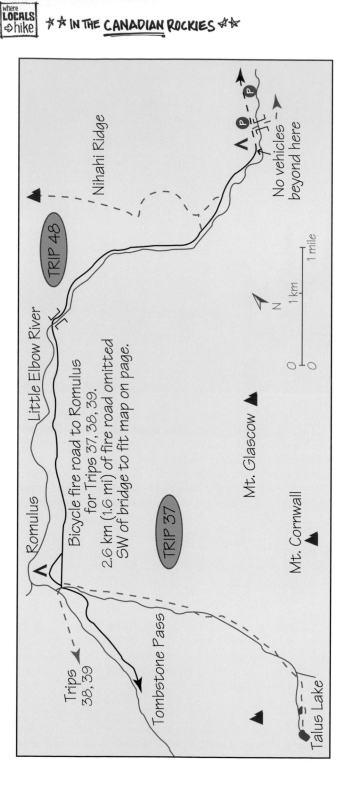

Nihahi Ridge

TRIP 48

Little Elbow River

Romulus

Bicycle fire road to Romulus
for Trips 37, 38, 39.
2.6 km (1.6 mi) of fire road omitted
SW of bridge to fit map on page.

TRIP 37

No vehicles
beyond here

N

0   1 km

0   1 mile

Mt. Glascow

Mt. Cornwall

Trips
38, 39

Tombstone Pass

Talus Lake

it undulates frequently and gains 207 m (680 ft). Moderately strong cyclists will do it in 1½ hours. The return, largely downhill, takes only about an hour.

From either the pullout or the parking lot, ascend the campground entrance road southwest. As it curves west, stay on the main road, continually bearing left where right spurs access campsites. Go around a couple metal gates, or through them if open. Vehicles are prohibited beyond a final trailhead parking lot that might also be gated.

In a couple minutes, pass a sign for Nihahi Ridge and Little Elbow trail. Cross a cattleguard. About ten minutes along, pass a trail forking right (northwest) into the forest; it also climbs to Nihahi Ridge (Trip 48). Keep following the road. It curves northwest now, on the Little Elbow River's north bank.

About 15 minutes along, cross the stony bed of **Nihahi Creek** (likely shallow or dry). A signed trail forks right, probing the creek canyon upstream (north-northwest). Keep following the road. Two minutes farther, cross a bridge to the Little Elbow River's south bank. The road now leads southwest, climbing a long, steep hill to 1755 m (5756 ft).

After cycling about an hour, pass a bench at a viewpoint on the left. Mt. Remus (cliffbands) is north-northwest, across the valley. Left of it (northwest) is Mt. Romulus (brown scree slopes). Soon cross a tributary streambed.

Pass a road forking right (west)—the first entrance to Mt. Romulus campground—after cycling nearly 1½ hours. Proceed southwest on the main road. A few minutes farther, at 1817 m (5960 ft), immediately before the **confluence of Talus Creek and South Fork Little Elbow River**, another road forks right (north). This is the second entrance to Mt. Romulus campground. The main road left climbs south over Tombstone Pass.

If your goal is Talus Lake, stop cycling here. Stash your bike, plus any cycling gear you won't need, in the forest—left (southeast) of the road, east of the Talus Creek drainage.

If your goal is the West Fork Little Elbow (Trip 39) or Paradise Pass (Trip 38), turn right (north) onto the campground's second entrance road. In two minutes, immediately before entering the campground, reach a four-way junction. Ahead (north) are the campsites. Right (east) is the first entrance road. Left (west) is the road you'll hike to either destination after stashing your bike. It quickly crosses the South Fork, then leads southwest, up the West Fork valley.

On Foot

The unsigned Talus Lake trail forks left (south-southeast) from the main road. Look for it opposite the campground's second entrance, east of Talus Creek, west of the Mt. Romulus campground sign.

Follow the trail across stony flats. In a few minutes, it climbs a steep, dirt bank, at the edge of pines. East, across Talus Creek gorge, you can see the road that ascends to Tombstone Pass. Soon dip into a mossy gully. Your general direction of travel is southeast. The trail undulates above the east wall of the creek gorge.

After about 20 minutes and little elevation gain, the trail descends a gentle ridge over stony ground, through pine and Engelmann spruce. Cross a bedrock stream gully. After a short, rough ascent, Talus Creek is visible and audible. The trail again undulates.

At 1930 m (6330 ft), cross another stream gorge with bedrock pools (possibly dry). A little farther, after hiking about 45 minutes, arrive at the east bank of **Talus Creek**. It too has large bedrock pools—inviting on a hot day. Just 15 meters (yards) upstream, the trail crosses to the west bank. In another minute, it re-crosses to the east bank and continues generally southeast. Ahead, the canyon opens. The long wall of Mt. Cornwall is left (east).

At 2.5 km (1.6 mi), 1915 m (6280 ft), immediately before a tributary stream joins Talus Creek, the trail climbs steeply left on scree, out of the drainage. The ascent eases on a terrace above the tributary's east bank. The trail heads south, then turns right (west), crosses the tiny tributary and enters trees. After swerving south again, it leads through open forest broken by grassy clearings.

Beyond the clearings, the trail curves right (west) and drops sharply to Talus Creek. Rockhop to the northwest bank. Head upstream. Follow a shallow depression beside trees, about 3 m/yd from the bedrock creekbed. In two minutes, where the tread is faint, go 5 m/yd right. Pick up a cairned route for the remaining short distance to **the forks**, at 3.7 km (2.3 mi), 2088 m (6850 ft).

Proceed west-southwest on a rocky route. A blocky peak (south) divides the two upper forks of Talus Creek. The route enters the southwest fork, right of the peak. Cairns offer guidance among giant boulders and rock heaps. Go through a dry gully. The faint route leads just below and right of the largest, cabin-size boulder visible ahead (west). Ascend among boulders, then on grass, toward the distant cirque. Cross another dry creekbed and ascend its left bank.

Reach a **shallow lakelet** at 2162 m (7090 ft). There's a pleasant campsite in a meadow on the north shore. It has a view of the headwall guarding Talus Lake.

A path rounds the lakelet's southeast side. Tag onto a trail ascending across the scree slope above a cascade in the gorge. Pass through tight krummholz. About 15 minutes from the lakelet, overcome the headwall. The northeast shore of **Talus Lake** is 10 m/yd below, at 2223 m (7290 ft). You've hiked 5 km (3 mi) from Mt. Romulus campground.

The teal lake is in a cirque whose walls are talus slopes rising to sheer cliffs. A grassy bench is left, above the lake. There's room for a single tent among trees on the right. The view northeast, out of the cirque, is dominated by Mt. Cornwall.

Arnica

TRIP 38
Paradise Pass

LOCATION	Elbow-Sheep Wildland Provincial Park Hwy 66, southwest of Bragg Creek
ROUND TRIP	20.8 km (13 mi) cycling, plus 17.4 km (10.8 mi) hiking
ELEVATION GAIN	207 m (680 ft) cycling, plus 787 m (2580 ft) hiking
KEY ELEVATIONS	trailhead 1610 m (5280 ft), pass 2576 m (8450 ft)
HIKING TIME	2½ hours cycling, plus 7 to 8 hours hiking
DIFFICULTY	moderate
MAPS	page 208; Gem Trek Bragg Creek and Elbow Falls Gem Trek Kananaskis Lakes

Opinion

Striding through florid meadows in Paradise Basin—with the summer sun overhead, the wondrous Opal Range looming above you on one side, the hulking Ripsaw towering above you on the other, immense Tombstone Mountain in view over your shoulder, and the prospect of a revelatory panorama from the pass just ahead—might make you think tolerating those wicked Canadian prairie winters is worth it.

The journey begins with a scenically motivating, 1½-hour bike ride on a rocky, undulating, old road. You'll leave your mechanical horse at Mt. Romulus backcountry campground. For peace of mind, secure it to a tree using a cable and lock. You'll likely want to wear a helmet, cycling shorts, gloves, and perhaps cycling shoes. Cache those along with your bike.

Then begin hiking. You'll still be on an old road, but one succumbing to entropy. Often narrow and overgrown, it feels more like a wide trail. Besides, it offers frequent views of the beautiful, steep-walled, mountain valley you're piercing. So you won't grouse about what's underfoot.

The final leg, on undeveloped trail, is where the ascent begins in earnest. The grade isn't Olympic. Just athletic. You'll escape the trees and enter sub-alpine meadows in 20 minutes. From there on, the hiking is five-stars premier: high on grassy slopes, across rolling meadows, with peaks surrounding you like a devoted entourage. Paradise Pass and the basin preceding it are a remote, sublime destination. Popular with locals, too. Watch for an elk herd in the meadows, or a flock of bighorn sheep on the crags above.

The trail to Paradise Pass continues beyond. It descends north, skirting small, forested Evan-Thomas Lake, which is visible from the pass. Then it curves northeast, intersecting the North Fork Little Elbow River trail at Evan-Thomas Pass. There, left leads generally north, then northwest, all the way to Hwy 40. Right leads southeast back to Mt. Romulus campground. "A loop!" you exclaim. But this loop has little to recommend it. The scenery north of Paradise Pass is uninspiring. Returning the way you came allows you to relive the splendour of the approach, plus it's shorter.

Before coming solely to visit Paradise Pass, consider that two other trips in this book—West Fork Little Elbow River (Trip 39), and Talus Lake (Trip 37)—entail cycling to Mt. Romulus campground. If you can muster three days, bring your tent and establish a basecamp at Romulus. Devote day one to Talus Lake, the shortest of the three excursions. On day two, trek all the way to Piper Pass via the West Fork Little Elbow. On day three, hike to Paradise Pass, then saddle up and ride out.

Another option is repacking on the morning of day two and moving your camp 5 km (3.1 mi) farther southwest, into the West Fork valley, just past where the West Fork and Paradise Pass trails split. That will save you from repeating the 9.4-km (5.8-mi) round trip between Mt. Romulus campground and the trail split. Hiking that in-and-out stretch only once, however, requires you to do it bearing a full load, rather than twice with just a daypack. A lonelier, more scenic campsite up the West Fork valley on night two tilts the scales in favour of moving camp.

Fact

Before your trip
Be aware that Hwy 66, from Elbow Falls to the trailhead, is closed December 1 through May 15.

By Vehicle
Follow the directions for Forgetmenot Ridge (Trip 47) to the end of Hwy 66, about an hour southwest of Calgary. Park just beyond the Elbow River campground entrance, in the small pullout on the right, at 33 km (20.5 mi), 1610 m (5280 ft). If the pullout is full, return to the spacious lot just outside the campground entrance.

By Bike
Follow the directions for Talus Lake (Trip 37). Turn right (north) onto the Mt. Romulus backcountry campground's second entrance road, at 1817 m (5960 ft). In two minutes, immediately before entering the campground, reach a four-way junction. Ahead (north) are the campsites. Right (east) is the first entrance road. Left (west) is the road you'll hike to Paradise Pass after stashing your bike. It quickly crosses the South Fork Little Elbow River, then leads southwest, up the West Fork valley.

On Foot
From the four-way junction immediately south of Mt. Romulus backcountry campground, take the road leading west. In a couple minutes, either ford or rockhop across the **South Fork Little Elbow River**. Follow the road southwest, ascending steeply through a corridor of trees.

You're entering the **West Fork Little Elbow River valley**. In about 15 minutes, where the road crests, pause before descending. Look west. You'll see where the route to Paradise Pass climbs right (northwest) behind a massive ridge. That's also where the main West Fork valley (Trip 39) curves south.

Mounts Hood and Packenham, from Paradise Pass trail

Continue generally southwest on the road. The valley's towering cliff walls are frequently visible. At 1820 m (5970 ft), about 20 minutes along, the road intersects the **river**. Don't ford. Follow the bypass trail left, upstream, along the south bank. Ascend briefly, then drop back to the road, bear left and resume up-valley.

At 1878 m (6160 ft), after hiking about an hour, reach a broad, rocky **streambed**. It's probably shallow, possibly dry. Hike in it, angling left. A minute or so farther, turn left (west) onto the road, through willow bushes and trees.

Ascend to a minor **fork**, at about 1¼ hours. Right descends to the river. Stay left (high) on a bench above the river. Immediately cross a rough gully. Within another five minutes, the road passes a **campsite** on the left and intersects the **river**. Either ford or rockhop to proceed southwest.

About seven minutes farther, reach a **cairn** in a grassy clearing at 1933 m (6340 ft). The overgrown road ends here. You've hiked 4.7 km (2.9 mi) from Mt. Romulus campground. About 15 paces beyond the cairn, the **Paradise Pass trail** forks right (northwest). The West Fork Little Elbow trail veers left, immediately crosses a creek, then leads south to Piper Pass.

The Paradise Pass trail soon splits. Right is easier. The paths rejoin shortly. A steep ascent on slippery dirt grants a superb view south, up the West Fork. The view is impressive but misleading, suggesting that Piper Pass is impassable. At a moderate grade, the trail leads west, then northwest. Views up the West Fork continue to expand. At 2064 m (6770 ft), about 20 minutes from the road's end cairn, the grade eases on grassy, bushy subalpine slopes.

Nearing Paradise Pass

About 35 minutes up, drop into a willowy draw with a creeklet. Then stay left on the main trail. Descend through tight trees to a reliable **creek** at 2159 m (7080 ft). It's a steep, slippery ascent out. The trail begins switchbacking on leafy meadows. You'll see broad-leaved willow-herb (fireweed), yarrow (fern-like leaves), and stands of krummholz.

At 2257 m (7403 ft), about an hour up, the trail curves north on a grassy ridge. Mounts Hood and Packenham punctuate the Opal Range, left (west). Proceed along the edge of a small but impressive stream gorge. Arrive in **Paradise Basin**. Continue north across grassy meadow for 10 to 15 minutes before ascending the final scree slope to the pass. Right (east) is a cirque beneath the striking peaks of The Ripsaw—unlabeled on most maps.

Reach 2576-m (8450-ft) **Paradise Pass** about 1½ hours from the road's end cairn. You've hiked 8.7 km (5.4 mi) from Mt. Romulus campground. West-northwest of the pass is 3097-m (10,158-ft) Mt. Evan-Thomas. North of it, the Opals diminish to a grassy ridge. Northwest, below the pass, is forested Evan Thomas Lake. Looking south-southwest, down the east wall of the Opal Range, you can see through Piper Pass (Trips 27 and 39) to Rae Glacier on Mt. Rae.

TRIP 39
West Fork Little Elbow River

LOCATION	Elbow-Sheep Wildland Provincial Park
	Hwy 66, southwest of Bragg Creek
ROUND TRIP	20.8 km (13 mi) cycling, plus 22 km (13.6 mi) hiking
ELEVATION GAIN	207 m (680 ft) cycling, plus 990 m (3247 ft) hiking
KEY ELEVATIONS	trailhead 1610 m (5280 ft), Piper Pass 2580 m (8462 ft)
HIKING TIME	2½ hours cycling, plus 8 to 9 hours hiking
DIFFICULTY	moderate
MAPS	Gem Trek Bragg Creek and Elbow Falls
	Gem Trek Kananaskis Lakes

Opinion

The farther out on a limb you go, the more exhilarating it feels coming back in. And Piper Pass via the West Fork Little Elbow River valley is definitely way out there. It's a positively Homeric journey if you pull it off in a single day. Mostly because of the marathon distance. But also because the sketchy route probing the upper West Fork valley requires navigational competence. And because the final ascent to the pass demands that you climb like a yak on a headwall so steep and rocky that even a yak would balk. You're swift as a Yeti pursued by photographers? A daytrip is possible. Start early on a bombproof-blue mid-summer day. Pack your headlamp in case of a late return. You'll be thrilled by the scenery, elated by the accomplishment. You're a mere mortal hiker? Keep reading. There are advantages, in addition to common sense, for making this a multi-day adventure.

The journey begins with a scenically motivating, 1½-hour bike ride on a rocky, undulating, old road. You'll tether your two-wheeled pony at Mt. Romulus backcountry campground. For peace of mind, secure it to a tree using a cable and lock. You'll likely want to wear a helmet, cycling shorts, gloves, and perhaps cycling shoes. Stash those along with your bike.

Then begin hiking. You'll still be on an old road, but one succumbing to entropy. Often narrow and overgrown, it feels more like a wide trail. Besides, it offers frequent views of the beautiful, cliff-sided, mountain valley you're piercing. So you won't grumble about what's underfoot.

From road's end, you'll veer into the secluded, upper West Fork valley. In the shadow of the worship-worthy Opal Range, an undeveloped trail glides across meadows, fades while climbing through subalpine forest, then zings into the alpine zone. Here the terrain turns feral, all but bearing its teeth. Steep grassy slopes give way to a riot of rock. The valley's upper reaches could have been dynamited from the constricting walls. Novices unnerved by this chaotic basin and the headwall's terrifying, vertical appearance should turn back at the tarn, justifiably proud of their achievement. Pushing onward and upward calls for strength and confidence. It's

West Fork Little Elbow River valley

not even a scramble, but the severe grade keeps the scree and talus unsteady. Experienced mountain freaks will revel in the challenge.

Piper Pass is a lonely, scenic perch among lofty, jagged peaks. It affords stirring views north and south. You'll see the trail continuing through Piper Creek basin, into Piper Creek canyon (Trip 27). Having previously attained Piper Pass via that southern approach should not discourage you from returning from the north, via the West Fork valley. Only atop the pass will the scenery be familiar. If traversing the pass on a backpack circuit appeals to you, read *Opinion* paragraphs six and seven in Trip 27.

Before coming solely to explore the West Fork Little Elbow River valley, consider that two other trips in this book—Paradise Pass (Trip 38), and Talus Lake (Trip 37)—entail cycling to Mt. Romulus campground. If you can muster three days, bring your tent and establish a basecamp at Romulus. Devote day one to Talus Lake, the shortest of the three excursions. On day two, trek all the way to Piper Pass via the West Fork Little Elbow. On day three, hike to Paradise Pass, then saddle up and ride out.

Another option is repacking on the morning of day two and moving your camp 5 km (3.1 mi) farther southwest, into the West Fork valley, just past where the West Fork and Paradise Pass trails split. That will save you from repeating the 9.4-km (5.8-mi) round trip between Mt. Romulus campground and the trail split. Hiking that in-and-out stretch only once, however, requires you to do it bearing a full load, rather than twice with just a daypack. A lonelier, more scenic campsite up the West Fork valley on night two tilts the scales in favour of moving camp.

Fact

Before your trip

Be aware that Hwy 66, from Elbow Falls to the trailhead, is closed December 1 through May 15.

By Vehicle

Follow the directions for Forgetmenot Ridge (Trip 47) to the end of Hwy 66, about an hour southwest of Calgary. Park just beyond the Elbow River campground entrance, in the small pullout on the right, at 33 km (20.5 mi), 1610 m (5280 ft). If the pullout is full, return to the spacious lot just outside the campground entrance.

By Bike

Follow the directions for Talus Lake (Trip 37). Turn right (north) onto the Mt. Romulus backcountry campground's second entrance road, at 1817 m

Final approach to Piper Pass, from West Fork Little Elbow River valley

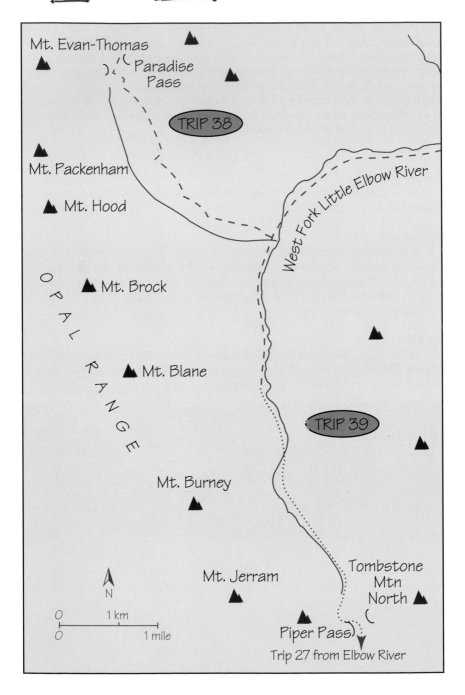

Mt. Evan-Thomas
Paradise Pass

TRIP 38

Mt. Packenham

Mt. Hood

West Fork Little Elbow River

O P A L   R A N G E

Mt. Brock

Mt. Blane

TRIP 39

Mt. Burney

N

0   1 km
0   1 mile

Mt. Jerram

Tombstone Mtn North

Piper Pass

Trip 27 from Elbow River

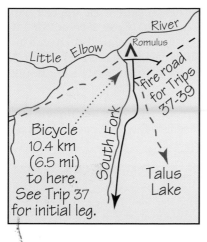

Bicycle
10.4 km
(6.5 mi)
to here.
See Trip 37
for initial leg.

(5960 ft). In two minutes, immediately before entering the campground, reach a four-way junction. Ahead (north) are the campsites. Right (east) is the first entrance road. Left (west) is the road you'll hike up the West Fork Little Elbow River valley after stashing your bike. It quickly crosses the South Fork Little Elbow River, then leads south-west.

On Foot

Follow the directions for Paradise Pass (Trip 38). In about 1½ hours, reach a **cairn** in a grassy clearing at 1933 m (6340 ft). The overgrown road ends here. You've hiked 4.7 km (2.9 mi) from Mt. Romulus campground. About 15 paces beyond the cairn, the trail to Paradise Pass forks right (northwest). Continue into the **upper West Fork Little Elbow River valley** by turning left (southwest) and immediately rockhopping across a small creek.

About ten minutes from the road's end cairn, the forest opens, granting you a view south into the upper West Fork valley, nearly to its end. The Opal Range forms the valley's right (west) wall. The rooty, hoof-beaten trail proceeds south for about 20 minutes through **meadow** bordered by trees. After briefly passing through **forest**, begin a gentle ascent. The trail narrows, crowded by willows.

Near 2165 m (7100 ft) the trail deteriorates in grass. Watch for faint traces. Ascend through tight, low trees. Follow **game paths** as needed to progress generally southeast, high above the left (east) bank of the West Fork Little Elbow River. Near 2204 m (7230 ft) go right, contouring south-southeast. Descend slightly. A **discernible route** now ventures onto **talus**. The view ahead is impressive but misleading. Piper Pass appears insurmountably steep. Don't be alarmed. It is indeed a pass.

At 2256 m (7400 ft) continue ascending **grassy slopes**. Follow the higher game path, staying well above the river's deep gorge. Wildflowers here include sawwort, scorpionweed, and yarrow. Piper Pass remains an hour distant. At the **head of the gorge**, proceed about 50 m (55 yd) then drop to cross a minor drainage. Continue on grassy slopes into the upper basin. Left (east) is an intimidating scree and talus slope rising to Tombstone Mtn North.

Reach the base of the **headwall** at 2405 m (7890 ft), about 2½ hours from the road's end cairn. Left, 12 m (40 ft) below you, is a tarn. South, above you, is your goal: Piper Pass, the low gap on the left. The final ascent is on a perceptible but arduously steep, rough route across loose, awkward talus and scree. It climbs through charcoal-coloured rock, then whitish, then chocolate.

Begin toiling upward on the far right (west) side of the upper basin. Ascend generally south, then angle left (southeast). Crest 2580-m (8462-ft) **Piper Pass** at the low edge of the chocolate rock. You've hiked 11 km (6.8 mi) from Mt. Romulus campground. The pass is flanked by 2997-m (9830-ft) Tombstone Mtn North (left / northeast), and 2997-m (9830-ft) Mt. Jerram (right / west-northwest).

South-southeast, on the horizon, is 3218-m (10,558-ft) Mt. Rae and its tiny glacier. The south approach to Piper Pass (Trip 27) is via Piper Creek canyon; the upper reaches of the trail are visible below, in Piper Creek basin. Southeast, directly below the pass, is a tarn.

Honey bee pollinating a plumed aven

Shoulder-Season Trips

Wasootch Ridge (Trip 43)

TRIP 40

Mt. Rundle, South Summit

LOCATION	Spray Valley Provincial Park
	Hwy 742, west edge of Canmore
ROUND TRIP	4 km (2.5 mi) to bench, 5.2 km (3.2 mi) to summit
ELEVATION GAIN	612 m (2007 ft) to bench, 852 m (2795 ft) to summit
KEY ELEVATIONS	trailhead 1688 m (5535 ft), bench 2300 m (7544 ft)
	summit 2540 m (8331 ft)
HIKING TIME	3 hours for bench, 4 to 5 hours for summit
DIFFICULTY	moderate to bench, challenging to summit
MAPS	page 217; Gem Trek Best of Canmore

Opinion

Life: if you do it right, it's exhausting.

Remember that truth when you arrive in Canmore, gaze up at the skyline-dominating wedge you're about to ascend, and your knees buckle. Because the south summit of Mt. Rundle affords a panorama and sense of achievement that more than compensate for the rigourous ascent.

The mountain's south summit is just one end of a hulking massif—so lengthy it also looms above Banff townsite. That's where the true summit is: farther north. But the south summit is an easier goal, more quickly attained, and competitively scenic.

The trail to the north summit is a viewless slog most of the way. The trail to the south summit is instantly captivating. Glimpses of big scenery quickly widen into sweeping vistas.

The immediate surroundings also vie for your attention. Multiple routes engage you in a kind of terrestrial tic-tac-toe. Loose rock on steep inclines calls for secure boot placement.

About halfway, you might wonder if the mountain ever relents. It does. Below the summit, a grassy, nearly-level bench invites you to drop your pack, relax, and gaze at the peak-studded horizon.

In summer, the bench is a flowery oasis in a stoney realm. Many people stop here, recline, nibble on lunch, devour the scenery, then descend, pleased with their accomplishment.

Resuming the ascent poses one challenge: a short burst of light scrambling through rockbands guarding the summit. Some hikers do it without using their hands, others grab rocks to steady themselves.

If you summit, you'll see distant giants, including Mt. Temple, near Lake Louise, and Mt. Assiniboine. To the south is a mountainous collage: chunky peaks pasted one on top of the next. And the aerial perspective of Canmore and the Bow Valley is engrossing.

The Mt. Rundle trail ascends above Whiteman's Pond.

Fact

By Vehicle

From downtown **Canmore**, follow signs leading uphill to the Canmore Nordic Centre. Reset your trip odometer to 0 at the Nordic Centre turnoff. Continue ascending on Smith-Dorrien / Spray Trail (Hwy 742). Pavement ends at 1.2 km (0.7 mi). The road levels in Whiteman's Gap—a pass between Ha Ling (left / east) and the south summit of Mt. Rundle (right / north). Proceed along the west side of Whiteman's Pond. Slow down. At 5 km (3.1 mi), 1688 m (5535 ft), park in the pullout on the left (east), at the south end of the pond, in front of a rock outcrop.

From **northern K-Country**, drive north on Smith-Dorrien / Spray Trail (Hwy 742). Reset your trip odometer to 0 at the Goat Creek trailhead parking lot, on the left (west). Ascend north into Whiteman's Gap. At 0.4 km (0.2 mi), 1688 m (5535 ft), park in the pullout on the right (east), at the south end of Whiteman's Pond, just after a rock outcrop.

On Foot

The trail departs the west side of the road, about 50 paces north of the pullout. It initially leads north, left of the double telephone-pole stanchion.

After veering left, begin switch-backing, ascending steeply into the trees, heading generally southwest. Here on the lower reaches of the mountain, the trail is distinct and easy to follow.

Ascending to Mt. Rundle summit block

On Mt. Rundle's summit ridge

Soon curve right (north). With only incidental variation, this will remain your general direction of travel until near the summit. The aggressive grade eases occasionally but only briefly.

You'll face more ambiguity the higher you go, because the trail splinters and braids. In general, bear right (closer to the sheer southeast face) until you've surmounted treeline and worked your way above rocky slopes to a broad, grassy, nearly-level **bench** at 2300 m (7544 ft). Punctuated by a prominent cairn, it's just below a scattering of stunted trees. The view from here is immense.

The final push to the summit block entails light scrambling on loose rock and narrow ledges. But there's no actual exposure. It's very steep but not sheer. If you go, remember that your sense of confidence and comfort is usually an accurate measure of your safety. Should you feel anxious or hesitant, turn back.

Proceeding? Stand near the prominent cairn and look up at the summit block. You'll see a peaklet north-northwest. Directly below it is a **tan rockband**. Immediately below that is a **black rockband**. A route pounded into the talus will lead you there. Then angle right, between those rockbands.

You'll be above the rockbands after ten minutes of scrambling. Resume hiking on another path pummeled into the talus by previous summiteers. Crest the **summit ridge** a mere three minutes farther. Suddenly you're peering down the other side of the mountain. Bear right, clamber over a couple head-high ledges, and Mt. Rundle's 2540-m (8331-ft) **south summit** is yours.

The Bow Valley is east-southeast. Mt. Temple is northwest, towering above Lake Louise. Mt. Assiniboine is southwest. Mt. Rundle's soaring buttresses—accessible only to climbers—rake the sky north-northwest.

After returning to the bench, remember to bear left on the remaining descent. Hugging the sheer southeast face will help you keep to the main trail.

TRIP 41
Ha Ling Peak

LOCATION	Bow Valley Wildland Provincial Park
	Hwy 742, southwest of Canmore
ROUND TRIP	5.4 km (3.3 mi)
ELEVATION GAIN	741 m (2476 ft)
KEY ELEVATIONS	trailhead 1666 m (5463 ft), summit 2407 m (7897 ft)
HIKING TIME	1½ to 4 hours
DIFFICULTY	moderate
MAP	Gem Trek Best of Canmore

Opinion

Before Canmore shapeshifted into a luxe resort village, it was a gritty coal-mining town. Back then, residents burrowed into the mountains. Today they clamber over them: the south summit of Mt. Rundle (Trip 40), Mt. Lady Macdonald (Trip 42), Middle Sister (Trip 1), and especially Ha Ling. The trailheads are all within a ten-minute drive of Main Street. But Ha Ling— the incisor jutting skyward from Canmore's southwest corner—is the most clambered over of the bunch, because it's the least arduous ascent.

Local outdoor athletes train here, bounding up to the summit in 50 minutes or less, careening back down in under 30. Those figures, however, attest only to the vigour of Canmore's elite, not to the ease of this hike. The Ha Ling trail begins switchbacking steeply through forest, then surges past treeline onto very steep talus and scree, where it fades to a route. Imagine a mix of ball bearings, marbles, and billiard balls on a 45° incline. Bring your trekking poles for added purchase on the way up, extra shock absorption on the way down, and more stability throughout.

How long will it take you to get up and down Ha Ling? That depends on your experience and ability. A woman we know who's retired, rarely hikes, and suffers from asthma, was keen to summit this striking mountain that she gazes up at every day from her Canmore home. Neighbours who are strong hikers offered to guide her. It took four hours up, but she made it. On top, deeply moved by the tremendous panorama and the thrill of accomplishment, she wept.

Allow yourself at least 45 minutes on the summit, to peer at Canmore far below and stare at the Canadian Rockies in every direction. And step cautiously up there. The crest of the mountain ends abruptly at the sheer northeast face.

Approaching summit of Ha Ling

Fact

By Vehicle

From downtown **Canmore**, follow signs leading uphill to the Canmore Nordic Centre. Reset your trip odometer to 0 at the Nordic Centre turnoff. Continue ascending on Smith-Dorrien / Spray Trail (Hwy 742). Pavement ends at 1.2 km (0.7 mi). The road levels in Whiteman's Gap—a pass between Ha Ling (left / east) and the south summit of Mt. Rundle (right / north). Proceed along the west side of Whiteman's Pond. The road then descends south. At 5.4 km (3.4 mi), where the road is again level, turn right (west) into the Goat Creek trailhead parking lot. Elevation: 1666 m (5463 ft).

On Foot

From the Goat Creek trailhead parking lot, go left (north) about 80 paces on Hwy 742. Turn right onto the gated service road and ascend south. At the top of the hill, cross the **bridged canal**. The easy-to-follow trail starts behind the **shed**, initially ascending southeast into forest. Switchbacks lead generally east-northeast. After gaining 400 m (1312 ft) in about 20 to 30 minutes, you'll see the Goat Range (southwest) through thinning forest.

At 2.3 km (1.4 mi), 2275 m (7462 ft), you're near treeline, just below the col between Ha Ling Peak (left / north) and Miner's Peak (ahead / east-southeast). Consider detouring to Miner's Peak on the return. For now, follow the route steeply left (north). It zigzags through talus on this final pitch to your now visible goal.

Canmore and Fairholme Range, from Ha Ling summit ridge

Reach Ha Ling's **summit** cairn at 2.7 km (1.7 mi), 2407 m (7897 ft). The entire route to the south summit of Mt. Rundle (Trip 40) is visible northwest. Left of and beyond Rundle is Mt. Temple—distant but recognizable. The Goat Range is southwest. Canmore sprawls below you (northeast) in the Bow Valley. The Fairholme Range, walling in the valley's far side, is cleaved by Cougar Creek canyon. Mt. Lady Macdonald (Trip 42) is left (north) of the canyon, Grotto Mtn is right (south).

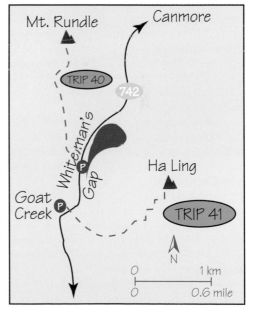

TRIP 42
Mt. Lady Macdonald

LOCATION	Bow Valley Wildland Provincial Park, northeast of Canmore
ROUND TRIP	6.6 km (4.1 mi) to shoulder 7.6 km (4.7 mi) to summit ridge
ELEVATION GAIN	917 m (3008 ft) to shoulder 1117 m (3664 ft) to summit ridge
KEY ELEVATIONS	trailhead 1383 m (4535 ft), shoulder 2300 m (7544 ft) summit ridge 2500 m (8200 ft)
HIKING TIME	4½ to 7 hours for shoulder 5½ to 8 hours for summit ridge
DIFFICULTY	moderate
MAP	Gem Trek Best of Canmore

Opinion

True Canadians love a snow-laden winter and all the sliding, gliding sports it allows. But come March, even the hardiest of us are sick of slush and ice and long to walk the earth again. In Canmore, we're tantalized, even tormented, by the sight of Mt. Lady Macdonald, whose sun-blasted southwest slope turns brown and advertises "spring!" long before winter has actually lost its grip on the Bow Valley. And year after year we're teased into charging up Lady Mac too soon, only to discover the trail's upper half remains thickly glazed and slick as a salesman. But the mountain usually sheds its frozen patina by April, so it's still among the earliest available shoulder-season hikes in this book, as well as one of the most challenging and rewarding.

Sticklers know Lady Mac is in the Fairholme Range, well outside even the loosest definition of K-Country. It's in this book nevertheless, because northeast Canmore is fastened like a barnacle to Lady Mac's lower slopes; the hike is immensely popular with locals as well as visitors; and the mountain is just across the valley from Mt. Rundle (Trip 40), Ha Ling Peak (Trip 41), Three Sisters Pass (Trip 3), Middle Sister (Trip 1), and West Wind Pass (Trip 4), all of which can legitimately claim to be K-Country residents.

It's ironic that Lady Mac's early availability is due in part to its steep incline. While it gives the entire slope good sun exposure, and causes snowmelt to run off rather than pool, it makes this an excruciating first hike of the season for anyone whose fitness level has slipped over the winter. Expect a muscle-straining ascent and joint-pounding descent. The lady is merciless. She'll generously reward you, however, with inspiring views. Within 30 minutes you'll overlook Cougar Creek canyon and survey much of the Bow Valley and its west-wall peaks. Chief among them is Mt. Rundle—

The shoulder of Mt. Lady Macdonald (upper center), just below the summit

a fantastically crenulated, fortress-like mountain stretching all the way from Canmore to Banff townsite. It's an awesome spectacle, especially from the aerial vantage of Lady Mac.

Though you can abandon the ascent midway up and feel compensated for your effort, try to reach level ground atop Lady Mac's 2300-m (7544-ft) south shoulder. It's a 2½-hour dash if you're swift, a 3½-hour plod if you're slow. Here, at 3.3 km (2 mi), you can lounge on the wooden platform intended to serve as a helipad for an aborted tourism venture. Nearby is the foundation for what would have been a teahouse unless Canmorites had said "no way!" Imagine helicopter flights constantly shuttling tourists between downtown and Lady Mac. The noise would have persecuted residents below. And the crowds would have been a pox on the mountain. What remains of the absurd teahouse is still a blight, but think of it as an encouraging symbol: sanity does occasionally prevail over destructive development.

The trail ends on the shoulder, so most hikers turn back there. But an obvious route, bootbeaten into the scree, continues beyond. It climbs 200 m (656 ft) in 0.5 km (0.3 mi) to Lady Mac's summit ridge. If you want more exercise, a heightened sense of adventure, and a bit better panorama, go for it. From the ridgecrest, you'll see the summit of Lady Mac farther north, at the end of a long, alarmingly sheer arête. Unless you're a fearless, black-belt scrambler, spare yourself the risk.

Before setting out for Lady Mac, fully hydrate yourself and pack a couple litres of water per person. It can get hot up there, you'll be working hard, and you'll encounter no water other than perhaps trickling snowmelt.

Wondering about the peak's aristocratic moniker? It was named in honour of Lady Susan Macdonald, wife of Canada's first prime minister, Sir John Macdonald. While iconoclasts rightfully resent the tradition of proffering mountains as tokens and demeaning them with irrational names that serve only to feed politicians' voracious egos, at least Lady Susan showed some enthusiasm for the Canadian Rockies. While traveling by train from Lake Louise to Golden via Kicking Horse Canyon, she rode—despite Sir John's adamant objection—in front of the locomotive, on the cow catcher, so she could better appreciate the stirring scenery.

Fact

By Vehicle

From **Calgary**, drive Trans-Canada Hwy 1 west. Take Exit 91, signed for Canmore and Hwy 1A. After curving to the stop sign, set your trip odometer to 0, and turn left (east) onto Bow Valley Trail / Hwy 1A. At 0.5 km (0.3 mi), turn left (north) onto Elk Run Blvd. Proceed uphill. At 1.8 km (1.1 mi), immediately after crossing the bridge over Cougar Creek, turn right into the paved parking lot, at 1383 m (4535 ft).

From **Canmore**, at the intersection of Railway Avenue and Bow Valley Trail, drive northeast over the Trans-Canada Hwy. Proceed uphill on Benchlands Trail into east Canmore. It curves right (southeast). Pass the store and café at Cougar Crossing, on the right. Just beyond, where the road forks near the eagle sculpture, bear right (south) onto Elk Run Blvd. Then immediately turn left into the paved parking lot. It's just before the bridge over Cougar Creek, at 1383 m (4535 ft).

On Foot

Follow the paved path north-northeast, between fenced backyards (left) and the deep Cougar Creek drainage (right). The creek is usually dry here, except for a brief spring flood.

Pavement soon ends. Proceed on smooth, packed dirt, then a broad, rocky path. Mt. Lady Macdonald is visible directly ahead (north). Grotto Mtn is east, beyond the creek.

Reach a signed junction within seven minutes. The Montane Traverse trail forks left (northwest) into forest. Continue straight (north-northeast) along the creek. One minute farther, go left onto an unsigned trail. Two minutes farther, reach a signed junction at 1.1 km (0.6 mi). Right follows the creek upstream (northeast). Go left (north) onto the Lady Macdonald trail and ascend out of the canyon.

About 20 minutes from the trailhead, ignore a faint left fork. Bear right. Ignore other sketchy spurs ahead. Keep to the obvious main trail, which ascends generally north.

At 1555 m (5100 ft), you can gaze out of the pine-and-fir forest, across the Bow Valley. Ha Ling Peak (Trip 41) is southwest. Mt. Rundle (Trip 40) is west. Cascade Mtn is northwest. A bit higher, you can appreciate the Three Sisters (Trip 1) to the south, and Mt. Lougheed south-southeast. After hiking 25 minutes from the trailhead, attain a view east-northeast deep into Cougar Creek canyon.

The forest is gradually opening. At 1848 m (6060 ft) pass an inviting **stone bench** that seats three. The trail proceeds along the edge of the slope, ascends a rockslide, then switchbacks up through boulders before briefly re-entering forest. At a chaotic **boulder pile**, the way forward is less evident. Slow down, look for cairns, and notice where hikers' boots have left dirt prints on the rock surfaces.

Trail soon resumes, with a short steep pitch leading to a sharp, **revelatory bend** at 2114 m (6934 ft). Mt. Lady Macdonald's summit ridge, and the level shoulder just below it, are now visible ahead (north). The view also extends northwest, across the mountain's southwest face, and up the Bow Valley.

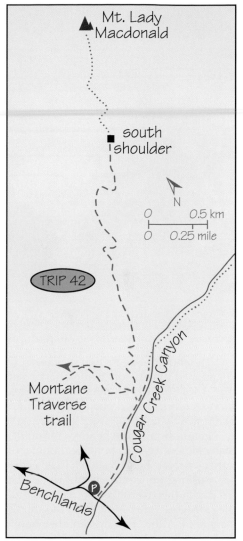

After a tight switchback, you might find the trail is again, momentarily, hard to discern. Stay left, out on the edge of the slope, then ascend through a couple, huge boulders to where obvious tread resumes. Traverse right (west-southwest) back toward the mountain's south side. The trail climbs gradually, then vaults steeply to the brink of a precipitous slope that plunges into Cougar Creek canyon. Turn left (north) here for the final approach.

Reach level ground atop the mountain's **south shoulder** at 3.3 km (2 mi), 2300 m (7544 ft). Strong hikers will be here 2½ hours after departing the trailhead and will complete the descent in 2 hours. Slow hikers will arrive in 3½ hours and will take nearly as long to descend.

Ascending Mt. Lady Macdonald. Mt. Rundle is across the Bow Valley.

The shoulder bears two structures. One is the foundation of a teahouse abandoned long before completion. Nearby is a spacious wooden platform that would have been the helipad for teahouse-bound passengers but now serves a more exalted purpose: comfortable sprawl space for hikers in need of a rest.

In addition to the nearby landmark mountains previously mentioned, many more are visible from the shoulder of Mt. Lady Macdonald. The western horizon reveals Banff National Park's peak-studded southern reaches.

Pushing on to the summit ridge? Though only 0.5 km (0.3 mi) farther, it's 200 m (656 ft) higher, so it's a significant slog. But the route, as well as the ridgecrest, are visible from the shoulder. It poses no obstacle other than steepness. Allow perhaps another hour to tag the 2500 m (8200 ft) crest, marvel at its vertiginous east face, and return to the shoulder.

From where you'll attain the **summit ridge**, it's a very challenging, 0.5-km (0.3-mi) scramble north along the crest to Mt. Lady Macdonald's 2605-m (8544-ft) summit. All but samurai mountaineers will be gripped by the exposure and should turn back.

TRIP 43

Wasootch Ridge

LOCATION	Elbow-Sheep Wildland Provincial Park, Hwy 40
ROUND TRIP	11 km (6.8 mi) to trail's end cairn
ELEVATION GAIN	1010 m (3315 ft)
KEY ELEVATIONS	trailhead 1433 m (4700 ft)
	trail's end cairn 2130 m (6986 ft)
HIKING TIME	4 to 6 hours
DIFFICULTY	moderate
MAP	Gem Trek Canmore and Kananaskis Village

Opinion

Ridges have ruffles. Though hikers persist in imagining themselves striding effortlessly along horizontal crests, the reality is that most ridges are severely serrated. In the craggy Canadian Rockies, ridges tend to plunge, swoop and soar as crazily as stunt pilots at an air show. So Wasootch Ridge is peculiar. Once the trail launches you steeply onto the crest, the few ups and downs are mellow all the way to trail's end. Yet views are nearly constant, and the scenery is remarkably stirring for a ridge whose front-range location makes it hikeably snow-free in spring and fall.

You'll soon be peering down into Wasootch and Porcupine creek canyons, and up at the long, north tentacle of Mt. McDougall. The venerable peaks west of Kananaskis Village will also compete for your attention. Among the trees you'll brush past along the crest are limber pines—gnarled, twisted beings who appear to be patience and tenacity incarnate. Wildflowers also grace the ridge. Look for lavendar Jacob's ladder, moss campion (tiny fuschia flowers in a green tuft), rock jasmine (tiny, white, with yellow centre), red roseroot, sawwort (dark-purple strands, thistle-like), purple saxifrage, and white mountain avens.

The trail on Wasootch Ridge was constructed by nothing more than continued foot traffic over the years, but you'll find it a competent hiking guide. It leads to a big cairn, one kilometer shy of the high point. Most ridge-walkers turn around at the cairn rather than scramble the rest of the suddenly intimidating ridge. The cairn is a fine place to relax, empty your boots, wiggle your toes in the breeze, and sip your Platypus full of lemonade. Remember: the ridge is dry. Pack more liquid than you think you'll need.

Fact

By Vehicle

From **Trans-Canada Hwy 1**, drive south on Hwy 40. Slow down after crossing signed Porcupine Creek. At 17 km (10.6 mi) turn left for Wasootch Creek day use area.

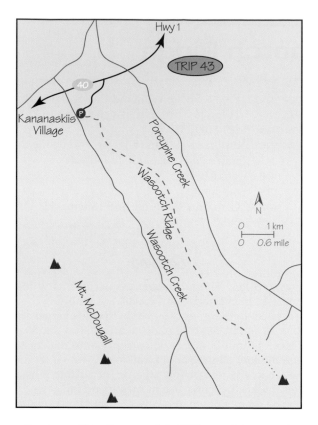

Or, from the turnoff to **Kananaskis Village**, drive north on Hwy 40. Slow down after crossing signed Wasootch Creek. At 23.1 km (14.3 mi) turn right for Wasootch Creek day use area.

From **either approach**, proceed 0.7 km (0.4 mi) to the road's end parking lot, at 1433 m (4700 ft).

On Foot

The trail departs the middle of the parking lot's east side. Ignore the signed, level trail going left (north-northeast) to Baldy Pass. Just beyond the signpost, go right (southeast) behind a few spruce trees to a small, gravel clearing. Ignore the game path (right). Between the two incorrect options, the Wasootch Ridge trail immediately rockets up-slope, east-northeast.

The initial ascent is very steep. It's soon apparent that the trail is heading southeast. This will remain your general direction of travel to the end of the ridge. Within three minutes, at 1483 m (4865 ft), rock slabs afford a view west to Mt. Allan (Trip 15) and northwest to Mt. Lorette. Where no trail is apparent, proceed south across the slabs. Within 12 m/yd, turn sharp left (east), pick up the trail again, and resume the taxing ascent.

Near 1555 m (5100 ft) the grade eases in young, open forest along the ridgecrest. Mount Baldy is visible left (north-northeast). The trail favours the right (west) side of the crest. Inspiring views continue.

Mt. Lorette, from Wasootch Ridge

About 30 minutes from the trailhead, mature trees restrict vision but grant shade. The trail veers left near a cairn at 1723 m (5650 ft), where a faint right fork is crudely blocked off.

Within 40 minutes, attain a view south-southeast up Wasootch Creek canyon. Much of the ridge is visible ahead. The canyon's right (west) wall is the long, north arm of 2726-m (8941-ft) Mt. McDougall. After a short drop, the trail rises into the open. Where it fades near 1829 m (6000 ft), look left (higher). It resumes near the crest, with views into Porcupine Creek canyon (left / east).

Looking south along Wasootch Ridge

Overall the ascent remains moderate. Your upward progress, however, is occasionally interrupted where the trail descends off minor summits before climbing to successively higher ones. Where the crest narrows, briefly follow a ledge on the right side before clambering around the left. Later, where the ridge broadens in the subalpine zone, the trail is less distinct, but the way forward remains obvious.

At 5.5 km (3.4 mi), 2130 m (6986 ft), reach **trail's end** on a rounded summit topped by a substantial cairn. Hiking time from the trailhead: about 2¼ hours. Mounts Sparrowhawk (Trip 6) and Bogart are visible west. The quadruple summits of Mt. Lougheed are west-northwest. Mt. Rundle (Trip 40) is northwest, beyond Skogan Pass.

Most of the ridge is now behind you. The remaining 1 km (0.6 mi) is only partially visible, but it's evident that pressing onward poses significantly more challenge. Proceed only if you're a capable scrambler who doesn't need guidance. Another 40 minutes of vigorous, occasionally hands-on effort is necessary to attain the **final summit** on Wasootch Ridge, at 6.5 km (4 mi), 2323 m (7619 ft).

TRIP 44
Old Baldy Ridge

LOCATION	Elbow-Sheep Wildland Provincial Park, Hwy 40
ROUND TRIP	16 km (10 mi)
ELEVATION GAIN	865 m (2837 ft)
KEY ELEVATIONS	trailhead 1520 m (4986 ft), ridge 2385 m (7823 ft)
HIKING TIME	5 to 6 hours
DIFFICULTY	moderate
MAPS	Gem Trek Canmore and Kananaskis Village
	Spray Lakes Reservoir 82 J/14

Opinion

You are a sensual creature. Your nose can catch the scent of berries in a forest, so you won't starve. Your ears can detect the distant snap of a twig, granting you a head start on a predator. Your eyes can leap far ahead of your feet, helping you bound across boulders without falling. But modern life—motionless work, cubicles, recycled air, artificial light—deprives your senses.

What we all need, every spring, is a retreat. A celebration of our sensuality and a reminder to cultivate it. For many of us, early-season hiking serves that purpose. In K-Country, an ideal retreat destination is Old Baldy Ridge.

An urbanite friend joined us here one June. Though the need to resuscitate our senses was unspoken, he obviously felt it. The hike exhilarated him. He jubilantly flung off his clothes and padded barefoot across Old Baldy Ridge, every pore gorging on the experience.

Old Baldy Ridge is a mellow, alpine hump well below 2728-m (8948-ft) Old Baldy Mtn. Ignored by motorists plying Hwy 40, Old Baldy Ridge is neither craggy nor towering. Its blunt top and forested flanks are nondescript. Singular peaks nearby hog all the attention: Mt. Lorette, Mt. Allan (Trip 15), Mt. Kidd, and The Wedge.

But Old Baldy Ridge is a fine grandstand from which to gaze upon those and other monumental mountains. The ridgetop is broad and, true to its name, treeless—perfect for napping, picnicking, dancing, or walking barefoot. Clothing optional, we've observed. Just remember there's not a scrap of shade, and even brief exposure to early-season sunshine can burn winter-white skin. Our friend suggests sunscreen. We prefer a hat, long sleeves, and pants.

Though the trip begins on an old road, it leads to an engaging, rugged trail—streamside for about an hour. Where it briefly deteriorates to a boot-beaten ledge climbing the gully wall, acrophobes will be unnerved. Beyond, a luxuriant subalpine gorge beckons, and the hiking is easy again. Upward progress is rewarded with startling over-the-shoulder views of The Fortress

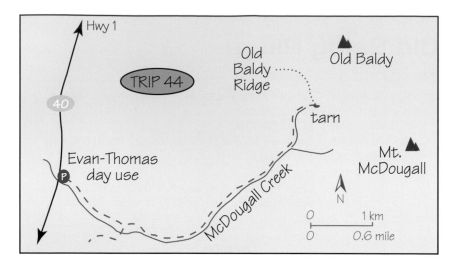

and The Wedge. The final, grassy-slope ascent is steep but increasingly scenic. On a clear, calm day, arrival atop the ridge can be euphoric.

If you don't visit Old Baldy Ridge in early summer, wait until fall. It's a premier shoulder-season trip, available sooner and later than others of similar elevation in central and north K-Country. Even in November, the stream you'll follow part way can still be flowing heartily. Late July to mid-September, however, choose another trip. One that's more gratifying initially, and aims farther and higher, so it's also more rewarding.

Fact

By Vehicle

From Trans-Canada Hwy 1, drive south 27.2 km (16.9 mi) on Hwy 40. Or, from Highwood Pass, drive north 40 km (24.8 mi) on Hwy 40. From either approach, turn east into the signed Evan-Thomas trailhead parking lot, at 1520 m (4986 ft). It's 0.4 km (0.25 mi) north of the bridge over Evan Thomas Creek.

On Foot

On the south side of the parking lot, right of the outhouse, begin on an old road—the **Evan-Thomas Creek trail**. Immediately reach a T-junction. Turn left (southeast). At 1.7 km (1.1 mi), about 25 minutes from the trailhead, reach a T-junction with the Wedge Connector from the south. Bear left (east-northeast), still on old road, ascending gradually.

About seven minutes later, the road curves right (south-southwest) and begins descending. In another 40 m/yd look for a **cairned trail** forking left into the trees. It departs the road at 1598 m (5240 ft), just before a creek. Hike the rough, narrow trail southeast, then east, gently ascending through forest. You're now following the left (north) bank of **McDougall Creek**, gradually curving northeast, upstream, into the drainage. Easily cross the creek a few times.

Old Baldy Mtn, from Old Baldy Ridge

At 1750 m (5740 ft), about an hour from the trailhead, the drainage narrows into a gorge as you pass **rocky outcroppings**. The path deteriorates, often clambering onto the eroding slope above the creek. Some stretches are just 25 cm (10 inches) wide, hanging above a sharp dropoff. But it's not an obstacle for anyone reasonably surefooted. Only when muddy or icy might it slow a capable hiker or deter others.

Beyond, the forest is more open, mixed with dwarf aspen. The Fortress and The Wedge are visible behind you (southwest). The trail continues ascending above the northwest bank of the creek. Near 1830 m (6000 ft), after hiking about an hour and 20 minutes, Old Baldy Mtn is visible ahead. Your goal is the ridge southwest of it.

Cross a minor **rockslide**, then negotiate several more precariously narrow sections. Entering forest in the upper drainage, the trail returns to more comfortable terrain. At 5.8 km (3.6 mi), 2037 m (6681 ft), reach the **creek forks**. Strong hikers will be here within two hours. The right (east) fork drops to the confluence in a series of cascades and pools. Follow the **left fork, curving north**, ascending moderately toward the hill of chunky rock. The swirling slopes of 2726-m (8941-ft) Mt McDougall are visible right (southeast).

Progressing up the grassy, flowery draw, you'll easily hop over the stream several times. The trail curves right (east) and climbs into trees. Cross a boggy meadow to a seasonal **tarn**. You're now at the mouth of a cirque walled-in by Old Baldy Mtn (north) and Mt. McDougall (southeast).

Marinating in the day's accomplishment atop Old Baldy Ridge

From the west end of the tarn, go left (north) up the steep, grassy slope. At 2385 m (7823 ft) crest rounded **Old Baldy Ridge** beneath 2728-m (8948-ft) Old Baldy Mtn (right, east-northeast). Follow the ridge left until the impressive view completely unfolds.

Mt. Collembola and Mt. Allan are visible northwest. Mt. Lougheed's four sharp peaks are left of Allan. Mt. Kidd is west-southwest. The Fortress is southwest. The Wedge is left of it, nearby southwest. Mt. Joffre is distant south.

Wildflowers adorn Old Baldy Ridge in early summer. Look for baby-blue alpine forget-me-not, red paintbrush, yellow succulent stonecrop, and magenta shooting star (see page 234).

Prairie crocus, or pasque flower, on Old Baldy Ridge in early June

TRIP 45
Jumpingpound Ridge

LOCATION	Powderface Trail, south of Hwy 68
SHUTTLE TRIP	17 km (10.5 mi) one way
ELEVATION CHANGE	640-m (2100-ft) gain / 976-m (3200-ft) loss
KEY ELEVATIONS	Jumpingpound trailhead 1835 m (6020 ft)
	Jumpingpound Mtn 2225 m (7300 ft)
	ridge lowpoint 1945 m (6380 ft)
	Dawson trailhead 1500 m (4920 ft)
HIKING TIME	6 to 8 hours
DIFFICULTY	easy
MAPS	Gem Trek Bragg Creek and Elbow Falls
	Bragg Creek 82 J/15,
	Jumpingpound Creek 82 O/2

Opinion

Dogs have to be walked. It's just universally understood that if you don't walk your dog, you're a negligent pet owner. So the statement "Gotta take the dog for a walk" clears your path of other obligations.

Saying "Gotta take my partner for a walk," however, doesn't elicit the same response. Not even close. Instead, you get raised eyebrows, concern, pity—all based on the assumption your spouse is an invalid.

How odd. Walking is tonic for relationships. Hiking—shared adventure—could prevent many couples from seeking a marriage counselor.

Only on the trail do we (Craig and Kathy) escape the locust-like swarm of details that devours us at home and work. Suddenly life is simple, fun, beautiful, and once again we relax into our love.

Yet it's not partner walking that's the national pastime. It's dog walking: being awkwardly tugged along behind a leash, stopping for an embarrassing butt sniff or humiliating poop scoop.

This must change. So here's one of Kananaskis Country's easiest, most convenient trails: a blessedly undemanding, scenically captivating, foothill ridgewalk available spring through fall. A mere hour from the city, the path will quickly loft you and your partner above the trees, where you can amble in harmony for most of a day.

Jumpingpound Ridge is popular with mountainbikers, but hiking is equally rewarding here. The broad, level, grassy ridgecrest often allows effortless striding. The views are vast—out across the prairie and deep into the Rockies' front range. Wildflowers, including moss campion, alpine forget-me-not, and rock jasmine, are abundant.

Jumpingpound Ridge can be hikeably snowfree as early as mid-May, when the Powderface Trail access-road opens. It's also a viable autumn destination through late October.

Ideally, at least two couples in two vehicles should arrange a shuttle, allowing both to complete the entire ridgewalk. Lacking a second vehicle, hitchhike between the trailheads; it's easy on weekends.

Given only half a day, Jumpingpound is still worth hiking because you can bail off the ridge early, to the Lusk Pass trailhead, where your total distance will be just 9.4 km (5.8 mi). This abbreviated trip still grants you, and your partner of course, 2.5 km (1.6 mi) of scenic ridgewalking. It also requires a shorter shuttle or hitch between trailheads.

Fact

Before your trip

Be aware that the Powderface Trail is closed near its north end, at Dawson trailhead, December 1 through May 15.

By Vehicle

From **Calgary**, drive the Trans-Canada (Hwy 1) west 32 km (19 mi) to the signed turnoff for Sibbald Creek Trail (Hwy 68). Follow this alternating paved and gravel road south then west. Reach a junction with the Powderface Trail in 23 km (14.3 mi).

From **Canmore**, drive the Trans-Canada (Hwy 1) east. Turn south onto Hwy 40 and reset your trip odometer to 0. In 7.7 km (4.8 mi) turn left onto

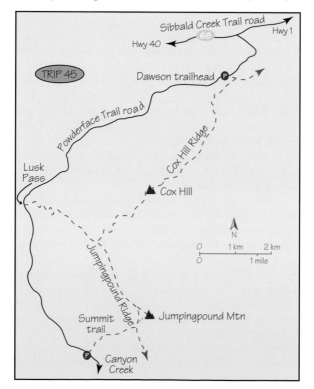

Jumpingpound Ridge trail

unpaved Sibbald Creek Trail (Hwy 68 East). At 21.7 km (13.5 mi) reach a junction with the Powderface Trail.

From **either approach**, reset your trip odometer to 0 and drive south on the Powderface Trail. In 3 km (1.9 mi) turn left into **Dawson trailhead**, at 1500 m (4920 ft). Park here, whether arranging a shuttle or hitchhiking, then continue southwest to **Jumpingpound trailhead** at 16.7 km (10.4 mi), 1835 m (6020 ft). Park in the small pullout on the right (southwest) side of the road.

On Foot

The Jumpingpound Summit trail starts on the northeast side of the road. Predominantly used by hikers, it's the most direct access to the ridgecrest. Equestrians favour the slightly longer access via Lusk Pass. Most mountain-bikers begin at the south trailhead, just north of Canyon Creek.

Enter spruce forest and begin ascending northeast—your general direction of travel until cresting the ridge. The well-engineered, moderately graded, switchbacking trail crosses several footbridges. At 1982 m (6500 ft) the ascent eases. Six minutes farther, a short spur leads southeast to a **bench** overlooking Elbow River Valley (southwest). The main trail steepens.

At 2.5 km (1.6 mi), 2135 m (7003 ft), top out on the **ridgecrest** and intersect Jumpingpound Ridge trail at a **signed junction**. Right descends the forested crest south toward Canyon Creek. Turn left and curve north through open forest. In a few minutes, bear right at a signed fork. Keep ascending the grassy slope northeast toward Jumpingpound Mtn.

Summit 2225-m (7300-ft) **Jumpingpound Mtn** at 3.3 km (2 mi). Fast hikers will arrive here one hour after leaving the trailhead. The panorama includes Cox Hill to the north, Moose Mtn east-southeast, and the Fisher Range southwest.

From Jumpingpound Mtn, bear right (northwest) and descend briefly. This shortcut is on a different trail than the one you ascended. Gradually curve north-northwest across the broad, nearly level, grassy ridgecrest. About half an hour beyond Jumpingpound Mtn, re-enter forest at 2160 m (7085 ft). The trail then contours just below the crest, on the right (east) side. A moderate descent ensues. You're still heading north-northeast.

At 5.9 km (3.7 mi), 2060 m (6757 ft), within one hour of leaving Jumpingpound Mtn, arrive at a **signed junction**. Go right (northeast) to continue the ridgewalk. Left (northwest) descends 3.5 km (2.2 mi) to the Powderface Trail at Lusk Pass. If you exit that way, your total hiking distance will be 9.4 km (5.8 mi) when you reach the road. On weekends, it should be easy to hitchhike south, back to the Jumpingpound trailhead.

Continuing the ridgewalk, the trail heads northeast and briefly ascends. It then drops through open, rocky terrain and plunges into forest. At 1945 m (6380 ft), the **lowpoint** of the trip, the trail begins climbing again. The ascent is initially steep but soon eases. Burst out of the trees onto grass at 2110 m (6921 ft).

The trail ascends northeast then north, rolling onto the broad, flat, 2195-m (7200-ft) summit of **Cox Hill** at 9 km (5.6 mi). Looking south, you can survey much of the ridgewalk you've completed thus far. Numerous peaks are visible in the distance. Northwest are Mounts Kidd, Bogart and Sparrowhawk.

North is Mt. Yamnuska, whose sheer cliffs attract rockclimbers. The prairie is northeast.

Depart Cox Hill northeast. The trail enters krummholz (stunted trees) then drops steeply into open, lodgepole-pine forest. A few short ascents remain, but you're generally descending now. Near the valley bottom, the trail passes a viewpoint where you can cool your brakes while gazing at the forested foothills.

After rounding the base of a clearcut, reach level ground and proceed east. Turn left at a signed junction, cross a footbridge over a creeklet, and arrive at **Dawson trailhead**. Elevation: 1500 m (4920 ft). You've hiked 17 km (10.5 mi) from Jumpingpound trailhead.

Shooting stars abound on Jumpingpound Ridge in early summer.

TRIP 46
Upper Kananaskis Lake

LOCATION	Peter Lougheed Provincial Park
LOOP	14.9 km (9.2 mi)
ELEVATION GAIN	negligible
KEY ELEVATIONS	trailhead and lakeshore 1725 m (5658 ft)
HIKING TIME	4½ to 6 hours
DIFFICULTY	easy
MAP	Gem Trek Kananaskis Lakes

Opinion

Sure, mountains are beautiful and noble and all that. But they can also be incontrovertible ogres. When have they ever stepped aside and made way for *you*? Probably never. Unless you've hiked around Upper Kananaskis Lake, where the mountains have magnanimously lumbered backward, allowing you unhindered passage. Though the trail ruffles their chest hairs, it gains little elevation. So it's not only easy, it's hikeable in shoulder-season. And the trail clings tenaciously to the shore of this ample body of water, so the hike is surprisingly long, frequently scenic, and best of all, a loop.

Because Trips 20 through 25 also begin at Upper Kananaskis Lake, and all grant alpine-zone access, the lakeshore trail is often ignored, as it should be in summer. But when the high country is snowbound, striding here feels like a gift. It's worth a try in early May, though you might encounter icy patches. And it usually remains a viable option through mid-November. Even when snow-covered, the trail is distinct, easy to follow. And as long as the snow is only inches deep, strong hikers can maintain a 4-kph (2.5-mph) pace without snowshoes.

Hiking the loop clockwise, as described below, has two important advantages: (1) It allows you to assess the snow-depth sooner, before you're committed to completing the entire trip. (2) If it gets dark before you finish, or someone in your party tires, you can eliminate the final 5.6 km (3.5 mi) by hitchhiking from the North Interlakes day use area, to your vehicle at the Upper Lake day use area. Bear in mind, however, this east-shore leg is mostly *on* the water, passes several beaches, and affords the best views. Try not to miss it.

As for snow, the initial south-shore leg will likely have less than the west shore. So if the snow seems too deep during the first 45 minutes, don't expect conditions to improve until you reach the north shore. The sunnier north and east shores should have the least snow.

Fact

By Vehicle

Follow the directions for Rawson Lake (Trip 25) to the Upper Lake day use area, on the southeast shore of Upper Kananaskis Lake. Park at the far south end of the unpaved lot, at 13.4 km (8.3 mi), near the trailhead sign for Kananaskis and Rawson lakes. Elevation: 1725 m (5658 ft).

On Foot

The wide trail leads southwest around the shore of Kananaskis Lake. Breaks in the forest grant views. Curve west within 15 minutes. Mt. Indefatigable (Trip 20) is visible north-northwest, across the lake.

At 1.2 km (0.75 mi), just past the bridge over **Sarrail Creek falls**, the signed Rawson Lake trail forks left (southwest). Bear right (west) and continue following the upper Kananaskis Lake shoreline.

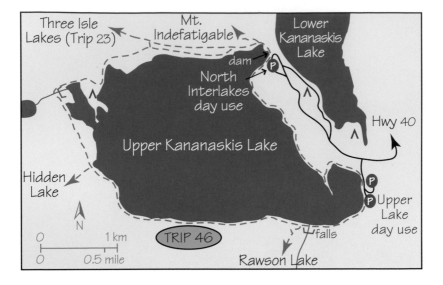

After curving northwest, pass a faint left fork at 5.2 km (3.2 mi). It leads southwest to Hidden lake. Proceed straight on the main trail, which now climbs above Upper Kananaskis Lake's west shore. In May or November, the snowpack will likely be heavier here than elsewhere around the lake, because Mt. Lyautey (left / west) blocks the afternoon sun.

Cross a bridge over the **Upper Kananaskis River** at 6.8 km (4.2 mi). Immediately downstream, Lower Kananaskis Falls tumbles over tiered ledges into a large pool. On the river's north bank, the trail veers right (northeast). Soon enter a field of angular boulders. Mt. Indefatigable is ahead (northeast). Left (west) is Mt. Putnik. Behind you (southwest) is Mt. Lyautey.

At 7.6 km (4.7 mi), 1740 m (5707 ft), pass a right (south) spur to **Point campground**. It has 20 tentsites with tables, fire pits, and bear-proof food storage. Proceed north on the main trail among more boulders.

At 8.8 km (5.5 mi) bear right where left ascends 100 m (110 yd) north to intersect the Three Isle Lake trail (Trip 23), which is a broad, rocky, fire road at that point. The lower, lakeshore trail affords more pleasant hiking because it's dirt, often covered with pine needles. Through the trees, Mounts Sarrail and Foch are visible right (south).

Intersect the Three Isle Lake trail at 10.2 km (6.3 mi) and bear right (east). At 10.7 km (6.6 mi), the trail ascending Mt. Indefatigable forks left. Proceed straight (east). At 11 km (6.8 mi), curve right and cross the **spillway bridge**. Follow the trail southeast atop the dam.

Just before the paved **North Interlakes parking lot**, reach the trailhead **kiosk**. Turn right here and continue southwest on the lakeshore trail, which for a brief stretch is just 6 m (20 ft) above the water. It soon drops to lake level, curving south then southeast. Pass a couple pebble beaches where deadfall has collected.

Upper Kananaskis Lake, from ascent to Invincible Lake (Trip 21)

Chipmunk

Approaching a small peninsula, the trail curves left (northeast), rounds a cove, then turns southeast again and passes the **White Spruce parking area**. Continue on a wide, gravel-topped dam. Beyond, cross the pavement and proceed over a small footbridge.

Arrive at the north, paved end of the **Upper Lake day use area**. Instead of walking through the long parking lot, go right. Resume on the lakeshore trail. Follow it south, past the picnic area. Reach the trailhead where your vehicle is parked—at the far, unpaved end of the lot—at 14.9 km (9.2 mi).

Forgetmenot Ridge

LOCATION	Don Getty Wildland Provincial Park, Hwy 66
ROUND TRIP	14 km (8.7 mi)
ELEVATION GAIN	715 m (2345 ft)
KEY ELEVATIONS	trailhead 1610 m (5280 ft)
	Forgetmenot Mtn 2330 m (7642 ft)
HIKING TIME	5 to 7 hours
DIFFICULTY	easy
MAPS	Gem Trek Bragg Creek and Elbow Falls
	Bragg Creek 82 J/15

Opinion

Legend holds that a courting couple admired a cluster of tiny, light-blue flowers beside a raging river. While picking them for his love, the man tumbled into the whitewater and was swept away. He tossed the flowers to her, calling his last words: "Forget me not!" This dainty flower, known as alpine forget-me-not, is a delight to behold. Its striking beauty is unforgettable. Many hikers consider it symbolic of their most memorable mountain experiences.

The rounded crest of Forgetmenot Ridge offers fulfilling yet relatively easy hiking. And, true to its name, the dryas-covered ridge burgeons with wildflowers June through early August. Look for cobalt gentian; pink-purple sweet vetch; purplish-blue harebells; purple dwarf larkspur; fuzzy, pale-yellow sulphur plant; succulent, deep-red stonecrop; white mountain-avens; purple-tipped, grey-fluffed sawwort; red-pink pods of inflated oxytropis; yellow cinquefoil; purple scorpionweed; and bluish-purple aster.

Views rapidly expand on the steep initial ascent. Then you'll enjoy a scenic, 3-km (1.9-mi), alpine cruise. High above Elbow River Valley, you'll parallel the Front Range—impressive opening act for the headlining main range farther west. You'll also overlook the foothills swelling from the east.

Forgetmenot Ridge, mid-June

Fording the Elbow River, to begin ascending Forgetmenot Ridge

Fact

Eager hikers training for an adventurous summer should besiege Forgetmenot Ridge in June. It will likely be snow-free then, while nearby peaks are still dramatically snow-laden. You can also hike here in October. The season is rapidly closing then, so venturing above treeline feels like sneaking in after hours.

Before your trip

Be aware that Hwy 66, from Elbow Falls to the trailhead, is closed December 1 through May 15.

By Vehicle

From Calgary, drive west on Trans-Canada Hwy 1. About 15 minutes beyond the city outskirts, exit right, following signs for Bragg Creek. Proceed on Hwy 22, south then southwest. Upon reaching the 3-way junction at the hamlet of Bragg Creek, reset your trip odometer to 0.

0 km (0 mi)

Bear left (south), following signs for Turner Valley and Elbow Falls.

3.3 km (2 mi)

Reach the junction of Hwy 22 and Hwy 66. Turn right (west) onto Hwy 66 (Elbow Falls Trail) and proceed generally southwest into K-Country.

22 km (13.6 mi)

Pass a left fork that quickly leads to Elbow Falls. The view is worth a brief detour.

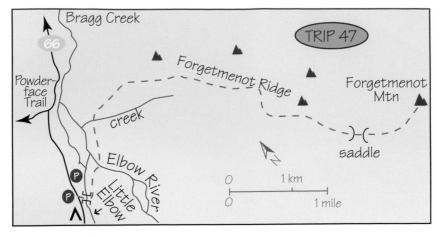

31 km (19.2 mi)
Go left. The unpaved road straight ahead is the Powderface Trail.

32 km (19.8 mi)
Pass Forgetmenot Pond day use area on the left. The north end of Forget-menot Ridge rises behind it (southeast).

32.3 km (20 mi)
Pass a spacious parking lot on the left. Proceed straight, through the Little Elbow River campground entrance.

33 km (20.5 mi)
Reach a small pullout on the right, at 1610 m (5280 ft). Park here for Forget-menot Ridge, Nihahi Ridge (Trip 48), Talus Lake (Trip 37), West Fork Little Elbow River (Trip 39), or Paradise Pass (Trip 38). If the pullout is full, return to the spacious lot just outside the campground entrance.

Alpine forget-me-not

On Foot
     From the small pullout, cross the road, head generally east-southeast, then cross the pink **suspension bridge** over Little Elbow River. From the spacious parking lot, follow the wide gravel path southwest 0.6 km (0.4 mi) along the river, then turn left and cross the suspension bridge. The bridge is the zero-point for distances.
     Having crossed the bridge to the south-east bank, drop back to the river. Pass a road forking right. Stay on the trail near the river. Five minutes beyond the bridge, follow the trail right, into forest. Soon reach a four-way, map-signed junction. Go left (east) on the

Forgetmenot Ridge from near its south end

Wildhorse Trail. Straight (south) is signed for Big Elbow, Threepoint, and Tombstone. Shrubby cinquefoil with yellow flowers brightens the ground cover. In a few minutes, cross a horse trail.

At 1 km (0.6 mi), cross the broad, stony channels of the **Elbow River**. In May, you might encounter only a trickle here. During summer, the water can be so high that crossing is dangerous. By fall, the river subsides underground, perhaps leaving the channels dry. On the east bank, continue northeast on the wide dirt trail.

At 1.8 km (1.1 mi), just past a tiny, **unnamed creek** (probably dry), turn right at a cairn onto a narrow, rough trail ascending east-northeast through forest above the creek drainage. At 3 km (1.9 mi) the trail heads northeast and continues ascending, though less steeply, near the left (west) edge of a northwest-jutting spur of Forgetmenot Ridge. After a brief level reprieve on the spur, go right (south-southeast) at a flagged fork. Visible north-northwest, across the Elbow River Valley, is Powderface Ridge rising above the Powderface Trail. Nihahi Ridge (Trip 48) is northwest. Mt. Remus is west.

The steep ascent continues on scree among scattered trees. Choose any of the bootbeaten paths. They stay close to together, heading generally southeast. All fade before reaching a saddle. Cairns indicate the route heading southeast through open forest. At 2128 m (6980 ft), about two hours from the trailhead, reach **grassy slopes** just beneath the ridge.

Continuing the now gentle ascent, pass a chaotic display of limestone karst. A bootbeaten path pierces a stand of trees before surmounting the **crest of Forgetmenot Ridge** at 4 km (2.5 mi). Fix this point in mind for your descent. A clump of rocks serves as a landmark.

Forgetmenot's north end is left, rising to 2240 m (7347 ft). Go right and follow the trail-less ridge south, contouring near 2204 m (7230 ft). The Front Range is visible west, across Big Elbow River valley. Starting at the north end of the range you can identify a lower, unnamed peak, then 2935-m (9629-ft) Mt. Glasgow. Just south of that, and slightly higher, is Mt. Cornwall.

Gentian

Next is Outlaw Peak. Just east of that is Banded Peak. On the northwest horizon are mountains beyond Hwy 1.

At 5 km (3 mi) a northeast-jutting arm of Forgetmenot Ridge invites exploration. It rises to 2256 m (7400 ft). But first continue south-southeast along the main ridge. While returning, you can decide if you have time and energy for the detour. On the main ridge you'll be closer to the bigger Front Range peaks rather than the foothills.

The ridge gently descends south-southwest. Drop to 2186 m (7170 ft) in a grassy, willowy saddle between shoulders. At 5.6 km (3.5 mi) the ridge veers west, rising 55 m (180 ft) to a **rocky knoll**. From the knoll's west edge, the ridge heads south. Choose the smoothest route through shattered rocks near the west side of the ridge. Abundant clearcuts fragment the forest below: southeast, east, and northeast. Desolate Moose Mtn is visible way north.

Proceed south-southeast, over dryas and rock slabs, past scattered trees. Reach the 2330-m (7642-ft) **summit of Forgetmenot Ridge** at 7 km (4.3 mi). Three Point Mtn is visible south-southwest. Beyond it, southwest, is 2863-m (9393-ft) Cougar Mtn. This section of the ridge is covered with black-lichen-splotched rock. Most dayhikers will want to turn around here.

Beyond the summit, the ridge dives 148 m (485 ft) to a saddle above the headwaters of Howard Creek and linked to Forgetmenot Mtn. It's an easy, grassy descent to the 2172-m (7125-ft) **saddle**, but there the hiking is tedious, over rough rock. The ascent resumes southeast, again mostly on grass. Top out on 2330-m (7642-ft) **Forgetmenot Mtn** at 9.6 km (6 mi). The view extends south of Threepoint Mtn and Mt. Rose to larger Bluerock Mtn. East of that is small Mt. Ware (Trip 49), a shoulder-season destination in the Sheep River Wildlife Sanctuary.

Return to where you first crested Forgetmenot Ridge. Descend from the landmark clump of rocks. Aiming for Forgetmenot Pond, go west toward trees. Flagging indicates where to enter the trees. The path then leads northwest along the spur jutting toward Powderface Trail. Continuing the descent, stay right of most trees. Maintain a course that would split Powderface Ridge and Forgetmenot Pond. But don't feel compelled to follow these directions precisely. Your goal is simply to get down the way you came up. Upon intersecting the Wildhorse Trail, turn left (southwest) and parallel the Elbow River. You're now on familiar ground.

If your vehicle is in the spacious parking lot just outside the campground entrance, consider a shortcut. Instead of hiking all the way back to the suspension bridge, leave the trail shortly after crossing the Elbow River's broad, stony channels. Angle right (northwest). Hike cross-country, ford the Little Elbow River, and shortly beyond you'll hit the parking lot—about half an hour sooner than via the trail.

TRIP 48
Nihahi Ridge

LOCATION	Hwy 66, southwest of Bragg Creek
ROUND TRIP	10 km (6.2 mi)
ELEVATION GAIN	735 m (2410 ft)
KEY ELEVATIONS	trailhead 1610 m (5280 ft)
	south summit 2345 m (7690 ft)
HIKING TIME	3 to 4 hours
DIFFICULTY	challenging
MAPS	page 198; Gem Trek Bragg Creek and Elbow Falls
	Bragg Creek 82 J/15

Opinion

"I love the Rockies," wrote Allan Fotheringham in *Maclean's* magazine. "Which, if you've ever seen the Alps, makes the Alps—you can drive through them in 30 minutes—look like a Hollywood backdrop from MGM." If you, too, love this great Canadian range, you'll want to get it under your boots as early as possible in the hiking season. An exciting place to do that is Nihahi Ridge.

Southwest of Calgary, Nihahi is precisely where the Rockies begin. To the east are foothills and prairie. To the west is "A world to be born under your footsteps." St. John Perse, 1960 Nobel Laureate in Literature, penned that phrase. It evokes the thrilling anticipation you might feel while straddling the crest of Nihahi Ridge in early June, gazing at snow-mantled peaks. Or come in October, when icy flourishes again accentuate the mountains' stature, yet the ridge itself is not yet white.

The first hour of this short trip is a cheery hike on an adequate but increasingly steep trail. During the final half hour to the ridge's south summit, however, you'll tussle with the rocky, airy cliffs that the Stoney Indian word *Nihahi* describes. Light scrambling is necessary. Mild exposure is unavoidable. At least one member of your party should be a strong, patient mountain goat who can assist and reassure the inexperienced.

Many hikers surmount Nihahi without previously scrambling anything but eggs. If you're wary but willing, give it a go. You can attain inspiring views without endangering yourself. Just turn around before the ridge outstrips your desire and ability. Beyond the south summit, the ridge is a tightrope walk that only skilled scramblers should attempt.

Little Elbow River valley, from Nihahi Ridge

Fact

Before your trip

Be aware that Hwy 66, from Elbow Falls to the trailhead, is closed December 1 through May 15.

By Vehicle

Follow the directions for Forgetmenot Ridge (Trip 47) to the end of Hwy 66, about an hour southwest of Calgary. Park just beyond the Elbow River campground entrance, in the small pullout on the right, at 33 km (20.5 mi), 1610 m (5280 ft). If the pullout is full, return to the spacious lot just outside the campground entrance.

On Foot

From either the pullout or the parking lot, ascend the campground entrance road southwest. As it curves west, stay on the main road, continually bearing left where right spurs access campsites. Go around a couple metal **gates**, or through them if open. Vehicles are prohibited beyond a final trailhead parking lot that might also be gated.

This road is the approach to Talus Lake (Trip 37), Paradise Pass (Trip 38), and West Fork Little Elbow River (Trip 39), but you'll be departing it soon. Pass a sign for Nihahi Ridge and Little Elbow trail. Cross a cattle-guard. About five minutes beyond the final gate, follow a **signed trail** forking right (northwest) to Nihahi Ridge. Enter forest and begin a gentle ascent. A couple minutes in, go left. About five minutes farther, reach a **fork**. Go right and ascend north, again following a sign for Nihahi Ridge.

At 1720 m (5642 ft), Nihahi Ridge is visible northwest. Also attain views southwest to Mounts Glasgow and Cornwall. About half an hour from the trailhead pullout, enter stunted, **open forest** and grassy **meadows**. After a brief, shallow descent, the stiff climb resumes northwest. The trail curves

Scrambling to Nihahi Ridge

left (west, then southwest) beneath rock bands, before veering right (north) to ascend the ridgecrest.

Reach a **fork** at 1845 m (6050 ft). Go right, ascending north. Mounts Romulus and Remus are visible west, above the Little Elbow River valley (Trips 37, 38, and 39). About 15 minutes farther, proceed up the open, rocky slope. At 2090 m (6855 ft), about an hour from the trailhead, the dirt trail is severely steep and scoured. It affords minimal traction. At least you're now on the east side of the crest, sheltered from the often fierce west wind.

At 2170 m (7118 ft) several routes lead upward. Left is the quickest ascent to the trail just right of the crest. Then go right one minute farther to the more gradual ascent along the escarpment beneath the crest. Choose either of two sections of trail that soon rejoin before ending beneath a short **scree gully** on the left. You've hiked 1⅓ hours from the trailhead pullout. You must now grapple with challenging terrain to reach the trip's climax.

Scramble 5 m (16 ft) up the vertical gully, then go left (northwest) to regain the **ridgecrest**. Continue on scree at a gentle grade for about ten minutes. Reach vertical rock slabs at 2293 m (7520 ft). What might appear to be a difficult scramble actually isn't—if you go left, around the chunky rocks.

Like steps, stone blocks allow you to work though a break in the craggy escarpment to 2310 m (7577 ft). Proceed northwest along the crest another five minutes to reach the **south summit of Nihahi Ridge** at 4 km (2.5 mi), 2345 m (7690 ft). Total hiking time: about 1½ hours.

Powderface Ridge is visible northeast, across Ford Creek valley. Forget-menot Ridge is southeast. Mt. Remus is west-southwest, and Mt. Fullerton is north of it. The massif comprising Mounts Glasgow and Cornwall, as well as Outlaw and Banded peaks, is south-southwest.

The crest of Nihahi Ridge, composed of angular rock slabs, is precipitously narrow. The right (east) side is vertical. The left (west) side is only slightly less sheer. All but advanced scramblers should turn around at the south summit. The north summit of Nihahi Ridge is 7 km (4.3 mi) northwest.

TRIP 49
Mt. Ware

LOCATION	Sheep River area, west of Turner Valley
ROUND TRIP	17.4 km (10.8 mi)
ELEVATION GAIN	533 m (1750 ft)
KEY ELEVATIONS	trailhead 1591 m (5220 ft), summit 2150 m (7052 ft)
HIKING TIME	5½ to 7 hours
DIFFICULTY	easy
MAPS	Gem Trek Bragg Creek and Elbow Falls Mount Rae 82 J/10

Opinion

An initiation into hardihood this isn't. The Sheep River country is equestrian heaven: rolling, forested foothills that tax hikers' patience more than their strength. But that's precisely what you need in shoulder season, so you can get out and stride instead of wading through snow. And this trip leads you above the equine zone, onto the trail-free slopes of Mt. Ware, for vast vistas unhindered by trees, and boundless tranquility seldom interrupted.

Numerous trails wiggle through the Sheep River country. This is the most rewarding because it accesses one of the area's few true mountains. With nothing nearby to overshadow Mt. Ware, the sun beats on it ceaselessly, promising you a snow-free ascent perhaps by late May. Though the climb is cross-country, the terrain and vegetation are amicable, the routefinding straightforward. From the summit, you'll admire the Front Range—a stirring sight, especially in May, June, or October, when snow highlights the peaks.

Certainly Mt. Ware is the trip's climax, but the approach is enjoyable too, or it wouldn't be in this book of premier trails. You'll hike through a coniferous forest frequently broken by meadows and stands of aspen. The spring limes and fall golds of the aspen contrast vibrantly with the dominant evergreens. Within an hour of the trailhead, you'll pass a delightful cascade where Gorge Creek glides over smooth bedrock. Because this is a low-elevation trail, it's hikeable as early as May, as late as November. Avoid it late June through August, or risk baking your brains to liquid. Besides, summer is precious, prime time for exploring higher and deeper in the main range.

Yet another reason to hike Mt. Ware is the drive from Turner Valley. The quiet highway swoops out of the prairie, toward the Rockies, granting constant views of the aspen-cloaked foothills. The beauty spikes in late September, when the aspen leaves are so brilliant yellow they appear to have absorbed every ray of summer sunshine. Either before or after the hike, you can also visit nearby Sheep River Falls—an unheralded K-Country marvel.

Between the trailhead and the base of Mt. Ware, expect to encounter mountainbikers, horseback riders, and cattle. Yes, road apples and cowpies

On Mt. Ware's north slope

are part of the scenery. And, true to its name, the Sheep River country is home to flocks of bighorn sheep, which contribute to the annual, spring outbreak of ticks. Be wary whenever you sit, and check your dark, secret recesses after the hike.

Fact

Before your trip
Be aware that Hwy 546, from just west of the Sheep River ranger station to the Gorge Creek trailhead, is closed December 1 through May 15.

By Vehicle
From Calgary, drive south on Hwy 2, then west on Hwy 7, to the town of Black Diamond. Reset your trip odometer to 0 at the junction of Hwys 22 and 546. Continue west on Hwy 546 toward Turner Valley.

0 km (0 mi)
Starting west on Hwy 546 from Black Diamond.

4 km (2.5 mi)
In Turner Valley, proceed straight on Hwy 546 where Hwy 22 goes right (north) to Millarville.

4.9 km (3 mi)
Bear right to continue following Hwy 546 west. Soon pass a sign stating that Blue Rock Recreation Area is 35 km (21.7 mi) ahead.

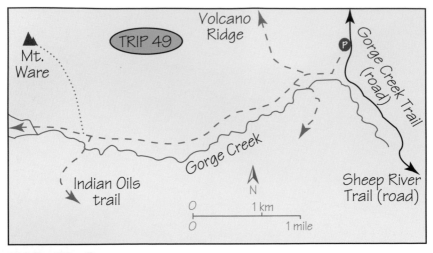

Volcano Ridge
TRIP 49
Mt. Ware
Gorge Creek Trail (road)
Gorge Creek
Indian Oils trail
Sheep River Trail (road)
N
0   1 km
0   1 mile

19.3 km (12 mi)
Enter Kananaskis Country.

22.4 km (13.9 mi)
Pass the Sheep River ranger station (public telephone) on the right.

25.8 km (16 mi)
Enter the Sheep River Wildlife Sanctuary.

33.5 km (20.8 mi)
Turn right and ascend on unpaved Gorge Creek Trail. Left descends, passes Sheep River Falls (worth a look) in 6 km (3.7 mi), soon reaches Bluerock campground and ends shortly beyond.

37.7 km (23.4 mi)
Turn left into the Gorge Creek trailhead parking lot, at 1591 m (5220 ft).

On Foot
Starting near the sign at the southwest corner of the parking lot, follow the Gorge Creek trail south-southwest through forest. It's a former road, broad and smooth. Within five minutes, enter a meadow among aspen. Descend into the creek drainage. Bear right on the trail.

Within 15 minutes, rockhop across shallow **Gorge Creek**. Just beyond is a **map-sign**. The Link Creek / Volcano Ridge trail proceeds straight (west-northwest). Turn left (south) for Gorge and South Gorge creeks. A minute farther, bear right (southwest) at the **fork**. Soon emerge from trees. Bluerock Mtn is visible west.

The Gorge Creek trail, still a former road, continues along the north edge of the gorge, occasionally overlooking the creek. About an hour from the trailhead, enter meadows and a grove of aspen. The road narrows to actual trail here. Watch for a **cascade** flowing through a smooth, rock trough, into deep pools. There's a small, sandy beach here.

Gorge Creek trail

About ten minutes farther, reach a **fork**. Left descends to a meadow. Bear right, ascending the main Gorge Creek trail toward an orange blaze. Soon pass through a **gate**, then descend to follow the creek.

At 6.2 km (3.8 mi), 1686 m (5530 ft), about 1½ hours from the trailhead, reach a **signed junction** in a clearing. The Indian Oils trail goes left (southwest) through the meadow and crosses Gorge Creek. Bear right (northwest) on the Gorge Creek trail. A minute past the junction, immediately before the trail grazes the creek, turn right onto a **game path** and ascend north through forest.

The game path leads between two pines. In 40 m/yd where the path splits, bear right and ascend steeply. About ten minutes above the Gorge Creek trail, reach a small, north-south **gully**. A narrow track parallels the right (east) bank. Pass old flagging as you contour north through scruffy lodgepole pine.

This description is detailed, because landmarks are few and discreet. But it's not necessary to follow our route precisely. If you have difficulty doing so, don't worry. You're travelling cross-country now. Just keep ascending generally north-northwest to the open slopes of Mt. Ware. The grade is only moderately steep. The terrain and vegetation pose little resistance. On the return, don't drop straight south off the mountain. An angling descent (left / southeast) will ensure that you intersect the Gorge Creek trail near where you first departed it.

Contouring north through scruffy lodgepole pine, the narrow track soon vanishes. At flagging, turn right and ascend through open forest. Angle slightly left. About four minutes farther, reach the base of a draw (shallower than the gully). Proceed along its left side to regain a path about 10 m/yd left (west) of the gully.

Aspen in Sheep River country

About half an hour above the Gorge Creek trail, the path curves left and climbs northwest. It soon disappears in the tall grass of an open forest. Keep ascending northwest, perhaps following traces of path, until you crest the broad, open, **southeast ridge** of Mt. Ware, at 1884 m (6180 ft). Visible west, across Gorge Creek valley, is 2790-m (9150-ft) Bluerock Mtn. Right (north-northwest) above you is Mt. Ware. Turn right and follow the ridgecrest toward your goal. Work your way over scree, across rock slabs, through grass and krummholz (stunted trees).

To begin circumambulating the mountain below its summit, gradually curve left (northwest). Pick up a game path traversing the southwest slope. After cresting the west ridge, contour right (east) across the north slope. The terrain gets rougher and steeper until after you round the mountain's east side. It takes about an hour to return to where you first arrived on the southeast ridge.

To summit the mountain, bear right (north-northeast) above the krummholz. The chunky rocks on the moderate east-southeast slope afford the easiest ascent route. Clamber upward wherever you're most comfortable. Top out on 2125-m (6970-ft) **Mt. Ware** about 2.5 km (1.6 mi), or 1¼ hours, from the Gorge Creek trail. You've hiked 8.7 km (5.4 mi) from the trailhead.

Calgary is visible northeast. Surveyor's Ridge is nearby north, below you. Mt. Rose is northwest. 2937-m (9633-ft) Mt. Burns is southwest. Gibraltar Mtn is distant southwest. The Sheep River Valley is southwest and south. Farther south is Junction Creek valley.

TRIP 50
Grass Pass / Bull Creek Hills

LOCATION	Highwood Junction
ROUND TRIP	15 km (9.3 mi) including Boundary Pine peninsula detour
ELEVATION GAIN	719 m (2358 ft)
KEY ELEVATIONS	trailhead 1460 m (4789 ft)
	highest hill 2179 m (7149 ft)
HIKING TIME	5 to 6 hours
DIFFICULTY	easy round trip, moderate loop
MAP	Gem Trek Highwood & Cataract Creek

Opinion

In the Canadian Rockies, fanatic local hikers ache most of the year. Not from hiking, but from the unfulfilled *desire* to hike. Winter lows plunge to -30° C (-22°F), even in the milder valley bottoms. The snowpack accumulates to 300 cm (118 in) among the peaks. That means hiking season—when it's rock, not ice, crunching beneath your boots on the high passes—is cruelly short. But there are a few special places in the easternmost foothills where snow-free hiking is possible nearly seven months a year. One of them is Grass Pass and the Bull Creek Hills.

This is the edge of the prairie, far from the stirring main range, but you'll see a couple junior peaks nearby and glimpse a more adventurous shoulder-season goal farther south: Mt. Burke (Trip 53). In spring, enough wildflowers flourish on these sun-baked hills to warrant bringing your identification book. Look for red stonecrop, and tiny, mauve cactus. In fall, you might still see lupine and purple harebells before the aspen trees turn brilliant yellow. Either time of year, Grass Pass and the Bull Creek Hills offer you the satisfaction of pounding your energy into the land for a full four to six hours—a veritable marathon for shoulder season. In summer, should a storm dash your alpine plans, retreat to these foothills where the weather is always more genial.

At Grass Pass, before ascending the Bull Creek Hills, take two scenic detours. First, spend a couple minutes proceeding through the pass for a view of Holy Cross Mtn and Mount Head. Then spend 30 minutes on a sidetrip to Boundary Pine peninsula, to overlook the Highwood River Valley and reconnoiter the Bull Creek Hills. Later, atop the hills, you'll have to choose: round trip, or loop? Your surveillance from the peninsula will help you decide. The round trip simply entails turning back at the third and highest hill. The loop, though only a skosh farther than the round trip, adds both challenge and tedium. Loopsters will continue on a rough route over

Bull Creek Hills

the fourth hill, descend cross-country, pick up a final spurt of trail to the highway, then endure a 40-minute road-walk to the trailhead unless they hitchhike or pre-arranged a shuttle.

Grass Pass / Bull Creek Hills is just one of several shoulder-season trips near Highwood Junction. The others are Junction Hill (Trip 51) and Mt. Burke (Trip 53). So if you car-camp at nearby Etherington Creek, you can enjoy two hikes on a weekend. Make it your pre-season training-camp jamboree.

Tick attack! All these trails are in sunny, grassy foothills: prime tick habitat. The nasty parasites are active early April to mid-June. Check yourself at lunch and again more thoroughly at day's end. Also bear in mind this isn't pristine wilderness. It's ranch country. Expect to see, and occasionally plod through, muddy, hoof-churned, manure-splotched terrain.

Fact

Before your trip

Be aware that Hwy 40, from Kananaskis Lakes Trail to Highwood Junction, is closed December 1 through June 14, preventing spring access to this trailhead from the north. During that time, drive here only from the east, via 541 out of Longview. Etherington Creek campground (on Hwy 940, just 6 km / 3.7 mi south of Highwood Junction) is open the first weekend of May through mid-October. Call (403) 558-2373 to confirm dates.

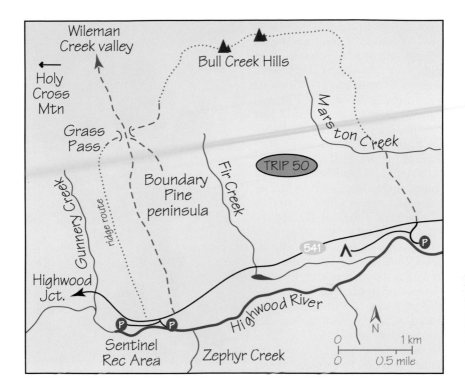

Wileman
Creek valley

←

Holy
Cross
Mtn

Bull Creek Hills

Grass
Pass.

Marston Creek

TRIP 50

Gunnery Creek

ridge route

Boundary
Pine
peninsula

Fir Creek

541

P

Highwood
Jct.

Highwood River

P   P

N

0   1 km

Sentinel
Rec Area

Zephyr Creek

0   0.5 mile

By Vehicle

From **Calgary**, drive Highway 22 south to Longview. Turn west onto Hwy 541 and continue 37.6 km (23.3 mi).

From **Trans-Canada Hwy 1**, east of Canmore, drive Hwy 40 south 105 km (65.2 mi) to Highwood Junction, where Hwys 40, 940 and 541 intersect. Continue east 5.4 km (3.3 mi) on Hwy 541.

From **either approach**, turn south into Sentinel Recreation Area. Park in the first parking lot, at 1460 m (4789 ft).

On Foot

From the trailhead parking lot, return to the highway. Cross to the far (north) side of the pavement. Turn right (east-northeast). Walk parallel to the highway on a path bootbeaten through the grass. Continue 250 m (250 yd). Pass the culvert and the sign SENTINEL PEAK facing westbound traffic. Turn left (north-northwest), away from the highway, onto the trail between big boulders. Begin a moderate ascent through mixed forest, on a wide, rocky track that used to be a road. A few big Douglas firs enhance the scenery.

Your general direction of travel will remain north-northwest all the way to **Grass Pass**, at 3.2 km (2 mi), 1880 m (6166 ft), about 50 minutes from the highway. Here you have four options. (1) A three-track trail ascends left (west), then southwest, to a rough-but-hikeable ridge that descends left (south-southeast) back to the trailhead. (2) Straight through the pass is a track descending north-northwest into Wileman Creek valley. A couple-minute detour in that direction reveals an impressive sight left (northwest). Contour above the trail for the optimal view of Holy Cross Mtn and, just past it, 2782-m (9126-ft) Mt. Head. (3) Right (northeast) is the trail ascending the Bull Creek Hills. (4) Sharp right (southeast) is a trail contouring to, and soon ending at, a superb vantage point.

Limber pine, Boundary Pine peninsula

Option four, to **Boundary Pine peninsula**, is a 30-minute round-trip digression. Take it. Traverse grassy slopes, proceed among stout, hearty, Limber pines, and within 12 minutes— about 1 km (0.6 mi) from the pass—attain a vista across the Highwood River Valley. The Zephyr Creek drainage is directly south. Its right (west) wall is the long, north ridge of Mt. Burke (Trip 53). The peninsula also grants a fine view of the Bull Creek Hills (north to northeast). Take time to study the hills from here, so you'll be oriented when they're underfoot.

Leaving the peninsula, follow the trail only about halfway back to Grass Pass, then abandon it for the faint shortcut path ascending directly north. It soon intersects the Bull Creek Hills trail, atop the minor hill ahead. If you're uncertain about this, retrace your steps all the way to Grass Pass, where the Bull Creek Hills trail starts.

From Grass Pass, the Bull Creek Hills trail ascends the open, gentle slope northeast. Above, dip briefly before continuing over two small bumps atop the **first minor hill**. Then drop 40 m (131 ft) into forest. Stay on the cow-trodden trail until, about 30 minutes from the pass, a swath of **scrubby meadow** opens to the right. Look for a large, blue spruce on the meadow's left side, about 20 m/yd up from the trail. That prominent spruce is your assurance that, yes, you're in the right place. Abandon the trail here. Go right (northeast) and begin a short, cross-country ascent through the meadow, among scattered trees, gaining 245 m (800 ft) to the ridge visible ahead.

When you can look right (east) and see no trees, angle in that direction. Just below the outcrop near the ridgecrest, among rock and gravel, pick up a defined route ascending left. Follow it north-northeast then east to the 2150-m (7052-ft) summit of the **second hill**. The panorama extends to the Great Divide on the southwest horizon, and Calgary's office towers northeast.

The route continues east, then fades. But the way is obvious, the terrain open, the hiking easy. Descend 30 m (98 ft), then ascend 61 m (200 ft), surmounting the **third and highest hill** at 6.5 km (4 mi), 2179 m (7149 ft), a mere 15 minutes from the second hilltop.

Okay, decision time. From the third hill, you can, of course, turn around and retrace your steps to the trailhead, where your total round-trip distance (including the Boundary Pine peninsula detour) will be 15 km (9.3 mi). But if you're eager and energetic, you can complete a loop by proceeding east along the ridge, then working your way generally southeast down to the highway. In that direction, it takes about 2 hours to hike the remaining 3.7 km (2.3 mi) to pavement, where you'll have to walk the highway 3.5 km (2.2 mi) back to your vehicle. The loop entails a 160-m (525-ft) drop—rough, rocky, requiring dexterity and concentration—prior to ascending the **fourth hill**. From there, you'll begin descending. The route becomes a more defined trail just south of where you must rockhop Marston Creek. It intersects **Hwy 541** at **Highwood River Recreation Area**. From there, turn right and follow the highway west-southwest to the trailhead parking lot at Sentinel Recreation Area, where your total loop distance will be 15.7 km (9.8 mi).

Attracted by the challenge of the loop but turned off by its tedious finale? Capable scramblers who are comfortable routefinding can descend to the highway from atop the second hill, thus reducing the road-walk by half. Begin by working your way south along an escarpment. It gradually relaxes into a mellow ridge; follow it southeast. After a nearly level stretch, the descent steepens again. Bear right (south, curving southwest). Then scope out the easiest final descent (generally south) to the highway, where you should be within 2 km (1.2 mi) of the trailhead—about a 20-minute walk.

Cut-leaf daisies

TRIP 51
Junction Hill

LOCATION	Highwood Junction
LOOP	8.5 km (5.3 mi)
ELEVATION GAIN	762 m (2500 ft)
KEY ELEVATIONS	trailhead 1510 m (4953 ft), summit 2233 m (7326 ft)
HIKING TIME	4 to 5½ hours
DIFFICULTY	challenging
MAP	Gem Trek Highwood & Cataract Creek

Opinion

A "junction" is a crossroads. An intersection. An opportunity to turn in a new direction. Junction Hill is exactly that. As early as mid-April, you'll find Junction Hill a surprisingly adventurous, robust hike that will spin your attention from "when will winter end?" to "hiking season is here!" Or, if you're interested in but apprehensive about hiking off-trail, Junction Hill is an easy yet intriguing introduction to routefinding. It might widen your scope of what's possible and enjoyable in the mountains.

Junction Hill rises immediately north of Highwood Junction, in southern K-Country. Though visible from the pavement, the hill is unimposing, ignored by hikers, therefore trail-less. But its lacklustre appearance belies the excitement of climbing it, the frequent views it affords, and its commanding summit panorama.

You'll quickly burst through a fringe of trees and stride onto grassy slopes. A sharp ascent leads to a breach in the cliffy southeast ridge, through which you'll attain the crest. Simply follow the rough, treed ridgecrest to the rocky summit. Then drop your pack, break out your Havarti cheese and organic corn chips, and marvel at the Great Divide—a mountainous, peak-studded wall spanning the western horizon.

Descending the south ridge, you'll be in trees only occasionally and briefly. The final descent is wide open, but you'll have to stop to admire the scenery, because the grade is watch-your-step steep. You'll complete the loop by sauntering about 20 minutes along the highway back to your vehicle.

"Hill" doesn't do this little peak justice. Though comparatively small, it *is* a mountain. If the unrelenting ascent doesn't convince you of that, the severe, final descent will. Wear sturdy hiking boots. Bring trekking poles. Start hydrated. Pack a couple litres of water per person, because you'll find none along the way. And carry a compass. The route will be obvious to veteran ramblers, but the compass references in our route description will aid less experienced hikers through sections that, to them, might otherwise seem obscure.

The High Rock Range, from Junction Hill

Don't worry. You won't be orienteering. You'll simply use the compass to confirm which way is north, south, east or west. Besides, the nearby highways are rarely out of sight. And though we haven't seen cows on top of Junction Hill, there's evidence of bovine summit bids high on both ridgecrests. Surely you can outclimb a cow.

Fact

Before your trip

Be aware that Hwy 40, from Kananaskis Lakes Trail to Highwood Junction, is closed December 1 through June 14, preventing spring access to this trailhead from the north. During that time, drive here only from the east, via 541 out of Longview.

By Vehicle

From **Calgary**, drive Highway 22 south to Longview. Turn right (west) onto Hwy 541 and continue 43.2 km (26.8 mi) to Highwood Junction, where Hwys 40, 940 and 541 intersect. Turn left (south) onto unpaved Hwy 940, then immediately turn right (west) into the Highwood House parking lot, at 1475 m (4838 ft).

From **Trans-Canada Hwy 1**, east of Canmore, drive Hwy 40 south 105 km (65.2 mi) to Highwood Junction, where Hwys 40, 940 and 541 intersect. Turn

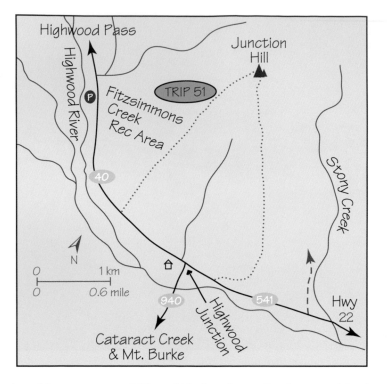

right (south) onto unpaved Hwy 940, then immediately turn right (west) into the Highwood House parking lot, at 1475 m (4838 ft).

On Foot

From the Highwood House parking lot, walk out to the intersection of Hwys 40, 940 and 541. Turn right (east) and walk uphill on Hwy 541. About 250 m (273 yd) from the intersection, pass a pullout on the right. Then be looking left for the trail departing the pavement. It's 15 m/yd before (west of) a white **road sign** warning west-bound motorists that Hwys 40 and 940 are ahead.

From the pavement, at 1510 m (4953 ft), head north on the unsigned trail, up the steep slope, into pine forest. You're ascending the left side of a drainage. In about four minutes, follow a faint path curving left (northwest).

About ten minutes up, at 1577 m (5174 ft), the Great Divide is visible west. South, below you, is unpaved Hwy 940. The gentle, **open slope** above is inviting. Angle right (north-northwest) and ascend cross-country.

Within 20 minutes, you'll be funneled into a narrowing **corridor of trees**. At a worn patch of dirt, where the forested slope ahead falls away steeply into a basin, turn right (northeast). Follow a game path through a stand of pines and, in a couple minutes, emerge onto another **open slope**. Ascend north-northeast. Highwood House is visible below.

After about 40 minutes, reach a **minor ridgecrest** at 1727 m (5665 ft). Its far (east) slope plummets steeply into the upper end of the drainage that

Nearing summit of Junction Hill

you began hiking next to when you departed the highway. Turn left and ascend north, just below the ridgecrest, on its gentler left (west) side.

Pick up a contouring cattle path angling right, around the far (north) end of the minor ridgecrest. When the path disappears, proceed right (northeast) onto a gentle **saddle** dividing two drainages. Right is the smaller drainage you began hiking beside and which you overlooked a short way back, from the minor ridgecrest. Left is a much larger drainage beneath Junction Hill (visible north). The larger drainage separates Junction Hill's right (southeast) ridge from its left (south) ridge.

Pause on the saddle to orient yourself. You'll ascend the right ridge to the summit, then descend the left ridge to Hwy 40. That means your immediate task is to surmount the right ridge. Though it has the forbidding appearance of a continuous cliff, directly above you is a breach through which even cattle have crested the ridge.

Carry on, northeast. The higher you ascend, the more apparent this **breach** will become. After side-hilling to the right, turn left and follow a natural ramp up between boulders. Finally, angle right between more boulders and you'll quickly top out in an open, level patch of grass on Junction Hill's **southeast ridge**. Total hiking time: about one hour.

Relax. Enjoy the view. You can now peer north-northeast into Stony Creek canyon and up at Holy Cross Mtn. The abandoned fire lookout atop Mt. Burke (Trip 53) is visible southeast. The mesa beyond it is Plateau Mtn. A continuous wall of peaks—the Great Divide—spans the southwest horizon. The Divide comprises sub-ranges. You're primarily looking at the High Rock Range. The Elk Range is west-northwest.

From here to the top of Junction Hill, your route is the **ridgecrest**. Just keep following it northwest. After a few, small (8-m/yd) ups and downs, the ascent is consistently moderate. Expect a pleasantly vigourous hike on rocky terrain, through pine forest, with frequent views. You'll encounter some deadfall that you'll have to clamber over or around, and a couple short, steep, hands-on pitches, but no exposure. Occasionally skirt right or left of the crest, whichever is easiest.

At 2018 m (6620 ft), about 1½ hours after departing the highway, negotiate tilted rock slabs left of the crest. About 2½ hours from the highway, hikers who've maintained a moderate pace will surpass the trees, proceed over a rocky bump, and arrive at the true, cairned summit of 2233-m (7326-ft) **Junction Hill**. Mt. Head is now visible north, in the Highwood Range. The Cat Creek Hills are below you, northwest. Much farther northwest is Mist Mtn (Trip 33).

Departing the cairned summit, drop to the bump, then descend southwest, initially over broken rock. Stay just right of the trees, along the upper edge of the right (northwest) slope. Proceed southwest as long as the grade remains comfortable. Just before it plunges, bear left (south) to continue descending less steeply.

Briefly work your way down through trees, then across a **boulder field** (large, charcoal-coloured slabs covered with black and green lichen). Below, to the south, is a knoll with a bald top. That's your immediate goal. It will often be in view as you descend.

After the boulder field, re-enter forest. The angle of descent steepens. Drop through trees for about eight minutes. Angle right and emerge onto an open, grassy slope. Keep descending south. At 1845 m (6050 ft), re-enter forest on a **cattle path**. It begins just 5 m/yd below (right of) a treed saddle. Follow it into a stand of aspen. A minute farther, where the path appears to end, proceed over rock slabs; you'll find it resumes, contouring right (west) of a knob. Thank goodness for those enterprising cows, eh?

About 1¼ hours from the summit, reach a small, grassy **saddle**. From here, a three-minute ascent through forest leads to the **bald-topped knoll** you've been aiming for. Keep descending south. Bear right, between stands of trees, where the grade is more gradual.

The terrain is open from here on, and the highway is in view, so you can complete the descent however you please. But this last slope tilts at an alarming angle. To avoid the steepest section, look left for a prominent, standing **snag** at 1768 m (5800 ft). It's on the edge of a 3-m (10-ft) **rock band**. Just below the snag is an easy place to scramble left, through the rock band, to the slightly more gradual slope below.

Proceed south, edging your way down precipitous dirt, rock and grass. After a joint-crunching final descent, step onto **Hwy 40** at 1558 m (5110 ft). Turn left and follow the pavement about 20 minutes east to where the 8.5-km (5.3-mi) loop ends, at Highwood House.

Kananaskis Country, mid-September

TRIP 52

Raspberry Ridge

LOCATION	Hwy 940, south of Highwood Junction
ROUND TRIP	9 km (5.6 mi)
ELEVATION GAIN	653 m (2142 ft)
KEY ELEVATIONS	trailhead 1707 m (5600 ft), summit 2360 m (7741 ft)
HIKING TIME	3 to 4 hours
DIFFICULTY	easy
MAPS	Gem Trek Highwood—South Kananaskis Country Mount Head 82 J/7

Opinion

A single Rocky Mountain thunderstorm can bombard these mountains with 600 lightning strikes. So you definitely want to check the weather forecast before hiking to a fire lookout—the very place where statistics like this are recorded. Three such lookouts crown southern K-Country summits: Hailstone Butte (Trip 54), Mt. Burke (Trip 53), and Raspberry Ridge. A head-spinning view awaits you atop each.

In spring and late fall, when your hiking options are limited, all three lookouts might be accessible. They're located in the front range, where snow accumulates later, less abundantly, and melts earlier than in the main range. So put them at the top of your shoulder-season list. Consider staying overnight at one of the nearby provincial-park campgrounds. You can tag two, possibly three lookouts on a weekend.

Don't hike Hailstone or Raspberry in mid-summer, however. These trips are too short, too easy. During prime hiking season, both are uneventful and anti-climactic compared to most destinations in this book. The Mt. Burke trail is longer, more varied, and its summit airier and therefore more exciting, but it still isn't a premier summertime objective. All three lookouts are far from the skyscraping crest of the Rockies.

Much of the Raspberry hike is on road reverting to trail. The ascent is gradual until the final, steep assault of the alpine ridgetop. The forest en route is unimpressive. But due to the broad track, neither is it claustrophobic. Views are frequent. Carry plenty of water; you'll find none on the ridge. Pack wind-proof clothing, so gusts won't chill you before you're ready to leave.

Ever wonder about hiking the Great Divide trail? If so, a reconnaissance trip to Raspberry could be enlightening. From here, you can see where a big chunk of the route bobs along below treeline. It might persuade you to opt for the *hit-and-run* tactic of selecting shorter trips to scenic highlights, like Raspberry Ridge, rather than slavishly plodding long distance.

En route to Raspberry Ridge in the distance

Fact

Before your trip

Be aware that Hwy 40—between Kananaskis Lakes Trail and Highwood Junction—is closed December 1 through June 15. So, spring access to Raspberry Ridge is via Hwy 22, southwest of Calgary.

By Vehicle

From **Highwood Junction**, drive south 11.4 km (7.1 mi) on Hwy 940. (Highwood Junction is where Hwys 40, 541 and 940 intersect. It's 43 km / 26.7 mi southwest of Longview; 105 km / 65.1 mi southeast of Trans-Canada Hwy 1.)

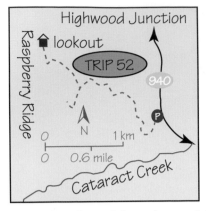

From **Hwy 532**, drive north on Hwy 940. Pass the entrance to Cataract Creek campground at 18.8 km (11.7 mi). Proceed north another 1.7 km (1.1 mi).

From **either approach**, look for the unmarked, gated, dirt spur on the west side of Hwy 940. Park in the pullout before the gate, at 1707 m (5600 ft).

On Foot

Follow the spur past the gate. In 40 m/yd, overgrown Raspberry Ridge road forks right. Follow it, ascending south-southwest. In a few minutes, at a **Y-junction**, bear right and ascend. The wider left track descends into Cataract Creek valley.

Above the Y-junction, the old road is rehabilitating to trail. It curves west, then north, through pines. At 1738 m (5700 ft), about 15 minutes from the trailhead, Raspberry Ridge is visible left (northwest). Drop into a **stream gully**, then ascend more steeply. After a gentle southward stretch, the trail bends north-northwest.

At 1939 m (6360 ft), about 50 minutes from the trailhead, you're approaching the southeast end of Raspberry Ridge. Visible southeast is Plateau Mountain. Mt. Burke is east, its abandoned, dilapidated fire lookout barely discernable. The Mt. Burke trail ascends through forest, then follows the open, rocky ridgeline left to the summit.

Reach a **cairned fork** at 1950 m (6396 ft) after hiking about one hour. Ignore the left fork—an old road descending west. Turn right (north-northwest) and ascend. Raspberry Ridge fire lookout is visible ahead, on the skyline. Continued upward progress soon grants you an overview of Cataract Creek valley.

After hiking about 1 hour and 15 minutes, the trail steepens at 2134 m (7000 ft). Strong striders will crest **Raspberry Ridge** in another 20 minutes. Turn right (north) for the final five-minute ascent to the **fire lookout** crowning the 2360-m (7741-ft) summit. Total hiking time: about 1 hour and 40 minutes.

Numerous clearcuts mar the scenery below. Above and beyond, however, is an engaging Rocky Mountain panorama. Mt. Head, at the south end of the Highwood Range, is north. The prominent, lone massif of Mist Mountain (Trip 33) is far north-northwest. Mist Ridge (Trip 35) is below it, northwest.

Nearby northwest and west are peaks of the High Rock Range. Fording River Pass is northwest. Mt. Armstrong (northwest) is the highest peak north of the pass. Baril Peak is directly west. Etherington is west-southwest. Multi-peaked Scrimger Ridge is south of Etherington. 2896-m (9500-ft) Mt. Farquhar is southwest. Crowsnest Mountain is way south. Calgary is north-northeast.

Mt. Burke

LOCATION	Hwy 940, south of Highwood Junction
ROUND TRIP	16 km (10 mi)
ELEVATION GAIN	935 m (3067 ft)
KEY ELEVATIONS	trailhead 1605 m (5264 ft), summit 2541 m (8333 ft)
HIKING TIME	5 to 7 hours
DIFFICULTY	moderate
MAPS	Gem Trek Highwood—South Kananaskis Country Mount Head 82 J/7

Opinion

Mt. Burke is the most exciting K-Country peak mere hikers can fling themselves at in shoulder-season and expect to summit. Its front-range location, sun-blasted west-facing trail, and barren, wind-ravaged upper reaches ensure you'll encounter a minimal snowpack.

It's startling how early you can get up here. Without gradually easing into the mountains on several lower-elevation rambles, a springtime ascent of Burke is like entering a theater mid-movie and being assaulted by explosions, celebrations, chase scenes: totally out of context, but sensational.

The derelict, ramshackle, fire-lookout cabin teetering atop Burke attests to the panorama awaiting you. You'll see much of southern K-Country: from Calgary and the prairie, to the Great Divide. It's just a long way up. This would be a lot to ask of indolent muscles if not for a most compassionate trail. The switchbacks are actually so languorous they might try your patience. That's why you're sure to at least achieve the vantage above tree-line. From there on, the slope is tantalizingly open and will re-ignite your resolve to prevail.

Need more inspiration? Last time we were hiking up, we met a 76-year-old bounding down. Regular exercise should enable most of us to remain summiteers into our 80's. Anyone under 50 better have a doctor's note if unable to surmount Burke. Even declining middle-agers can reclaim their natural vitality and stamina. That's what our hero said he did after retiring early from his career.

While you're clacking across scree on the slim summit ridge, imagine the bug-eyed, heart-racing terror of the hapless pack horses forced to carry supplies to the fire-lookout attendant. Cliff bands plunge into Salter Creek canyon 854 m (2800 ft) below. The lookout was manned every summer from 1929 until 1953, then superseded by Raspberry Ridge lookout (Trip 52) to the west.

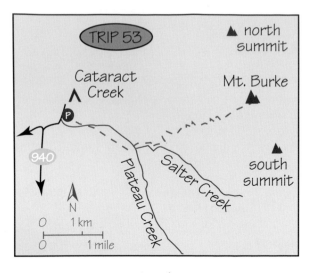

Fact

Before your trip

Be aware that Hwy 40—between Kananaskis Lakes Trail and Highwood Junction—is closed December 1 through June 15. So, spring access to Mt. Burke is via Hwy 22, southwest of Calgary.

By Vehicle

From **Highwood Junction**, drive south 13 km (8.1 mi) on unpaved Hwy 940. (Highwood Junction is where Hwys 40, 541 and 940 intersect. It's 43 km / 26.7 mi southwest of Longview; 105 km / 65.1 mi southeast of Trans-Canada Hwy 1.)

From the **junction of Hwys 940 and 532**, drive north 18.8 km (11.7 mi) on unpaved Hwy 940.

From **either approach**, upon reaching Cataract Creek day use area, turn east onto the Cataract Creek campground access road. Cross Salter Creek bridge in 0.7 km (0.4 mi). Just 100 m (110 yd) farther, turn right into the trail-head parking lot, at 1605 m (5264 ft). From here, Mt. Burke is in full view east, from its forested lower slopes to the scree-covered summit.

On Foot

Make sure you've packed plenty of water for the dry ascent that lies ahead. Then follow the road back to **Salter Creek bridge**. On the north side of the bridge, turn left (east) onto the grass-covered imprint of an old road paralleling the creekbed. In several minutes, cross the rubbly, usually dry creekbed and continue generally southeast. Proceed briefly through a stand of aspen and pine. Where the trail vanishes, follow a faint cattle track between berms. Then pick up an old two-track road and go left (east) toward Mt. Burke.

Within 20 minutes, cross a creekbed. Follow another scrap of trail, then a cobbly stretch. At 2.7 km (1.7 mi), 1704 m (5590 ft), about 25 minutes from

Mt. Burke summit ridge

the trailhead, reach the **confluence of Salter and Plateau creeks**—both probably dry. Plateau Creek enters via the narrow, steep-walled gorge immediately ahead. Don't go that way. Turn left (east) and cross Salter Creek's main channel. On the far side, ascend an old road northeast into forest. In a minute, ignore the cairned route forking left (north-northwest) upslope. Keep following snippets of trail and eroded road along the boulder-strewn bed of Salter creek. The old road favours the left side of the drainage.

At 1698 m (5570 ft), about ten minutes above the Salter/Plateau confluence, arrive at a **yellow sign**. Just beyond is a **metal pipe** protruding from the ground, perhaps creatively adorned by previous hikers. Turn left (north) here onto the **steep trail ascending the west-facing slope**, initially through scruffy, scaly Engelmann spruce and skinny lodgepole pine. You've begun the switchbacking ascent of Mt. Burke.

Near 1980 m (6495 ft), about 1¼ hours from the trailhead, attain views through the forest. Raspberry Ridge is visible west-northwest, beyond Cataract Creek valley. Alpine fir now beautify the forest. A bootbeaten path rockets directly up the fall line, shortcutting the switchbacks. But it's easier to keep to the main trail and cruise briskly. On the descent, zooming down the direct route does save time.

Swift hikers will emerge above the 2186-m (7170-ft) **treeline** about 1¾ hours after departing the trailhead. The Highwood Range is visible northwest. Mist Mtn (Trip 33) is just beyond. The Great Divide runs the length of the western horizon. Plateau Creek canyon is southwest. South, across Salter Creek Canyon, is the oddly flat expanse of unmistakable Plateau Mtn. Underfoot, yellow shrubby cinquefoil brighten the grey rock. Surprisingly, purple monkey's pod also survives in this desolation.

The trail zigzags upward through chunky rock. At 2287 m (7500 ft), you can see your destination east-northeast: the Mt. Burke fire-lookout cabin. The trail gets more exciting as it switchbacks up the north side of the south-west-jutting summit ridge. A short stretch is just four meters (yards) wide. The final ascent is just below the crest of the **narrow summit ridge**, on the right (south) side, 550 m (1800 ft) above Salter Creek canyon.

Speedy hikers will drop their packs on the 2541-m (8333-ft) **summit of Mt. Burke** about 2¾ hours after departing the trailhead. Total distance: 8 km (5.1 mi).

Stay out of the abandoned, dilapidated fire-lookout cabin. It's unsafe. The Livingston Range is visible north-northeast. Calgary is northeast, beyond Longview. Sentinel Peak is nearby southeast, just left of Plateau Mtn. Hailstone Butte (Trip 54) is past Sentinel. On the Great Divide, Baril Peak is west, and Mt. Armstrong is northwest.

It's possible to be back at the trailhead within 1¾ hours, if you gallop at race pace.

Lichen

TRIP 54
Hailstone Butte

LOCATION	Hwy 532, southeast edge of K-Country
ROUND TRIP	4 km (2.5 mi)
ELEVATION GAIN	327 m (1073 ft)
KEY ELEVATIONS	trailhead 2037 m (6680 ft), summit 2364 m (7753 ft)
HIKING TIME	2 to 3 hours
DIFFICULTY	easy
MAPS	page 277; Langford Creek 82 J/1

Opinion

The serendipitous combination of alpine slopes, exposure to the snow-melting warmth of our sacred star, and a nearby, high-elevation trailhead, distinguishes Hailstone Butte as a premier early-season destination. The fire lookout garnishing the summit affords a panoramic vista that can make a hiker's winter-dormant heart palpitate with possibilities.

Available as early as May or as late as November, Hailstone's prime time is spring, when the grass is verdant and the frequently ferocious winds are less frigid. Whenever you come, pack your toque, gloves, and windproof shell. Gusts up to 150 kph (93 mph) have been clocked at the fire lookout. Imagine hunkering down all night with a gale like *that* battering your door.

Enhance your exploration of southern K-Country by reading the description of Windy Peak Hills (Trip 55), which shares the same trailhead as Hailstone Butte. You should hike both, perhaps in a single day, while you're here. Also read Raspberry Ridge (Trip 52) and Mt. Burke (Trip 53). They're in Hailstone's neighbourhood, are likewise crowned with fire lookouts, and will reward you with grand views. You can bag two, possibly three lookouts on a weekend.

Coming from Calgary? Be sure to drive unpaved Hwy 532 (off Hwy 22) at least one way. It rolls through beautiful, lush foothills blanketed with aspen. Lightly traveled, mostly by those working the land, the area has a soothing, pre-bustle atmosphere. And don't worry, the road's maintained. You won't hurt the Acura.

Paintbrush

Ascending Hailstone Butte

Something else you need not be concerned about is the word *scramble* in the *On Foot* description. Attaining Hailstone Butte entails a quick, easy, no-exposure scramble near the top. Anyone who can hang on while lifting knees to chin for a couple steps will slither up, no problem.

Fact

Before your trip

Be aware that Hwy 40—between Kananaskis Lakes Trail and Highwood Junction—is closed December 1 through June 15. So, spring access to Hailstone Butte is via Hwy 22, southwest of Calgary.

By Vehicle

Following directions for Windy Peak Hills (Trip 55), drive Hwy 532 to a pass called *The Hump*. A roadside pullout here affords trailhead parking: south of the Texas gate, beside the small pond, at 2037 m (6680 ft).

On Foot

From the south side of the Texas gate, head southwest, cross the road, and walk up the short slope. Then go northwest through a grassy gully. You'll see two trails. The upper one soon ends. Follow the lower one around the low, grassy ridge, into the upper drainage. The fire lookout atop Hailstone Butte is visible northwest. You'll be ascending just left of it. Keep that in mind, because you'll be unable to see the lookout when you're below it, farther up the **drainage**.

When the lower trail fades in willows and along the creeklet, proceed northwest. Ascend the **grassy slope** just left of where the lookout is perched atop the butte. Above this slope, the rock band is thin and broken, granting an easy scramble onto the crest.

Nearing the **rock band**, there's a gully between grassy ribs. Ascend northwest between them. Surmounting the first 3 m/yd of the rock band requires athleticism. Above that you'll find easier stairstep ledges. Strong hikers will top out on **Hailstone Butte** within 30 minutes of leaving the road.

Turn right (north) and follow the path just below the left (west) side of the crest to reach the now visible **fire lookout** in a couple minutes, at 2364 m (7753 ft). The butte extends farther northwest. A fire road descends the west side. Calgary is visible northeast. Sentinel Peak is nearby north. Mt. Burke is northwest. Plateau Mtn is west-northwest. Windy Peak is southeast, and beyond it is Mt. Livingston.

Time permitting, enjoy striding south about 1.5 km (0.9 mi) along the open butte before returning the way you came.

Ascending Windy Peak Hills (Trip 55). Upper left ridge is Hailstone Butte.

TRIP 55
Windy Peak Hills

LOCATION	Hwy 532, Southeast edge of K-Country
LOOP	9 km (5.6 mi)
ELEVATION GAIN	500 m (1640 ft)
KEY ELEVATIONS	trailhead 2037 m (6680 ft)
	Windy Peak 2250 m (7380 ft)
HIKING TIME	3½ to 5 hours
DIFFICULTY	easy
MAP	Langford Creek 82 J/1

Opinion

Hiking is a conversation with the earth. The greening-up of the land in spring indicates that it's ready to talk again and is inviting you to listen. The Windy Peak Hills is a fine place to respond.

These front-range hills green-up early and can be hikeable by May. Granted, they're merely hills, not mountains—not by the Canadian Rockies standard anyway—but they're beautiful and offer a varied, vigorous loop hike with constant views. If you're lucky, you'll witness the pre-summer burst of wildflowers featuring lavender harebells and brown-eyed susan.

Further burnishing the hills' appeal is another premier hike, Hailstone Butte (Trip 54), sharing the same trailhead. Plus, you'll find officially sanctioned free camping nearby. So this is an ideal destination for your first hiking/camping weekend of the season. Or your last. The Windy Peak Hills are attractive in autumn too, when snowfall dampens your more vigourous dialogue with the main range alps.

You'll swoop up and down the emerald hills by following a faint, boot-beaten trail that occasionally vanishes. It sometimes reappears as a cattle track or barely distinguishable route. Easy navigation is briefly necessary in a few places. But no worries. You're frequently on or near a crest, so the whole area is often in view, and the way forward is usually obvious. You'll also have our precise directions.

The loop is a tour of five hills (ridgeline bumps, really), plus Windy Peak—the last and highest promontory in this compact group and the only one with a name. From Windy, you'll descend a forested slope, cross a clearcut-cum-pasture, then intersect a dirt highway. The final 1.8 km (1.1 mi) is a road-walk back to your vehicle. Don't let this deter you from completing the loop. You'll likely encounter little or no traffic on this remote road, so the home stretch is pleasant enough. If a vehicle does appear, hitch a ride.

Windy Peaks Hills

About those cattle tracks. Expect to see the lumbering beasts and their splatterings. It's a minor blemish on an otherwise superlative hike during shoulder-season—the time of year when you feel fortunate to be hiking at all. In summer, however, you want to be much higher in the Rockies, stepping over grizzly-bear scat, not bovine offal.

Fact

Before your trip

Be aware that Hwy 40—between Kananaskis Lakes Trail and Highwood Junction—is closed December 1 through June 15. So, spring access to Windy Peak Hills is via Hwy 22, southwest of Calgary.

By Vehicle

From **Highwood Junction**, drive southeast 31.8 km (19.7 mi) on Hwy 940. (Highwood Junction is where Hwys 40, 541 and 940 intersect. It's 43 km / 26.7 mi southwest of Longview; 105 km / 65.1 mi southeast of Trans-Canada Hwy 1.) Upon reaching Hwy 532, go left (northeast) another 4 km (2.5 mi) to a pass called *The Hump*, where a roadside pullout affords trailhead parking: south of the Texas gate, beside the small pond, at 2037 m (6680 ft).

Or, from **southwest Calgary**, drive south on Hwy 22 to Longview. Proceed another 28.5 km (17.8 mi) to the junction with Johnson Creek Trail (Hwy 532). Reset your trip odometer to 0 and follow Hwy 532 southwest. Enter K-Country in 8.2 km (5.1 mi). At 11.8 km (7.3 mi) a sign RANDOM CAMPING AREA marks a potholed, dirt road (prohibitively muddy when wet) descending left to free camping. Just after crossing Johnson Creek, pass Indian Creek campground on the right at 13.3 km (8.2 mi). (Dependable access, but camping here will cost you.) At 18.5 km (11.5 mi) the Windy Peak Hills are visible left (south). Ahead you can also see Hailstone Butte (Trip 54) above and beyond the road you're about to traverse. At 22 km (13.6 mi) reach a pass called *The Hump*, where a roadside pullout affords trailhead parking: south of the Texas gate, beside the small pond, at 2037 m (6680 ft).

On Foot

From the north side of the Texas gate, ascend southeast on the remains of an old road. In 20 m/yd it dwindles to trail. Soon climb over a barbed-wire fence. Proceed where the trail disappears. It resumes on the south side of the first bump. Where it fades again, stay left. About 30 minutes from the trailhead, surmount the 2174-m (7130-ft) **first bump**. You can now see that lichen-adorned rock covers much of these slopes, though from a distance they appeared grassy. Dwarf lupine and other colourful wildflowers are abundant here in spring and early summer.

Faint trail resumes just below the first bump's summit. Continue southeast about ten minutes along the obvious ridge to the 2146-m (7040-ft) **second bump**. Trail resumes below, to the right. Descend through krummholz five minutes to a junction in Timber Creek Pass. Left (northeast) leads to Johnson Creek. Keep following the ridgeline southeast. The route crosses small rock slabs, skirting the **third bump** on its right (southwest) side. Hailstone Butte is visible northwest.

Drop to the **second pass** at 2030 m (7040 ft). You're now 3 km (2 mi) from the trailhead, having hiked about 50 minutes. A cattle track descends right (southwest) across meadow into the forest of South Twin Creek. It offers a shortcut exit, intersecting Hwy 532 just 1.8 km (1.1 mi) below (south of) The Hump. But if you want to resume the loop, ascend the trail southeast along a fence.

Swift hikers will surmount the 2125-m (6970-ft) **fourth bump** about ten minutes above the col. Visible south-southwest is rounded Windy Peak. Behind it is Mt. Livingston. Way beyond, the prominent, lone peak is 2787-m (9140-ft) Crowsnest Mtn. Saddle Mtn is southeast. Chain Lakes Reservoir is partially visible east.

The trail now rounds the head of the draw down which you can see the two-track trail on the right side of the meadow. Curve briefly southeast, then south-southwest toward Windy Peak. About 1½ hours from the trailhead, descend a bit to reach the bottom of a **third pass**, at 2085 m (6840 ft). Ascend a bit more, passing below and just west of the **fifth bump** (two bumps close together). Do not follow the road-trail descending between the fourth and fifth bumps to a meadow between forested slopes.

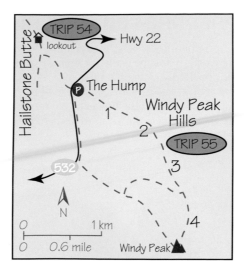

Where the trail disappears, aim for the far end of the fifth bump. Within minutes, pick up a well-defined rock-and-dirt trail through trees. It soon veers northwest, ascending through more trees. The trail traverses a slope, then pops out onto Windy Peak's open, gentle, summit ridge. Turn left (south) and stride uphill across grass and heather to quickly surmount 2250-m (7380-ft) **Windy Peak**. You're now 4.8 km (3 mi) from the trailhead, having hiked nearly two hours.

From the summit, retrace your steps down the generally northwest-trending ridge. Pick up a faint trail as you descend, initially curving north. Then bear north-northwest over rock and grass, on the left (west) side of the ridge. If you're experienced at cross-country navigation, skip the detailed directions below and sniff out your own route down to the tussocky meadow, then northwest to Hwy 532.

Re-enter trees about 15 minutes below the summit of Windy Peak. Look left (rather than down the center of the ridge) for the easiest descent route: a one-meter-wide (one-yard-wide) **swath cut through the trees** long ago. Follow it west. About five minutes below treeline, drop through a meadow and angle right. Pick up traces of cattle track. Continue down northwest through forest broken by grassy clearings. The going is easy so far.

About ten minutes below treeline, reach the edge of willowy **South Timber Creek drainage** at 1951 m (6400 ft). Go right (northwest) to take advantage of a broad cattle-track. Tiptoe through a bog and hop a creeklet. On the low slope just above the bog, follow a trail northwest through the cutblock. Progress is briefly impeded in the tussocky, willowy, muddy bog of North Twin Creek. Stretches of cattle track are helpful. Cross a creeklet twice before finally intersecting **Hwy 532** at 1907 m (6255 ft). Total hiking time: about three hours. Turn right and walk the road north 1.8 km (1.1 mi) back to your vehicle parked at The Hump.

PREPARE FOR YOUR HIKE

Hiking in the Canadian Rockies is an adventure. Adventure involves risk. But the rewards are worth it. Just be ready for more adventure than you expect. The weather here is constantly changing. Even on a warm, sunny day, pack for rain or snow. Injury is always a possibility. On a long dayhike, be equipped to spend the night out. If you respect the power of wilderness by being prepared, you'll decrease the risk, increase your comfort and enjoyment, and come away fulfilled, yearning for more.

Mt. Robertson, on the Great Divide

The following recommendations will help you know what's best to pack for mountain conditions. If you don't own or can't afford some of the things listed, make do with what you have. Just be sure to bring warm clothing that insulates when wet: synthetic or wool fabrics, not cotton. When buying new equipment, consult this section so you don't waste money on something inefficient or inappropriate.

You Carry What You Are

Even with all the right gear, you're ill-equipped without physical fitness. If the weather turns grim, the physical capability to escape the wilderness fast might keep you from being stuck in a life-threatening

Guard your gear. Salt from sweat attracts animals.

situation. If you're fit, and a companion gets injured, you can race for help. Besides, if you're not overweight or easily exhausted, you'll have more fun. You'll be able to hike farther, reach more spectacular scenery, and leave crowds behind. So if you're out of shape, work on it. Everything else you'll need is easier to acquire.

Travel Light

Weight is critical when backpacking. The lighter you travel, the easier and more pleasant the journey. Carrying too much can sour your opinion of an otherwise great trip. Some people are mules; they can shoulder everything they want. If you'd rather be a thoroughbred, reduce your load and get lighter gear. You might have to sacrifice a little luxury at the campsite in order to be more agile, fleet-footed and comfortable on the trail, but you'll be a happier hiker.

Weigh your pack when it's empty. Switching to a newer, lighter model might shave a couple pounds off your burden. A palatial dome tent is probably overdoing it. Check out the smaller, lighter, anthropomorphic designs. A down sleeping bag will weigh less, stuff smaller and last longer than a synthetic-filled bag that has the same temperature rating. You can also cut weight and volume with a shorter, inflatable sleeping-pad instead of a full-length one made of thick foam. Forget that heavy, bulky, fleece jacket. If you get really cold at camp, wear your raingear over other insulating layers. And on any trek less than four days, it's possible to pack only real food and leave all that clunky cooking equipment at home. Try it. Hot meals aren't necessary. Playing outdoor chef and dishwasher is a time-consuming ordeal. It also makes it harder to leave no trace of your visit, and it can attract bears. Select the right foods and you'll find they weigh no more than a stove, fuel, pots, and pre-packaged meals.

These reductions long ago revitalized our interest in backpacking. Now we revel in going light. Lighter equipment is more expensive because the materials are finer quality and the craftsmanship superior. But it's definitely worth it. Consult reputable outdoor stores for specific brands.

Rawson Lake and Mt. Sarrail (Trip 25)

Unnecessary Stuff

We once encountered two men labouring up a trail, bound for a distant, back-country lake, pushing wheelbarrows piled with camping "necessities." They had a cooler, tackle box, hatchet, lawn chairs, even a radio. They also had sore hands, aching spines, and a new appreciation for backpacks and minimal loads.

Unless you're in terrific shape, have a high pain threshold, or don't mind creeping along at a slug's pace, think about everything you pack. Jettisoning preconceptions will lighten your burden.

You don't need the entire guidebook. Take notes, or photocopy the pages of your book. Carrying the whole thing is like lugging a rock in your pack. Even an iPod is questionable, and not just because of the added weight. Toting tunes into the outdoors will deny you the delight of birdsong, windsong, riversong. Wearing headphones blunts your awareness, increasing the likelihood of a bear encounter.

An extra pair of shoes? No way. Even sandals are heavy. For in-camp comfort, bring a pair of beach flip-flops. The cheap, $1.99 variety are almost weightless, and their treadless soles are easy on the environment.

Jeans are ridiculous. They're heavy, restrictive, and don't insulate. Cotton sweatpants are almost as bad. Anything 100% cotton is a mistake, as explained on the next page.

Layer with Wool and Synthetics

Don't just wear a T-shirt and throw a heavy sweatshirt in your pack. Cotton kills. It quickly gets saturated with perspiration and takes way too long to dry. Wet clothing saps your body heat and could lead to hypothermia, a leading cause of death in the outdoors. Your mountain clothes should be made of synthetic or wool fabrics that wick sweat away from your skin, insulate when wet, and dry rapidly. Even your hiking shorts and underwear should be at least partly synthetic. Sports bras should be entirely synthetic.

There are now lots of alternatives to the soggy T-shirt. All outdoor clothing companies offer short-sleeve shirts in superior, synthetic versions. Unlike cotton T-shirts, sweat-soaked synthetics can dry during a rest break.

For warmth, several layers are more efficient than a single parka. Your body temperature varies constantly on the trail, in response to the weather and your activity level. With only one warm garment, it's either on or off, roast or freeze. Layers allow you to fine tune for optimal comfort.

In addition to a short-sleeve shirt, it's smart to pack two long-sleeve tops (zip-T's) of different fabric weights: one thin, one thick. Wear the thin one for cool-weather hiking. It'll be damp when you stop for a break, so change into the thick one. When you start again, put the thin one back on. The idea is to always keep your thick top dry in case you really need it to stay warm. Covered by a rain shell (jacket), these two tops can provide enough warmth on summer dayhikes. You can always wear your short-sleeve shirt like a vest over a long-sleeve top. For more warmth in camp, consider a down or lofty-synthetic sweater. But don't hike in down clothing; it'll get sweat soaked and cease to insulate.

For your legs, bring a pair of tights or long underwear, both if you're going overnight. Choose insulating wool or synthetic tights that have a small percentage of lycra for stretchiness. These are warmer and more durable than the all-lycra or nylon/lycra tights runners wear. Tights are generally more efficient than pants. They stretch, conforming to your movement. They're lighter and insulate better. You can wear them for hours in a drizzle and not feel damp.

Anticipating hot weather? Mosquitoes? Exposure to intense sun? You'll want long pants and a long-sleeve shirt, both made of tightly-woven synthetics and as lightweight as possible. Make sure they fit loosely enough to be unrestrictive. The shirt, designed for vigourous activity, should have a stand-up collar and a button front. Most outdoor clothing manufacturers offer them.

Raingear

Pack a full set of raingear: shell and pants. The shell (jacket) should have a hood. Fabrics that are both waterproof and breathable are best, because they repel rain *and* vent perspiration vapor. Gore-tex is the fabric of choice, but there are alternatives— less expensive and nearly as effective.

Don't let a blue sky or a promising weather forecast tempt you to leave your raingear behind. It can be invaluable, even if you don't encounter rain. Worn over insulating layers, a shell and pants will shed wind, retain body heat, and keep you much warmer.

Coated-nylon raingear might appear to be a bargain, but it doesn't breathe, so it simulates a steam bath if worn while exercising. You'll end up as damp from sweat as you would from rain. You're better off with a poncho, if you can't afford technical raingear. On a blustery day, a poncho won't provide impervious protection from rain, but at least it will allow enough air circulation so you won't get sweat soaked.

Boots and Socks

Lightweight fabric boots with even a little ankle support are more stable and safer than runners. But all-leather or highly technical leather/fabric boots offer superior comfort and performance. For serious hiking, they're a necessity. Here are a few points to remember while shopping for boots.

If it's a rugged, quality boot, a light- or medium-weight pair should be adequate for most hiking conditions. Heavy boots will slow you down, just like an overweight pack. But you want boots with hard, protective toes, or you'll risk a broken or sprained digit.

Grippy outsoles prevent slipping and falling. Sufficient cushioning lessens the pain of a long day on the trail. Lateral support stops ankle injuries. And stiff shanks keep your feet from tiring. Stiffness is critical. Grip the toe of a boot in one hand, the heel in your other hand. If you can bend the boot easily, don't buy it.

Out of the box, boots should be waterproof or at least very water resistant, although you'll have to treat them often to retain their repellency. Boots with lots of seams allow water to seep in as they age. A full rand (wrap-around bumper) adds an extra measure of water protection.

The key consideration is comfort. Make sure your boots don't hurt. If you wait to find out until after a day of hiking, it's too late; you're stuck with them. So before handing over your cash, ask the retailer if, after wearing them in a shopping mall, you can exchange them if they don't feel right. A half-hour of mall walking is a helpful test.

Socks are important too. To keep your feet dry, warm and happy, wear wool, thick acrylic, or wool/acrylic-blend socks. Cotton socks retain sweat, cause blisters, and are especially bad if your boots aren't waterproof. It's usually best to wear two pairs of socks, with a thinner, synthetic pair next to your feet to wick away moisture and alleviate friction, minimizing the chance of blisters.

Duct tape can help prevent blisters.

Gloves and Hats

Always bring gloves and a hat. You've probably heard it, and it's true: your body loses most of its heat through your head and extremities. Cover them if you get chilled. Carry thin, synthetic gloves to wear while hiking. Don't worry if they get wet, but keep a pair of thicker fleece gloves dry in your pack. A fleece hat, or at least a thick headband that covers your ears, adds a lot of warmth and weighs little. A hat with a long brim is essential to shade your eyes and protect your face from sun exposure.

Trekking Poles

Long, steep ascents and descents in the Canadian Rockies make trekking poles vital. Hiking with poles is easier, more enjoyable, and less punishing to your body. If you're constantly pounding the trails, they could add years to your mountain life.

Working on a previous guidebook, we once hiked for a month without poles. Both of us developed knee pain. The next summer we used Leki trekking poles every day for three months and our knees were never strained. We felt like four-legged animals. We were more sure-footed. Our speed and endurance increased.

Studies show that during a typical 8-hour hike you'll transfer more than 250 tons of pressure to a pair of trekking poles. When going downhill, poles significantly reduce stress to your knees, as well as your lower back, heel and forefoot. They alleviate knee strain when you're going uphill too, because you're climbing with your arms and shoulders, not just your legs. Poles also improve your posture. They keep you more upright, which gives you greater lung capacity and allows more efficient breathing.

The heavier your pack, the more you'll appreciate the support of trekking poles. You'll find them especially helpful for crossing unbridged streams, traversing steep slopes, and negotiating muddy, rooty, rough stretches of trail. Poles prevent ankle sprains—a common hiking injury. By making you more stable, they actually help you relax, boosting your sense of security and confidence.

Don't carry one of those big, heavy, gnarled, wooden staffs, unless you're going to a costume party dressed as Gandalf. They're more burden than benefit. If you can't afford trekking poles, make do with a pair of old ski poles. They're not as effective or comfortable as poles designed specifically for trekking, but they're better than hiking empty handed. If at all possible, invest in a pair of true trekking poles with a soft anti-shock system and adjustable, telescoping, easy-lock shafts. We strongly recommend Lekis.

Trekking poles could add years to your mountain life.

When backpacking, protect your trekking poles by keeping them inside your tent at night. Otherwise, the grips and straps—salty from your perspiration—will attract critters, such as porcupines, who will quickly chew them to shreds.

First Aid

Someone in your hiking party should carry a first-aid kit. Pre-packaged kits look handy, but they're expensive, and some are inadequate. If you make your own, you'll be more familiar with the contents. Include an anti-bacterial ointment; pain pills with ibuprofen, and a few with codeine for agonizing injuries; regular bandages; several sizes of butterfly bandages; a couple bandages big enough to hold a serious laceration together; rolls of sterile gauze and absorbent pads to staunch bleeding; adhesive tape; tiny fold-up scissors or a small knife; and a compact first-aid manual. Whether your kit is store bought or homemade, check the expiration dates on your medications every year and replace them as needed.

Instead of the old elastic bandages for wrapping sprains, we now carry neoprene ankle and knee bands. They slip on instantly, require no special wrapping technique, keep the injured joint warmer, and stay in place better.

Bandanas

A bandana will be the most versatile item in your pack. You can use it to blow your nose, mop your brow, or improvise a beanie. It makes a colourful headband that will keep sweat or hair out of your eyes. It serves as a bandage or sling in a medical emergency. Worn as a neckerchief, it prevents a sunburned neck. If you soak it in water, then drape it around your neck, it will help keep you from overheating. Worn Lawrence-of-Arabia style under a hat, it shades both sides of your face, as well as your neck, while deterring mosquitoes. For an air-conditioning effect, soak it in water then don it á la Lawrence. When shooing away mosquitoes, flicking a bandana with your wrist is less tiresome than flailing your arms. Carry at least two bandanas when dayhiking, more when backpacking.

Small and Essential

Take matches in a plastic bag, so they'll stay dry. It's wise to carry a lighter, too. A fire starter, such as Optimus Firelighter or Coghlan FireSticks, might help you start a fire in an emergency when everything is wet. Buy the short ones (finger size), not the barbecue wands.

Pack an emergency survival bag on dayhikes. One fits into the palm of your hand and could help you survive a cold night without a sleeping bag or tent. The ultralight, metallic fabric reflects your body heat back at you. Survival bags, which you crawl into, are more efficient than survival blankets.

Also bring several plastic bags in various sizes. Use the small ones for packing out garbage. A couple large trash bags could be used to improvise a shelter.

A headlamp is often helpful and can be necessary for safety. You'll need one to stay on the trail if a crisis forces you to hike at night.

Most people find mosquito repellent indispensable. If you anticipate an infestation, bring a mesh head-net.

For those dreaded blisters, pack Moleskin or Spenco jell. Cut it with the knife or scissors you should have in your first-aid kit.

Wear sunglasses for protection against glare and wind. A few hours in the elements can strain your eyes and even cause a headache. People who don't wear sunglasses are more prone to cataracts later in life. Also bring sunscreen and a hat with a brim. High-altitude sun can fry you fast.

And don't forget to pack lots of thought-provoking questions to ask your companions. Hiking stimulates meaningful conversation.

Keep It All Dry

Most daypacks and backpacks are not waterproof, or even very water resistant. To protect your gear from rain, organize it in ultralight, waterproof bags made by Sea To Summit. For extra assurance, use a waterproof pack cover. Rain is a constant likelihood, so always start hiking with your gear in bags. That's much easier than suddenly having to wrestle with it on the trail, in a storm.

Water

Drink water frequently. Keeping your body hydrated is essential. If you're thirsty, you're probably not performing at optimal efficiency. But be aware of giardia lamblia, a waterborne parasitic cyst that causes severe gastrointestinal distress. It's transported through animal and human feces, so never defecate or urinate near water. To be safe, assume giardia is present in all surface water. Don't drink

any water unless it's directly from a source you're certain is pure, like meltwater dripping off glacial ice, or until you've boiled, disinfected or filtered it.

Boiling water is a time-consuming hassle, especially along the trail, before reaching your campsite. Boiling also requires you to carry a stove and extra fuel, making it the heaviest method of ensuring safe water.

Killing giardia by disinfecting it with iodine tablets can be tricky. The colder the water, the longer you must wait. Iodine also makes the water smell and taste awful, unless you use neutralizing pills. And iodine has no effect whatsoever on cryptosporidium, an increasingly common cyst that causes physical symptoms identical to giardiasis.

Carrying a small, lightweight filter is a reasonable solution. Some filters weigh just 240 grams (8 ounces). To strain out giardia cysts, your filter must have an absolute pore size of 4 microns or less. Straining out cryptosporidium cysts requires an absolute pore size of 2 microns or less.

After relying on water filters for many years, we've switched to *Pristine* water purification droplets. The *Pristine* system comprises two 30 ml bottles with a total combined weight of only 80 grams (2.8 ounces). It purifies up to 120 litres (30 gallons) of water. The active ingredient is chlorine dioxide, which has been used for more than 50 years in hundreds of water treatment plants throughout North America and Europe. You'll find *Pristine* at most outdoor stores. Using it is simple: mix two solutions, wait five minutes, then add it to your water. You can drink 15 minutes later knowing you won't contract giardia. Treating for cryptosporidium requires a higher dosage and/or longer wait.

Body Fuel

When planning meals, keep energy and nutrition foremost in mind. During a six-hour hike, you'll burn 1800 to 3000 calories, depending on terrain, pace, body size, and pack weight. You'll be stronger, and therefore safer and happier, if you fill up on high-octane body fuel.

A white-flour bun with a thick slab of meat or cheese on it is low-octane fuel. Too much protein or fat will make you feel sluggish and drag you down. And you won't get very far up the trail snacking on candy bars. Refined sugars give you a brief spurt that quickly fizzles.

For sustained exercise, like hiking, you need protein and fat to function normally and give you that satisfying full feeling. The speed of your metabolism determines how much protein and fat you should eat. Both are hard to digest. Your body takes three or four hours to assimilate them, compared to one or two hours for carbohydrates. That's why a carb-heavy diet is optimal for hiking. It ensures your blood supply keeps hustling oxygen to your legs, instead of being diverted to your stomach. Most people, however, can sustain athletic effort longer if their carb-heavy diet includes a little protein. So eat a small portion of protein in the morning, a smaller portion at lunch, and a moderate portion at dinner to aid muscle repair.

For athletic performance, the American and Canadian Dietetic Association recommends that 60 to 65% of your total energy come from carbs, less than 25% from fat, and 15% from protein. They also say refined carbs and sugars should account for no more than 10% of your total carb calories.

Toiling muscles crave the glycogen your body manufactures from complex carbs. Yet your body has limited carb storage capacity. So your carb intake should be constant. That means loading your pack with plant foods made of whole-grain flour, rice, corn, oats, legumes, nuts, seeds, fruit and vegetables.

Dining Out

Natural- or health-food stores are reliable sources of hiking food. They even stock energy bars, which are superior to candy bars because they contain more carbs and less fat. Whether dayhiking or backpacking, always bring extra energy bars for emergencies.

On dayhikes, carry fresh or dried fruit; whole-grain pita bread filled with tabouli, hummus, avocado, cucumbers and sprouts; whole-grain cookies made with natural sweeteners (brown-rice syrup, organic cane-sugar, fruit juice, raw honey); whole-grain crackers; or a bag of organic tortilla chips (corn or mixed-grain) prepared in expeller-pressed safflower or canola oil. Take marinated tofu that's been pressed, baked, and vacuum-packed. It's protein rich, delicious, and lasts about three days. Omnivores have other excellent protein options: hard-boiled eggs, wild-salmon jerky, free-range bison jerky, and tuna with mayonnaise in a vacuum-packed, tear-open bag. Don't rely solely on cheese for protein; beyond small amounts, it's unhealthy.

For a backpacking breakfast, spread butter, maple syrup and cinnamon on whole-grain bread, or in pita pockets. Or why not whole-grain cookies in the morning? They're like cereal, only more convenient. The backpacking lunch menu is the same as for dayhiking. For dinner, try bean salad, rice with stir-fried

Entering James Walker Creek canyon (Trip 13)

veggies, or pasta with steamed veggies and dressing, all cooked at home and sealed in plastic. Bean burritos made ahead of time, then eaten cold on the trail, are great too. Fresh veggies that travel well include carrots and bell peppers.

For a one- or two- night trip, don't adhere blindly to tradition. Carry a stove only if cooking significantly increases your enjoyment. Real meals are heavier than pre-packaged, but they make up for it by eliminating the weight of cooking equipment and the bother of cooking and cleaning. Plus they're tastier, more filling, cheaper, and better for you. Fresh food tends to be too heavy, bulky and perishable for trips longer than three days. Then it makes sense to pack a stove and dehydrated food. Fast-and-easy options are soup mixes, lentils, and quick-cooking pasta or brown rice.

The best tasting, most nutritious pre-packaged meals we've found are made by Mary Jane's Farm: www.backcountryfood.org. They're dehydrated, so they retain more nutritional value than freeze-dried food. Mary Jane's wide range of delicious soups, pan breads, and dinners (pasta- or grain-based) have kept us from yearning for grocery stores and restaurants, even after a week on the trail. For breakfast, we recommend Mary Jane's Outrageous Outback Oatmeal. For dinner, each of us eats a soup as well as a main course. While visiting her website, read Mary Jane's life story. It's both interesting and inspiring. She was one of the first female wilderness rangers in the U.S. She later homesteaded, became an organic farmer, then created her organic backpacking food company.

INFORMATION SOURCES

For EMERGENCY 24-hour response, including Mountain Rescue assistance, call 9-1-1. To phone provincial park offices toll-free within Alberta, first dial 310-0000.

Hiking

Barrier Lake
Visitor Information Centre
ph (403) 673-3985

Bow Valley Provincial Park
ph (403) 673-3663

Elbow Valley
Visitor Information Centre
ph (403) 949-4261

Friends of Kananaskis
Suite 201, 800 Railway Avenue
Canmore, AB T1W 1P1
ph (403) 678-5508
www.kananaskis.org
friends@kananaskis.org
trails@www.kananaskis.org
   for trail maintenance

Peter Lougheed and Spray Valley
provincial parks
Visitor Information Centre
ph (403) 591-6322
www.Kananaskis-Country.ca

Sheep River District Office
ph (403) 933-7172
Fridays through Tuesdays

Camping

Backcountry Permit Desk
Kananaskis Country
ph (403) 678-3136

Bow Valley Park Campgrounds
ph (403) 673-2163

Elbow River Valley
ph (403) 949-3132
www.kananaskiscountry
campgrounds.com

Frontcountry Camping
Peter Lougheed Provincial Park
ph (403) 591-7226, or 1-866-366-2267
www.kananaskiscountry
campgrounds.com

Highwood / Cataract campgrounds
ph (403) 558-2373
www.campingalberta.com
gocamp@telusplanet.net

Mount Kidd RV Park
ph (403) 591-7700
www.mountkiddrv.com

Accommodation

Alpine Club of Canada
P.O. Box 8040, Indian Flats Road
Canmore, AB T1W 2T8
ph (403) 678-3200
fax (403) 678-3224
www.alpineclubofcanada.ca
info@alpineclubofcanada.ca

Canmore Bed & Breakfast Assoc.
P.O. Box 8005, Canmore, AB T1W 2T8
ph (403) 609-7224
www.bbcanmore.com

Kananaskis Wilderness Hostel /
Ribbon Creek
ph (403) 591-7333, or 1866-762-4122
www.hihostels.ca

INDEX

The Authors

Kathy and Craig are dedicated to each other, and to hiking, in that order. Their second date was a 32-km (20-mile) dayhike in Arizona. Since then they haven't stopped for long.

They've trekked through much of the world's vertical topography, including the Himalayas, Patagonian Andes, Pyrenees, French Alps, Scottish Highlands, Dolomites, Sierra Nevada, North Cascades, Colorado Rockies, New Zealand Alps, and canyons of the American Southwest. In 1989, they moved from the U.S. to Canada, so they could live near the Canadian Rockies—the range that inspired the first of their refreshingly unconventional guidebooks.

While living in Vancouver, British Columbia, they explored the Coast Mountains and the North Cascades, then wrote hiking guidebooks on each of those ranges. Later, while living in a cabin on Kootenay Lake, they researched and wrote two more hiking guidebooks: one on the West Kootenay, the other on the premier trails of southern B.C.

Kathy and Craig have since returned to the Canadian Rockies and now live in Canmore, Alberta. Their desire to hike, however, keeps them travelling constantly. For example, they migrate each spring and fall to the high-desert canyon country of southern Utah. Their guidebook *Hiking from Here to WOW: Utah Canyon Country* is especially stimulating and beautiful.

Canadian Rockies

Exploring canyon country in 1978

The Authors

Other Titles from hikingcamping.com

The following titles—boot-tested and written by the Opinionated Hikers, Kathy & Craig Copeland—are widely available in outdoor shops and bookstores. Visit www.hikingcamping.com to read excerpts and purchase online.

Don't Waste Your Time in the Canadian Rockies®
The Opinionated Hiking Guide

ISBN 978-0-9783427-5-3 Even here, in a mountain range designated a UNESCO World Heritage Site for its "superlative natural phenomena" and "exceptional natural beauty and aesthetic importance," not all scenery is equal. Some destinations are simply more striking, more intriguing, more inspiring than others. Now you can be certain you're choosing a rewarding hike for your weekend or vacation. This uniquely helpful, visually captivating guidebook covers Banff, Jasper, Kootenay, Yoho and Waterton Lakes national parks, plus Mt. Robson and Mt. Assiniboine provincial parks. It rates each trail *Premier, Outstanding, Worthwhile,* or *Don't Do,* explains why, and provides comprehensive route descriptions. 138 dayhikes and backpack trips. Trail maps for each hike. 544 pages, 270 photos, full colour throughout. Sixth edition July 2009.

Where Locals Hike in the West Kootenay
The Premier Trails in Southeast B.C. near Kaslo & Nelson

ISBN 978-0-9689419-9-7 See the peaks, glaciers and cascades that make locals passionate about these mountains. The 50 most rewarding dayhikes and backpack trips in the Selkirk and west Purcell ranges of southeast British Columbia. Includes Valhalla, Kokanee Glacier, and Goat Range parks, as well as hikes near Arrow, Slocan, and Kootenay lakes. Discerning trail reviews help you choose your trip. Detailed route descriptions keep you on the path. 272 pages, 130 photos, trail locator maps, full colour throughout. Updated 2nd edition April 2007.

Camp Free in B.C.

ISBN 978-0-9735099-3-9 Make your weekend or vacation adventurous and revitalizing. Enjoy British Columbia's scenic byways and 2WD backroads—in your low-clearance car or your big RV. Follow precise directions to 350 campgrounds, from the B.C. Coast to the Rocky Mountains. Choose from 80 low-fee campgrounds similar in quality to provincial parks but half the price. Find retreats where the world is yours alone. Simplify life: slow down, ease up. Fully appreciate B.C.'s magnificent backcountry, including the Sunshine Coast, Okanagan, Shuswap Highlands, Selkirk and Purcell ranges, Cariboo Mountains, and Chilcotin Plateau. 544 pages, 200 photos, 20 regional maps, full colour throughout. Updated 4th edition July 2009.

Gotta Camp Alberta

ISBN 978-0-9735099-0-8 Make your weekend or vacation adventurous and revitalizing. Enjoy Alberta's scenic byways and 2WD backroads—in your low-clearance car or your big RV. Follow precise directions to 150 idyllic campgrounds, from the foothill lakes to the Rocky Mountains. Camp in national parks, provincial parks, and recreation areas. Find retreats where the world is yours alone. Simplify life: slow down, ease up. Return home soothed by the serenity of nature. Approximately 400 pages, 170 photos, and 18 maps. Full colour throughout. First edition March 2010.

Bears Beware!
How to Avoid an Encounter

The 30-minute MP3 that could save your life. Download it at hikingcamping.com (>Guidebooks >Hiking >Rockies). In bear country, ignorance = risk. Learn simple, specific strategies for safer hiking, especially how to use your voice on the trail to warn away bears. Endorsed by the wardens at Jasper and Waterton national parks.

Hiking from Here to WOW:
North Cascades
50 Trails to the Wonder of Wilderness

ISBN 978-0-89997-444-6 The authors hiked more than 1,400 miles through North Cascades National Park plus the surrounding wilderness areas, including Glacier Peak, Mt. Baker, and the Pasayten. They took more than 1,000 photos and hundreds of pages of field notes. Then they culled their list of favourite hikes down to 50 trips—each selected for its power to incite awe. Their 264-page book describes where to find the cathedral forests, psychedelic meadows, spiky summits, and colossal glaciers that distinguish the American Alps. And it does so in refreshing style: honest, literate, entertaining, inspiring. Like all *WOW Guides*, this one is full colour throughout, with 180 photos and a trail map for each dayhike and backpack trip. First edition May 2007.

Hiking from Here to WOW:
Utah Canyon Country
90 Trails to the Wonder of Wilderness

ISBN 978-0-89997-452-1 The authors hiked more than 1,600 miles through Zion, Bryce, Escalante-Grand Staircase, Glen Canyon, Grand Gulch, Cedar Mesa, Canyonlands, Moab, Arches, Capitol Reef, and the San Rafael Swell. They took more than 2,500 photos and hundreds of pages of field notes. Then they culled their list of favourite hikes down to 90 trips—each selected for its power to incite awe. Their 480-page book describes where to find the redrock cliffs, slick-rock domes, soaring arches, and ancient ruins that make southern Utah unique in all the world. And it does so in refreshing style: honest, literate, entertaining, inspiring. Like all *WOW Guides*, this one is full colour throughout, with 220 photos and a trail map for each dayhike and backpack trip. First edition July 2008.

Done in a Day: Banff
The 10 Premier Hikes

ISBN 978-0-9783427-0-8 Where to invest your limited hiking time to enjoy the greatest scenic reward. Choose an easy, vigourous, or challenging hike. Start your adventure within a short drive of town. Witness the wonder of Banff National Park and be back for a hot shower, great meal, and soft bed. 136 pages, 90 photos, trail maps for each trip, full colour throughout. First edition December 2007.

Done in a Day: Calgary
The 10 Premier Road Rides

ISBN 978-0-9783427-3-9 Where to invest your limited cycling time to enjoy the greatest scenic reward. Spring through fall, southwest Alberta offers cyclists blue-ribbon road riding: from alpine passes in the Canadian Rockies, to dinosaur-country river canyons on the edge of the prairie. And this compact, jersey-pocket-sized book is your guide to the crème de la crème: the ten most serene, compelling, bike-friendly roads in the region. Start pedaling within a short drive of Calgary. At day's end, be back for a hot shower, great meal, and soft bed. 120 pages, 80 photos, road maps for each ride, full colour throughout. First edition December 2007.

Done in a Day: Jasper
The 10 Premier Hikes

ISBN 978-0-9783427-1-5 Where to invest your limited hiking time to enjoy the greatest scenic reward. Choose an easy, vigourous, or challenging hike. Start your adventure within a short drive of town. Witness the wonder of Jasper National Park and be back for a hot shower, great meal, and soft bed. 128 pages, 75 photos, trail maps for each trip, full colour throughout. First edition December 2007.

Done in a Day: Moab
The 10 Premier Hikes

ISBN 978-0-9735099-8-4 Where to invest your limited hiking time to enjoy the greatest scenic reward. Choose an easy, vigourous, or challenging hike. Start your adventure within a short drive of town. Witness the wonder of canyon country—including Arches and Canyonlands national parks—and be back for a hot shower, great meal, and soft bed. 160 pages, 110 photos, trail maps for each trip, full colour throughout. First edition May 2008.

Done in a Day: Whistler
The 10 Premier Hikes

ISBN 978-0-9735099-7-7 Where to invest your limited hiking time to enjoy the greatest scenic reward. Choose an easy, vigourous, or challenging hike. Start your adventure within a short drive of the village. Witness the wonder of Whistler, British Columbia, and be back for a hot shower, great meal, and soft bed. 144 pages, 80 photos, trail maps for each trip, full colour throughout. First edition December 2007.